Building Legislative Coalitions for Free Trade in Asia

What accounts for the large reduction in trade barriers among new democracies in Asia after World War II? Using new data from Japan and Thailand, this book provides a surprising answer: politicians, especially party leaders, liberalized trade by buying off legislative support with side payments such as pork barrel projects. Trade liberalization was a legislative triumph, not an executive achievement. This finding challenges the conventional "insulation" argument, which posits that insulating executives from special interest groups and voters is the key to successful trade liberalization. By contrast, this book demonstrates that party leaders built open economy coalitions with legislators by feeding legislators' rent-seeking desires with side payments rather than depriving their appetites. This book unravels the political foundations of an open economy.

Megumi Naoi is an associate professor of political science at the University of California, San Diego. Her work has been published in such journals as *American Journal of Political Science*, *Comparative Political Studies*, and *International Organization*, where she serves as an editorial board member. She has been a visiting research Fellow at Keio University and Waseda University in Tokyo; Chulaongkorn University in Bangkok, Thailand; and a predoctoral Fellow at Princeton's Neihaus Center for Globalization and Governance.

Building Legislative Coalitions for Free Trade in Asia

Globalization as Legislation

MEGUMI NAOI
University of California, San Diego

CAMBRIDGE
UNIVERSITY PRESS

32 Avenue of the Americas, New York, NY 10013-2473, USA

Cambridge University Press is part of the University of Cambridge.

It furthers the University's mission by disseminating knowledge in the pursuit of
education, learning, and research at the highest international levels of excellence.

www.cambridge.org
Information on this title: www.cambridge.org/9781107037038

© Megumi Naoi 2015

This publication is in copyright. Subject to statutory exception
and to the provisions of relevant collective licensing agreements,
no reproduction of any part may take place without the written
permission of Cambridge University Press.

First published 2015

A catalog record for this publication is available from the British Library.

Library of Congress Cataloging in Publication Data
Naoi, Megumi, 1973–
Building legislative coalitions for free trade in Asia : globalization as legislation /
Megumi Naoi.
    pages   cm
Includes bibliographical references and index.
ISBN 978-1-107-03703-8 (hardback)
 1. Political planning – Japan.   2. Political planning – Thailand.   3. Political leadership –
Japan.   4. Political leadership – Thailand.   5. Free trade – Political aspects – Japan.
6. Free trade – Political aspects – Thailand.   7. Finance, Public – Japan.   8. Finance,
Public – Thailand.   9. Japan – Appropriations and expenditures.   10. Thailand –
Appropriations and expenditures.   I. Title.
JQ1669.P53N36   2015
328.52′0746–dc23   2015003325

ISBN 978-1-107-03703-8 Hardback

Cambridge University Press has no responsibility for the persistence or accuracy of URLS
for external or third-party Internet Web sites referred to in this publication and does not
guarantee that any content on such Web sites is, or will remain, accurate or appropriate.

To My Family
感謝をこめて

Contents

List of Figures and Tables	*page* viii
Acknowledgments	xi
Abbreviations	xv

PART I BUILDING OPEN ECONOMY COALITIONS

1	Optimal Use of Pork, Policy, and Institutional Reforms	3

PART II EMPIRICAL EVIDENCE

2	Use of Pork as a Side Payment	35
3	Pro-Loser Policy during Hard Times	82
4	Helping Co-Partisan Legislators Survive Elections: Use of Institutional Reforms	120
5	Japanese Legislators in Rival Regions	141
6	Thai Legislators' Position-Taking on Foreign Retail Investment Liberalization	160

PART III DISCUSSION

7	The Political Foundations of an Open Economy: Discussion	183

References	191
Index	207

vii

Figures and Tables

Figures

1.1	Postwar Trade Liberalization	*page* 4
1.2	Unilateral versus Multilateral Trade Liberalization, 1983–2003	5
1.3	No Systematic Effects of Regime Types and Electoral Systems on Tariff Reduction (Weighted)	6
1.4	Initial Levels of Tariff Predict 92 Percent of the Variance in Tariff Reduction (Weighted)	7
1.5	Legislators' Position-Taking in the World of Trade Theorems	16
1.6	The GL and Legislators' Position-Taking	21
1.7	Pork Becomes Too Expensive with Diffused Losers	24
2.1	Fence-Sitters Were Exposed to Trade Liberalization in Japan, 1960–1964	47
2.2	The Number of Tariff Legislations and Side-Payment Legislation	55
2.3	Liberalization Index and Predicted Probability of Pork Allocations	61
2.4	Changes in the Levels of Agricultural Protection (Nominal Rates of Assistance) in Thailand, Selected Commodities, 1981–1988	72
3.1	Japanese Government's Budget Allocation to Diffused versus Organized Interests, 1955–2012	93
3.2	Thai Government's Budget Allocation to Diffused Losers, 1980–2005	104
3.3	Percentile Urban Constituencies for Ministers of Agriculture and Cooperatives in Thailand, 1982–2005	111
3.4	Percentile Urban Constituencies for Ministers of Agriculture in Japan	112

Figures and Tables   ix

4.1 Trade Exposure and the Incidence of Trade Policy Testimony
     before Japan's Lower House, 1950–2002   129
4.2 Proportion of Protectionist Testimony before Diet Committees
     (%), 1950–2002   130
5.1 Towel Industry – Predicted Legislator Positions   142
5.2 Tatami Mat Industry – Predicted Legislator Positions   143
6.1 Predicted Legislators' Position-Taking and Side-Payment
     Allocation   161

Tables

1.1   Predictions for Japanese and Thai Cases   14
2.1   The Determinants of the Planned Liberalization in
      Four Phases, 1960   49
2.2   The Determinants of Actual Trade Liberalization
      (Implementation)   52
2.3   Prefectures that Received Side Payments, 1960–1964   58
2.4   Side-Payment Allocations and Mean Liberalization Index   59
2.5   Liberalization Index and Side-Payment Allocations in Japanese
      Prefectures   60
2.6   Nominal Rates of Protection for Manufacturing Industries   66
2.7   The Determinants of Manufacturing Trade Liberalization in
      Thailand, 1975–1985   68
2.8   The Determinants of Agricultural Trade Liberalization in
      Thailand, 1981–1988   71
2.9   Side-Payment Allocations and the Depth of Manufacturing
      Liberalization   77
2.10 Trade Liberalization and Pork Allocations in Thai Provinces   78
A2.1 Provincial-Level Tariff Reduction, Weighted by Labor Force
      Composition   81
3.1   Predictions for Pork versus Policy   83
3.2   Government's Budget Allocation before and after the
      Energy Crises   91
3.3   The Japanese Government's Spending Allocation to Diffused
      Interests (%), 1955–2012   98
3.4   Policies to Support Economic Losers during and post-1997
      Financial Crisis in Thailand   108
3.5   Multiparty Coalition Suppresses Social Spending (%) –
      Thailand, 1980–2005   116

4.1	Major Corruption Scandals Involving Business and Legislators in Postwar Japan	123
4.2	The Predicted LDP Legislators' Voting Decisions on the 1975 Political Finance Bill	125
4.3	Who Defected? Access to Donation and Rural Safe Seats	125
4.4	Frequency of Trade Policy Testimony by Types of Interest Groups, 1950–2002	129
4.5	Testing for a Trend Shift in Protectionist Lobbying at Different Break Dates	132
4.6	Major Political Corruption Scandals Involving Business and Ministers in Thailand	135
4.7	Political Finance Reforms in Japan (1975 and 1994) and Thailand (1999)	136
5.1	Protectionism Was Chosen for Non-LDP, Single-Member Districts	158
6.1	Major Infrastructure Projects and the Electoral Competition under Thaksin's Cabinet (Approved in 2004)	175
6.2	Probability of Party Switching to Thai Rak Thai, 2003–2005 by Region	176

Acknowledgments

This project has taken me on a long and wonderful journey from its conception to completion, during which I have flown over the Pacific Ocean many, many times. During this journey, I have accumulated many intellectual and personal debts.

First and foremost, I thank my dissertation advisors, Helen Milner and Gerald Curtis. Although this book has evolved far from the dissertation, they have substantially influenced the ways in which I try to make sense of the world. Helen was the best advisor one could think of – critical and profound, yet encouraging and practical. She also showed unwavering support during the ups and downs of my scholarly career, which gave me renewed energy to work harder and move forward. I would not have been where I am without her support and encouragement. Professor Curtis always encouraged me to be a better scholar and redefined my understanding and appreciation for "tough love." I was continuously challenged by his knowledge of Japan, and I am not surprised that after all these years of my "soaking and poking," I found his interpretation of Liberal Democratic Party (LDP) survival, which emphasized policy adaptation, to be most convincing. I am grateful for insightful comments provided by my other dissertation committee members, David Epstein, David Weinstein, and Pablo Pinto.

I have been fortunate to have wonderful and supportive colleagues at UCSD. My warmest thanks go to Miles Kahler, whose mentoring, encouragement, and patience were indispensable. Miles also generously gave me funds to hold an author's book workshop, which helped me substantially improve the manuscript. David Lake and Peter Gourevitch have been terrific colleagues and mentors, and I have benefited tremendously from their sage advice and discussion. Discussions with Gary Cox, Keith Poole, and Matt McCubbins were critical in my effort to bring legislators to the center stage in the study of the politics of globalization. Keith Poole's multidimensional scaling course also taught

xi

me ways to think about legislators' policy positioning in the global economy. I learned much about Thai political economy from Krislert Samphantharak. I am thankful to Kaare Strom for his friendship and his research assistance (!) with the data on Norwegian agricultural ministers, which did not make it to this book owing to space constraints.

I have learned much from conversations with political economy scholars at UCSD: Lawrence Broz, Steph Haggard, Eddy Malesky (now at Duke), Christina Schneider, and Krislert Samphantharak. Also at UCSD, Japan scholars Ellis Krauss, Takeo Hoshi (now at Stanford), and Ulrike Schaede have been constant sources of inspiration and I feel very fortunate to be around them. "Going to school" has always been fun and something to look forward to thanks to Marisa Abrajano, Claire Adida, Scott Desposato, Karen Farree, James Fowler, Erik Gartzke, Clark Gibson, Zoli Hajnal, Thad Kousser, Sebastian Saiegh, Christina Schneider, and Branislav Slantchev, conversations with whom over lunch and coffee gave me energy and new ideas. My research assistants at UCSD, Celeste Beesely, Michael Plouffe, Matt Kearney, Maya Duru, Justin Reeves, and Yusaku Narita, provided incomparable data, figure, and editorial assistance. Krantarat Krongsiriwat and Chayathorn Termariyabuit at Chulalongkorn University provided fantastic research assistance on Thai data. I also learned much about Thai statistics from discussions with Doungdao Mahakitsiri in the Economics Department at UCSD.

At the author's book workshop, Gary Cox, Steph Haggard, Miles Kahler, David Lake, Mike Thies, and T. J. Pempel read the entire manuscript and provided invaluable comments. The workshop was the best intellectual experience I have ever had, and I was humbled by how much I learned from them. Special thanks go to Gary Cox for coming up with the concept of "Globalization as Legislation," which effectively communicates the central contribution of this book. Peter Gourevitch, Sam Popkin, and Phil Roeder also read the entire manuscript and helped me clarify its key contribution. Susan Shirk and Sam Popkin nourished me and my family with great food and wine over the years. I also thank Sam for cheering me up with his pep talks when I most needed them.

Outside of UCSD, Margarita Estevez-Abe, Kent Calder, Christina Davis, Allen Hicken, Horiuchi Yusaku, Saito Jun, Len Schoppa, Mike Thies, and Nita Rudra provided comments on different parts of manuscript, often in the form of conference papers, and I am grateful for their generosity and friendship. Pablo Pinto has offered superb comments to "flip the puzzle" (see Chapter 1) at the International Political Economy Colloquium (IPEC) at the University of Pittsburgh, where I also presented the manuscript. On the other side of the continent, in Japan and Thailand, I have enormously benefited from conversations with Kume Ikuo, Tatebayashi Masahiko, Fukumoto Kentaro, Okazaki Tetsuji, Pitch Pongsawat, and Veerayooth Kanchoochat. I am also thankful to Professor Fukumoto for sharing his legislation data (Figure 2.2, Chapter 2) and Professor Okazaki for generously sharing his Japanese commodity-level

Acknowledgments xiii

liberalization data used in Chapter 2. I am grateful to Allen Hicken and his research assistant for making individual names of candidates in the CLEA dataset available to me. Thai scholars, especially Ajarn Pitch Pongsawat at Chulalongkorn University and his juniors were generous with their time and support. Pitch's family and relatives in Chonburi and Suphan Buri were generous hosts during my fieldwork in these provinces. Pitch answered countless questions about Thai politics and guided me through the labyrinth of Thai legislators. Christian Sano also provided a place to stay during my fieldwork in Thailand. This book would have not been possible without the generosity of legislators, bureaucrats, and interest group leaders in Japan and Thailand who agreed to be my interviewees.

I have also incurred many institutional debts. A Fulbright scholarship allowed me to pursue a Ph.D. in the United States in the first place. The Tokyo Foundation and Columbia's East Asian Institute provided summer research funds to conduct fieldwork in Thailand. The Japan Society for the Promotion of Science provided a generous fund to conduct field research in Japan hosted by my alma mater, Keio University. Princeton's Center for Globalization and Governance (currently the Niehaus Center for Globalization and Governance) offered wonderful intellectual and nonintellectual (i.e., free lunches and espresso) support. UCSD's Committee of Research provided a grant for the final stage of book writing.

In the earlier years of my undergraduate and graduate studies at Keio University in Tokyo, Professor Yakushiji Taizo shaped my interests in political economy. He has opened so many doors for me that I don't know how to thank him enough. He taught me the nuts and bolts of social science research during my undergraduate years and encouraged me to pursue a Ph.D. in the United States.

Finally, my personal debts are the greatest.

I thank my family, Atsushi, Michiko, and Nozomi for all their support, love, and incomparable sense of humor when they were most needed. My other family in Austin, Texas, and Cherry Hill, New Jersey, William and Melissa Hornung, Frances Toepperwein Hornung Magee, Chet Hornung and Sunni Brown, Elissa Goss, and Stephen Magee always make me feel at home. I am grateful for the ease and warmth of Iwato-cho Committee members, Kim Chang-Ran, Kenji Hall, Iwamura Mari, and Kurasawa Naoki.

As an empiricist, I have noticed that there are two types of spouses thanked in acknowledgments of books: one who "reads and comments on the manuscript" (i.e., an academic spouse) and another who "helps keep things in proper perspective" (i.e., a nonacademic spouse). Bill Hornung has done an amazing job at both. I can always count on his irritatingly honest criticisms of my work and writing, and more importantly, he has been an anchor in my life. Kai and Ellie Hornung joined us, and their laughter and spontaneity have been a constant source of energy. To all, my deepest thanks and appreciation. Arigatou!

Abbreviations

ECONOMIC DATA

ERP	Effective Rate of Protection
GDP	gross domestic product
NRA	Nominal Rate of Assistance
NRP	Nominal Rate of Protection

ELECTORAL SYSTEMS AND COALITION-BUILDING

GL	Globalization as Legislation
MMD	multimember district
MR	majority requirement in legislature
PR	proportional representation
SMD	single-member district
SNTV	single nontransferable vote

INTERNATIONAL ORGANIZATIONS

GATT	General Agreements on Tariffs and Trade
IMF	International Monetary Fund
OECD	Organisation for Economic Co-operation and Development
WTO	World Trade Organization

JAPAN

CGP	Clean Government Party (*Kōmeitō*)
DPJ	Democratic Party of Japan (*Minshutō*)
JCP	Japan Communist Party (*Kyōsantō*)

xvi

JETRO	Japan External Trade Organization
LDP	Liberal Democratic Party (*Jiyū-Minshutō*)
MAFF	Ministry of Agriculture, Forestry and Fisheries
METI	Ministry of Economy, Trade and Industry
MITI	Ministry of International Trade and Industry
MOF	Ministry of Finance

THAILAND

NESDB	National Economic and Social Development Board
SAP	Social Action Party
TRT	Thai Rak Thai Party

A NOTE ON CONVENTIONS

Throughout this book, Japanese personal names are written as family name followed by given name, Thai names follow the Western convention.

PART I

BUILDING OPEN ECONOMY COALITIONS

1

Optimal Use of Pork, Policy, and Institutional Reforms

What accounts for the dramatic reduction in barriers to foreign trade after World War II? Postwar trade liberalization is a puzzle because governments initiated liberalization in places and at times that appeared the least likely: in newer, politically in flux democracies with strong legacies of import-substitution strategies. Governments around the world, especially in East Asia and Latin America, that faced pressures from new electoral competition and vested interest groups have reduced barriers to trade. What makes the postwar liberalization even more puzzling, moreover, is that the bulk of the liberalization was achieved unilaterally – that is, governments lowered trade barriers without bilateral or multilateral trade agreements that rest on the principle of reciprocity.[1] This book unravels political foundations of free trade.

Figure 1.1 documents the dramatic reduction in countries' barriers to trade, measured by simple average tariff rates from 1981 to 2010 for developing and industrialized countries (World Bank 2011). Figure 1.2 shows Martin and Ng's (2004) estimates of the proportion of unilateral versus multilateral trade liberalization that had contributed to overall tariff reduction for a set of developing economies that constituted more than 90 percent of import values around the world between 1983 and 2003. It shows that, on average, governments' unilateral liberalization contributed to 73 percent of tariff reduction between 1983 and 2003, while the Uruguay Round negotiations of the World Trade Organization (WTO) contributed 27 percent (Martin and Ng 2004; Baldwin 2010).[2] Two further patterns stand out. First, contrary to the conventional

---

[1] Rodrik (1994); Milner (1999); Baldwin (2010).

[2] Unilateral liberalization includes tariff reduction via loan agreements with the International Monetary Fund (IMF) and tariff reduction via WTO accession. Figure 1.2 does not imply that General Agreements on Tariff and Trade (GATT) or WTO did not have substantial effects on international trade. Goldstein et al. (2007) and Tomz et al. (2007) show that membership in

3

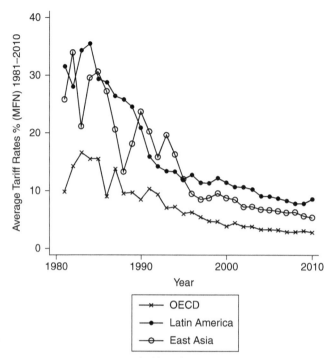

FIGURE 1.1. Postwar trade liberalization.
Source: World Bank, Francis K. T. Ng (2011), "Trends in Average MFN Applied Tariff Rates in Developing and Industrialized Countries, 1981–2010." Available at World Bank's Data Bank.
Note: Tariff rates are calculated by unweighted, simple average. East Asia includes China, South Korea, Indonesia, Japan, Laos, Malaysia, Mongolia, Philippines, Singapore, Taiwan, Thailand, and Vietnam. Latin America includes Argentina, Belize, Bolivia, Brazil, Chile, Colombia, Costa Rica, Cuba, Dominican Republic, Ecuador, El Salvador, Guatemala, Honduras, Jamaica, Mexico, Nicaragua, Paraguay, Peru, Uruguay, and Venezuela. Missing data are excluded from the mean calculation.

wisdom that political institutions affect countries' *levels* of trade protection (Nielson 2003; Kono 2006), political institutions have very little to do with the magnitudes of tariff *reduction over time*. Countries with or without democratic elections and countries with candidate-centered or party-centered electoral systems (Figure 1.3) similarly reduced the bulk of their trade barriers over time.

Second, the best predictor of the magnitude of tariff reduction over time is the countries' initial levels of applied tariff (weighted) as of 1983, which

---

GATT and WTO increased dyadic trade flows among members when membership includes colonial states and such, whereas Rose (2007) shows that members and nonmembers did not differ systematically regarding their dyadic trade flows. My point here is simply that WTO was not the main locus of tariff reduction for major developing economies since 1983.

Optimal Use of Pork, Policy, and Institutional Reforms

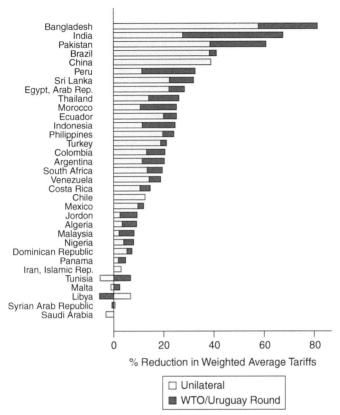

FIGURE 1.2. Unilateral versus multilateral trade liberalization, 1983–2003.
Source: The author made this figure using data used in Martin, Will and Francis Ng (2004), "A Note on Sources of Tariff Reductions in Developing Countries, 1983–2003," Background paper for Global Economic Prospects 2005 – Trade Regionalism, and Development. Washington, DC: World Bank.
Note: Martin and Ng used changes in weighted average of tariffs using United Nations Conference on Trade and Development (UNCTAD)'s Trade Analysis Information System (TRAINS) data from 1983 to 2003 and calculated the proportion of tariff reduction for each of the three sources: unilateral, preferential trade agreements, and WTO Uruguay Round. The figure omits tariff reduction by preferential trade agreements, because it constituted only an average 0.22 percent point reduction in weighted average tariffs during this period. Unilateral liberalization includes tariff concession through the International Monetary Fund (IMF)'s loan programs and tariff reduction preceding WTO accession. See Martin and Ng (2004) for details.

accounts for greater than 90 percent of cross-national variations in the magnitudes of tariff reduction (Figure 1.4). In other words, major importing countries eventually got rid of most, if not all, of their initial tariff barriers.

The patterns of postwar trade liberalization described in the preceding text force us to redefine the puzzles scholars have sought to solve. First, the real

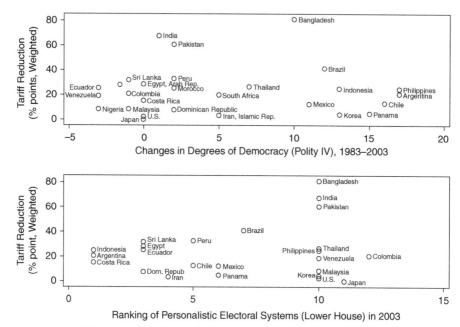

FIGURE 1.3. No systematic effects of regime types and electoral systems on tariff reduction (weighted).

Source: Tariff data are from Figure 1.2 and I added data for South Korea, Japan, and the United States. Polity IV data are from Marshal and Jagger, Version 2010, available at http://www.systemicpeace.org/inscr/inscr.htm (accessed June 2012) and I calculated change between 1983 and 2003 for each country. Positive values mean that a country became more democratic, negative values indicate that a country became more authoritarian, and zero indicates no changes. Personalistic electoral system ranking is from Wallack et al. (2003) and ranges from 0 to 12. The higher the number, the more candidate-centered the electoral system was in 2003. Bivariate regressions show that changes in regime types have no systematic effects on the magnitudes of tariff reduction (coefficients, 0.035; standard errors, 0.589; and *t*-statistics, 0.06) and candidate-centered electoral system ranking as of 2003 has no systematic effects, either (coefficients, 0.795; standard errors, 1.025; and *t*-statistics, 0.78 for 2003). The bivariate results for electoral system ranking hold the same for 1983 data.

variance to be explained is the liberalization over time, not cross-national variance in levels of trade protection. Second, we should be asking *how* these countries achieved trade liberalization, rather than to what extent. How did these newer democracies, which were exposed to electoral competition and vested interests after World War II, achieve this? Not only did these governments initiate liberalization, but they have also shown remarkable commitment to an open economy and provoked very little backlash against globalization during hard times, such as the energy crises in the 1970s and financial crises in the 1980s and the 1990s.

Optimal Use of Pork, Policy, and Institutional Reforms

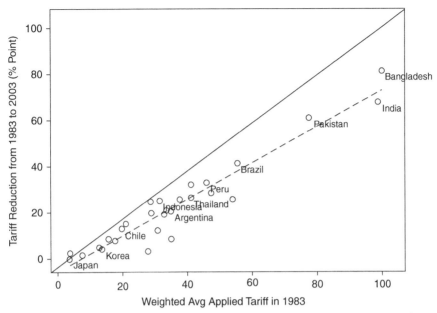

FIGURE 1.4. Initial levels of tariff predict 92 percent of the variance in tariff reduction (weighted).

Note: Data are the same as in Figure 1.3, which includes 28 countries (country labels shown selectively). The solid black line at 45 degrees indicates a hypothetical scenario where the initial levels of tariff explain 100 percent of variance in tariff reduction between 1983 and 2003. The dotted line is fitted from a linear regression and indicates the actual pattern of reduction, which still explains 92 percent of the variance (coefficients, 0.790; standard errors, 0.045; and *t*-statistics, 17.48).

Despite the high magnitude of liberalization after World War II, scholars have paradoxically invested more effort toward explaining the cross-national and cross-industry levels of protectionism, not the shift over time to an open economy. Economists have probably led this lopsided attention to the study of protectionism, as they found governments' choice to limit trade puzzling given the conventional wisdom that free trade increases the general welfare of citizens.[3] The majority of studies on protectionism emphasize the collective action capacity of interest groups – that losers from liberalization are concentrated and well-organized, while beneficiaries are diffuse.[4] Reelection-seeking legislators, studies have further shown, are more likely to respond to the protectionist demands from losers because they lobby harder. These explanations,

---

[3] Milner (1999).
[4] Schattschneider (1935); Olson (1965); Magee, Block, and Young (1978); Grossman and Helpman (1994); Baldwin and Nicoud (2007).

8   *Building Open Economy Coalitions*

however, are of little help in making sense of how governments were able to shift toward policies favoring an open economy. I thus flip the economists' puzzle and ask: How did newer democracies achieve postwar liberalization when protectionism seemed politically optimal? This book thus seeks to understand better the relatively unknown political foundations of the open economy.

Three theories have sought to explain when governments initiate and commit to an open economy. The first focuses on the role of reciprocity embedded in supranational institutions and international agreements, such as the General Agreements on Tariff and Trade (GATT), in mobilizing pro-trade interests. The second argument emphasizes the role of external pressures to open the market, coming from major exporters such as the United States or financiers of economic development, such as the International Monetary Fund (IMF).[5] Although these external actors provided a powerful impetus for postwar liberalization, these accounts fail to address the fact that the bulk of postwar liberalization occurred unilaterally. The third account turns to domestic politics and emphasizes the role of delegation of trade policymaking power from legislators to the executive branch (such as the president) and the bureaucracy.[6]

What these theories have in common is twofold. First, they consider politicians to either play a trivial role in, or serve as an obstacle to, the process of liberalization. They view politicians to be powerlessly entrenched in a web of special interest groups and voters. Second, these studies accordingly emphasize the importance of governments' abilities to insulate the trade policymaking process from interest groups and from rank-and-file legislators through a mechanism of delegation.

These insulation arguments, however, miss one of the key ingredients of democracy: policy changes, such as lowering tariffs and signing trade and investment agreements with foreign countries, require majority approval from legislators.[7] Even in the extreme cases in which bureaucrats or the executive branch set policies without legislators' input, the majority of legislators still need to pass these bills into law. If legislators are powerless and captured by protectionist interests, as the insulation arguments have portrayed, how do they build majority support for an open economy on the floor?

I argue that legislators serve two essential functions: constituency service and law making. The insulation arguments, however, consider legislators' jobs to be only about constituency service, with the implication that legislators respond sincerely to districts' demands. As Gilligan (1997:1) succinctly summarizes American trade policy before the New Deal: "import-competing industries asked for protection, legislators gave it to them." Legislators, however, also take policy positions to make laws. They often push liberalization

---

[5] Schoppa (1993, 1997).
[6] Goldstein (1986), Gilligan (1997), and Hiscox (1999) on the United States; Ramseyer and Rosenbluth (1993) on Japan.
[7] Gilligan (1997); McGillivray (1997); Mansfield, Milner, and Rosendorff (2000).

Optimal Use of Pork, Policy, and Institutional Reforms

bills that provide collective benefits to the party, the government, or general citizens in the long run, while hurting their own districts' interests at least in the short run. How do legislators achieve this?

This book develops a novel approach, *Globalization as Legislation* (hereafter GL), that provides an answer to this puzzle. GL views trade liberalization as a series of "general interest legislation"[8] – that is, policies that collectively increase the general welfare of citizens and raise the government's resources for political mobilization over the long run (Evans 2004).[9] The collective benefits to citizens and the parties in power, however, come with the private costs of liberalization (i.e., income loss of industries and voters) imposed on some electoral districts, and hence on some legislators, but not on others. Thus, legislating globalization presents a classic collective goods dilemma for politicians: legislators are collectively better off committing to liberalization, but the distribution of costs and benefits across districts makes their collective action difficult. How do legislators overcome this collective action problem and build a majority coalition that commits to an open economy?

I argue that party leaders can overcome this collective goods dilemma and build an open economy coalition by distributing side payments to buy off individual legislators. These side payments to legislators can take various forms: subsidies, public work projects, personnel appointments, and broader compensation policies. These side payments from the party leaders serve two interdependent goals of legislators: political survival and legislating policies. The first function of side payments is to mitigate the costs of liberalization imposed on some legislators to help them survive future elections. As shown in detail later, these side payments all work as substitutes for tariff protection by compensating for the electoral loss that some legislators incur from liberalization. Second, party leaders distribute side payments to bring swing legislators who are on the fence about liberalization into the majority coalition for an open economy. Side payments are thus used to entice legislators who might otherwise oppose liberalization.[10]

---

[8] This argument builds on Evans (2004), but differs from hers in considering party leaders' choices across three strategies of coalition building, which I call *Pork*, *Policy*, and *Institutional Reforms* (described later in this chapter). This book also considers the distributional implications of these diverse strategies, which Evans (2004) leaves out. I elaborate on my argument in greater detail in the text that follows.

[9] I fully substantiate why we can view trade and investment liberalization as "general interest legislation" in the text that follows. Abolishing tariffs and licensing regulations reduces the government's fiscal revenue. Yet globalization can also increase governments' revenues through other mechanisms, such as economic growth, increasing imports, and new investment entries. See Keen and Baunsgaard (2005) for a survey of the literature. Ebrill, Stotsky, and Gropp (1999) have found that trade liberalization led to increased trade revenues when it was associated with increased imports and thus some governments can liberalize trade without worrying too much about the revenue implications. See also Krueger (1974) and Milner and Kubota (2005).

[10] Mayer (1992) and Friman (1993) studied the role of domestic side payments in facilitating international cooperation, yet their focus was on compensation for domestic industries that

This argument breaks away from the insulation arguments in three important ways. First, contrary to the conventional view of legislators as powerless and entrenched, my approach considers the role of party leaders in building the majority coalitions essential to liberalization. Globalization gives a renewed and powerful role to party leaders as builders of open economy coalitions through their use of side payments.

Counterintuitively, side payments can entice legislators to support liberalization because of the presence of interest group capturing and the entrenchment of legislators, not despite these pressures. In the presence of interest group pressure, legislators have greater rent extraction opportunities over the allocation of side payments than in the absence of such pressure. For example, legislators extract rents through influencing which construction company to use for a newly obtained public work project from the party leaders. Party leaders were thus able to channel legislators' rent-seeking incentives into majority coalition building for an open economy in allocating side payments. In Evans's term (1994), side payments grease the wheels of policymaking. The argument defies the conventional wisdom that interest group capture contributes to protectionism, not to free trade.

Second, the GL approach accordingly predicts how party leaders allocate side payments to achieve the majority coalitions. The approach predicts that governments distribute side payments based on the political needs of the party or legislators in power, *not* on the sheer economic needs of industries or voters who are hurt by liberalization, or their collective action capacity. I show that because the government uses side payments to bring fence-sitting, swing legislators into majority coalitions, the distribution favors legislators representing small net losers of globalization (i.e., those who incur marginal income loss), not big net losers. The prediction differs from the widely claimed and tested "compensation hypothesis," which predicts that big net losers of globalization, when they are sufficiently well-organized, obtain compensation (Cameron 1978; Garrett 1998; Rudra 2008).

Finally, the GL predicts party leader choices across a wide range of side payments for the purposes of majority coalition building. In particular, I focus on leader choices across three distinct forms of side payments, which I call *Pork, Policy,* and *Institutional Reforms. Pork* refers to legislator- and district-specific projects such as personnel appointments for legislators and public work projects for districts, in which benefits are excludable to other legislators or electoral districts. *Policy* refers to side-payment legislation that benefits broader constituents, such as social welfare policies and income compensation programs for depressed industries. Unlike Pork, the benefits of Policy are not contained in particular districts or directed to individual legislators; many districts

---

might have vetoed the ratification, not legislators. Goldstein and Martin (2000) consider the side-payment legislations as a consequence of increasing transparency in the multilateral negotiations, rather than as an instrument for building the pro-trade coalition.

Optimal Use of Pork, Policy, and Institutional Reforms 11

and legislators share Policy benefits and its credit-claiming opportunities.[11] *Institutional Reforms* refers to changing the rules of the game in politics to help backbenchers survive future elections, such as political finance reform. Unlike Pork or Policy, Institutional Reforms change the rules in which political or distributional battles are fought, as opposed to how government allocates its resource. This book's focus on the strategic choices of party leaders differs from the literature, which only considers the levels of pork or welfare programs (Policy) as bargaining deals struck between governments and citizens in the global economy.

Understanding party leader choices across different coalition-building strategies is important, because they have different welfare implications for citizens and legislators – whether side payments benefit urban versus rural constituents, narrow versus broad constituents (i.e., the choice between Pork or Policy), or whether they change how legislators mobilize votes and rents (Institutional Reforms). These strategies also differ in the longevity and renewability of the initial arrangement; generally, Pork's income and electoral effects are more short term than Policy,[12] and Institutional Reforms are stickier and their effects tend to be longer term than those of *Pork* or *Policy*.

This book shows that a country's political institutions, especially whether its party systems are centralized or decentralized, affect the party leader's choice across these three strategies by changing the costs of intra-elite bargaining over resources. Under decentralized party systems defined by the higher number of parties in a ruling coalition, such as multiparty coalition governments, *Pork* is the dominant choice. Under centralized party systems defined by fewer parties in a coalition, such as one-party majority governments, *Policy* and *Institutional Reforms* are optimal choices. Centralized vs. decentralized party systems are associated with different strategies of coalition-building, because these strategies require different levels of legislator coordination and collective action. Pork requires less coordination and collection action among legislators than Policy or Institutional Reform.

I further demonstrate that electoral systems are neither a necessary nor sufficient explanation for the party leaders' choice across Pork, Policy, or Institutional Reforms.[13] Although electoral systems can influence the disciplinary power of

---

[11] *Policy* as defined here can be universal, such as a universal unemployment insurance scheme, or its benefits are diffused to many electoral districts.

[12] Saito (2010) shows that once complete, party leaders cannot withdraw infrastructural projects and thus pork is not "renewable." I agree with him that once complete, infrastructural projects are not renewable, but the lack of renewability is not an issue in the context of my research, where party leaders use pork to "cushion" temporarily income shocks from liberalization (and electoral loss of a given legislator). My definition of "Pork" also differs from his in that "Pork" is defined as a district- or legislator-specific benefit, including personnel appointments and subsidies (that are renewable in a short time frame).

[13] To the extent to which party systems often correlate with electoral systems (e.g., proportional representation [PR] systems are more likely to produce multiparty coalitions), electoral systems also indirectly affect the party leaders' coalition-building strategies. I return to this point later.

party leaders over backbenchers (i.e., the strength of "stick"), what ultimately matters for the coalition building is the party leaders' abilities to distribute side payments ("carrot") to buy off legislative support. Because variations in party systems affect the costs of intra-elite bargaining over resources, party systems carry more weight than electoral systems in influencing the party leaders' choice of coalition-building strategies.

The remainder of this book develops the GL approach and tests its observable implications using the case of two Asian economies with entrenched legislators, Japan and Thailand. The conventional approach, designed to answer the "economists' puzzle" (of why protectionism prevails when the open economy is economically optimal), is to hold the level of economic development (or factor endowment) constant and differentiate legislators' incentives for protectionism shaped by different political institutions. In this book, by contrast, the puzzle is redefined, asking under what conditions party leaders are able to build majority coalitions for an open economy when protectionism seems politically optimal. Accordingly, I flip the conventional research design. I hold "protectionism-friendly" political institutions relatively constant between the two countries, and instead vary their levels of economic development (i.e., factor endowment). Japan transitioned from a developing to a developed economy around the mid-1960s,[14] while Thailand has been a developing economy throughout the postwar period.

This design allows me to demonstrate the validity of the GL approach over the economic approaches to party leader coalition-building strategies. First, it shows that party leaders in developed and in developing economies face similar obstacles when building majority coalitions for an open economy. Moreover, the approach reveals that a similar logic of buying off legislators' support prevails in party leader choices among strategies, regardless of differences in the respective countries' levels of economic development. Second, the research design allows me to show that, for party leaders, the marginal utility of the three instruments for coalition building and political survival (Pork, Policy, and Institutional Reforms) does not differ between developed and developing economies. Rather, the instrument choice is a function of how much legislative support party leaders can buy with the fiscal resources at hand, given the costs of coordination and bargaining among elites.

I chose Japan and Thailand to test the validity of the GL approach because they nicely fit the "flipped" research design described previously. Both have had quintessential "protectionism-friendly" electoral institutions, that is, multimember district (MMD) systems with high district magnitudes, until the mid-1990s. The two countries went through similar electoral reforms in the

---

[14] In 1964, the Japanese government joined the Organisation for Economic Co-operation and Development (OECD) and has accepted the International Monetary Fund's Article VIII obligations (which are the general rules prohibiting currency restrictions and stating payment and transfer responsibilities for full members). Both constituted the "official" beginning of Japan's developed country status. See Simmons (2000).

Optimal Use of Pork, Policy, and Institutional Reforms 13

mid-1990s, instituting a combination of the closed-list PR system and the single-member district (SMD) system that centralized decision-making power away from backbenchers toward party leaders. Political parties in the two countries are also characterized as decentralized and weak with a prevalence of factions, that is, intraparty groups formed by legislators with whom they shared ideology, policy agendas, and/or political financiers (McCubbins and Thies 1997; Chambers 2008). There has been a general lack of strong ideological or programmatic party platforms that bind voters and politicians. Labor unions in both societies are also decentralized or enterprise based, which has made the embedded liberalism bargain (i.e., the exchange of welfare expansion for supporting the open economy) more difficult to achieve. These common structural characteristics make party leaders' task to build majority coalitions equally challenging in the two countries.

Despite all of these indicators for "protectionism-friendly political institutions," party leaders in Japan and Thailand were able to build and maintain majority coalitions for an open economy. The two newer democracies are the poster children of the broader postwar shift from closed to open economies and government commitment to liberalization throughout a series of economic crises.[15] How did they do it? The characteristics listed earlier make Japan and Thailand puzzling and comparable cases.

The two countries, however, differ in how party leaders built the open economy coalitions. Although party leaders in both Japan and Thailand extensively used Pork to build the majority coalition under their MMD system,[16] Japan's Liberal Democratic Party (LDP) was able to use Policy for diffused losers and Institutional Reforms to help backbenchers survive in the 1970s under the exact same electoral system. By contrast, Thailand rarely used Policy, which favors diffused losers, or Institutional Reforms, which helped backbenchers win elections under the MMD system. It was not until 2001, when the Thai Rak Thai Party assumed a single-party majority, that the Thai government used Policy favoring diffused losers to keep its commitment to an open economy. This book argues that party systems, in particular the effective number of parties in government, account for the stark difference in coalition-building strategies between Japan and Thailand. More centralized party systems, such as Japan's single-party majority government (1955–1993), are more likely to use Policy or Institutional Reforms, owing to lower costs of intra-elite bargaining over resource and over new rules of the game. Decentralized party systems, such as Thailand's multiparty coalition governments until 2001, are more likely to resort to the use of Pork owing to difficulty in striking Policy or Institutional Reform bargains among elites.

Table 1.1 summarizes the key similarities and differences between the Japanese and Thai cases, as well as the predictions for their respective coalition-building strategies.

---

[15] Calder (1988); World Bank (1993); Haggard and Webb (1994); Stiglitz and Yusuf (2001).
[16] Japan before 1996, Thailand before 2001.

TABLE 1.1. *Predictions for Japanese and Thai Cases*

	Electoral Systems	Party Systems	Electoral System Prediction	GL Prediction	Outcome
Japan I. 1955–1960s	Multi-member District System (Candidate-centered)	One-party Dominance (Decentralized LDP)	Pork	Pork	Pork
II. 1970–1979 (Fiscal Constraints)		One-party Dominance (Centralized LDP)		Policy & Reform	Policy & Reform
III. 1980–1993				Policy	Policy
IV. 1994–2012	Single-member District System + Closed-list PR (Party-centered)	Coalitions (Decentralized)	Policy	Pork	Pork
Thailand I. 1982–1988 Semi-Democracy (Non-elected PM)	Multi-member District System (Candidate-centered)	Multi-party Coalitions	Pork	Pork	Pork
II. 1988–2001 Democracy (Elected PM)					
III. 2001–2005 Democracy/Thaksin cabinet	Single-member District System + Closed-list PR (Party-centered)	One-party majority (Centralized; Thai Rak Thai)	Pork	Policy	Policy

LDP, Liberal Democratic Party; PR, proportional representation.

Optimal Use of Pork, Policy, and Institutional Reforms

The remainder of this book proceeds as follows. The next section develops the GL approach and derives testable hypotheses. Chapters 2 through 4 test the optimal Use of *Pork* (Chapter 2), *Policy* (Chapter 3), and *Institutional Reforms* (Chapter 4) that are defined in this chapter. Each of these three chapters compares Japan and Thailand during the time periods considered. Chapter 2 compares Japan's and Thailand's coalition-building strategies during and after their accession to GATT. Chapter 3 compares their Pork and Policy responses to energy crises in the 1970s and recessions in the late 1990s and 2000s. Chapter 4 compares Japan's institutional reform that helped ruling party legislators survive elections to Thailand's lack of such reforms. Chapters 5 and 6 expand on case study evidence from legislators' position-taking in "rival" regions in Japan and Thailand. These chapters show that legislators supported an open economy despite protectionist lobbying in their districts, due to party leaders' use of Pork to offset the legislators' electoral costs of supporting liberalization. Chapter 7 discusses the broader implications of this study and lays out a future research agenda.

THE OPTIMAL USE OF PORK, POLICY, AND INSTITUTIONAL REFORMS

The Conventional Approach: Legislator Position-Taking in the World of Trade Theorems

The major work on legislator position-taking on foreign trade considers legislators as simple transmitters of their districts' positions. Consider a single dimensional policy space on globalization (x-axis of Figure 1.5), ranging from protectionist (the left side of dimension x) to pro-liberalization (toward the right side of dimension x). Assume a democratic country divided by electoral districts n, which consist of a number of geographic units n. Voters in each district elect between one (in a SMD system) to multiple (in a MMD system) candidates. Each electoral district is located on this single policy dimension x according to their median voters' policy positions toward trade liberalization, which reflect their economic interests.[17]

The y-axis indicates the size of the income benefits and losses that an electoral district i incurs from liberalization. The solid black line illustrates how the costs and benefits of liberalization are distributed across districts. I assume that a government cannot adopt a policy change that brings only the benefits of liberalization without the costs. This is due to either the reciprocity principle

---

[17] Whether median or majority voters' policy position determines legislators' trade policy position depends on electoral systems. Mayer (1984). For analytical simplicity here, I do not assume the existence of voting restrictions (e.g., owners of certain factor are excluded from voting) or substantial voting costs, both of which could change the economic profile of median voter, and hence his or her trade policy position.

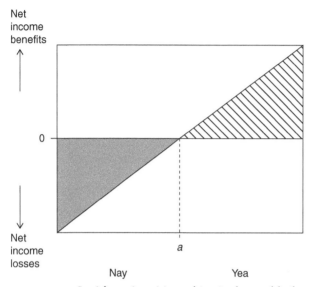

FIGURE 1.5. Legislators' position-taking in the world of trade theorems.

of trade agreements (if liberalization occurs through bilateral or multilateral agreements) or the fear of provoking retaliation from foreign governments by pursuing export liberalization without any reciprocal opening of its own markets (if liberalization occurs unilaterally). The sizes of costs and benefits are conversely correlated. The point a is where a district derives no net benefits or costs from a given policy change.

Note that in the world of trade theorems, a district's policy position is derived solely from the predicted effects of liberalization on the districts' income benefits or loss, nothing else. Thus, as shown in Figure 1.5, a district's policy position on the protectionism–liberalization dimension (x-axis) should correlate with the net income benefits or costs that the district incurs from liberalization (y-axis). Districts that reap net income gains from liberalization ("winners") are located to the right of point a, and districts that are net income losers of liberalization are located to the left of point a ("losers").

If legislators simply transmit their districts' interests that are derived from the trade theorems, then point a should be located on the dividing line between Yea (pro-liberalization) and Nay (protectionism) votes on the floor (Figure 1.5). Indeed, studies on legislator position-taking on trade and foreign investment have mostly tested how district economic characteristics, operationalized as factor-endowment and industry make-up, affected legislators' roll-call votes in the United States (Broz 2005; Milner and Tingley 2011). These empirical tests have shown the overall validity of the Stolper–Samuelson theorem, that a district's endowment of skilled and unskilled labor is the best predictor of a legislator's position-taking on trade with some support for other factors such

Optimal Use of Pork, Policy, and Institutional Reforms

as industry's financial contributions to the legislator and the ideology of legislators and district voters.

The Electoral Disconnection

Despite the theory, legislator position-taking often deviates from district interests (see Chapters 5 and 6). There are multiple explanations for this deviation. The most fundamental challenge to the model is the contention that income effects of liberalization might not determine the policy positions of electoral districts or legislators (i.e., no or imperfect correlation between a district's policy position on the x-axis and the size of net benefits or costs on the y-axis). Instead, ideological heuristics, such as people's association of globalization with anti-patriotism or legislators' ideological pre-dispositions, might dictate citizens' and legislators' position-taking (O'Rourke and Sinnott 2001; Milner and Tingley 2011). A less damning challenge to the model is to say that people are not fully rational or informed. With limited information and cognitive capacity, industries, citizens, and legislators are not necessarily fully aware of the income effects of liberalization and consequently make errors of a narrow or wide margin (Guisinger 2009; Mansfield and Mutz 2009; Naoi and Urata 2013).

My critique of the trade theorem approach, however, concerns its internal validity. Even if we accept its premise that income effects drive legislator position-taking, the conventional approach misses two key realities; (1) democratic governments need to legislate liberalization with majority support on the floor and (2) the government's income compensation programs can substitute for protectionism. I will elaborate each point below.

First, legislators serve to perform two functions: constituency service and law-making. Both activities can increase or decrease a district's income and thus are consistent with the income premise of the "trade theorem" approach to legislator position-taking. Yet, the trade theorem approach considers legislator position-taking as an effort to respond sincerely to district interests and demands, like constituency service. Legislators, however, also take policy positions to make laws. This neglect of law-making is problematic, because almost all policy changes in democracies, including those that pertain to globalization, require majority support from legislators to become law. Electotral disconnection can occur partly due to the legislators' law-making incentives.

Second, supporting an open economy versus closed economy is not a dichotomous policy choice where industries will inevitably win or lose – that is, a middle ground exits, which combines the open economy with income compensation for losers. The middle ground is possible, because interest groups' and legislators' protectionist positions are mutable as long as opposition to globalization concerns income losses (as opposed to ideological positions). Tariffs and income compensation programs (e.g., subsidies or taxes), for instance, can then serve as substitutes for import-competing industries in assisting their survival

(Rodrik 1986). Accordingly, governments can buy off losers' support for an open economy by packaging liberalization with compensation programs.[18] Yet, the trade theorem approach does not predict when governments strike such a middle ground.

Instead, I build the GL approach on the literature about the general welfare ranking of trade policy instruments (tariffs vs. subsidies) developed in trade economics. This research program suggests that a legislator's choice of tariff vs. compensation (subsidies) depends on two conditions: (1) what the legislator seeks to maximize – social welfare, votes, government's revenues, or rents; and (2) whether an import-competing sector is a monolithic actor or comprises multiple firms. It has been established that rent- and vote-seeking legislators should prefer subsidies with open economy to tariffs as long as an import-competing industry comprises multiple firms (as opposed to a monolithic actor) (Rodrik 1986).[19] Under the two conditions, a legislator's preference for subsidies over tariffs arises as a result of free-riding problems among import-competing firms. When lobbying for tariffs, import-competing firms face a free-rider problem because firms can equally benefit from the tariff protection without participating in lobbying efforts. Firms can overcome this free-rider problem with subsidies because it is easier for legislators to target subsidies to some firms or localities, while excluding others. This means that import-competing firms have stronger incentives to lobby for subsidies rather than tariffs, which leads to rent-seeking legislators preferring subsidies to tariffs for greater rent extraction (e.g., organized votes or campaign contribution).[20]

In sum, the two limitations of the trade theorem approach call for a new approach to legislators' position-taking on trade.

---

[18] I built my argument on the literature on welfare ranking on trade policy instruments in trade economics, because it allows me to analyze both broad and narrow forms of policy instruments for income substitution (e.g., welfare spending vs. pork barrel projects), and to consider legislator behavior under different utility assumptions, i.e., whether they are vote-, policy-, or rent-seeking. The literature on embedded liberalism is built on the similar logic of income substitution, yet is narrower in its theoretical and empirical scope than the literature on welfare ranking. The embedded liberalism literature concerns the expansion of the welfare state as a "grand compromise" between governments seeking an open economy and vulnerable labor, and tend to assume "policy-seeking" leaders.

[19] Until the publication of Rodrik's 1986 article, the conventional wisdom in trade economics was that direct subsidies are welfare-superior to tariffs because the former is associated with lower deadweight losses (Bhagwati and Ramaswami 1963; Johnson 1965; Acemoglu and Robinson 2001). If legislators are social welfare maximizers, they should thus prefer direct subsidies to tariffs. This established argument hinges on the two assumptions that diverge from the real policymaking process: (1) tariffs or subsidies are set exogenously (i.e., politics and industry lobby do not play a role), and (2) the import-competing sector is a monolithic actor (not comprising multiple firms). By contrast, Rodrik (1986) shows this welfare ranking can be reversed if legislators are rent-seeking and an import-competing industry comprises multiple firms.

[20] In some countries, campaign finance law prohibits that firms that receive government subsidies to give campaign contributions to legislators or parties. Japanese Political Finance Law is one

The Approach of This Book: Globalization as Legislation

This book develops a novel perspective on globalization, viewing trade liberalization as a series of "general interest legislation" – policies that collectively increase the general welfare of citizens and thus raise the government's resources for redistribution as well as the reputation of the party in the long run.

Three well-established premises justify viewing liberalization as general interest legislation (i.e., public goods for the economy and the party). First, free trade increases the overall welfare of citizens in the long run, especially consumer welfare, through lowering the prices of goods. Second, the improvement of citizens' economic welfare, in turn, is a good predictor of incumbents' political survival globally, and especially in democracies (Duch and Stevenson 2006; Gandhi and Przeworski 2007). This means that if incumbent party leaders care about long-term political survival and building their party's reputation, they should prefer an open economy to protectionism. Finally, although an autarky might be politically optimal in the short run (because of the rents it generates for import-competing industries), a closed economy stagnates economic growth and dissipates a government's resources for redistribution and political mobilization in the long run.[21] If citizens' economic welfare is even partially associated with political survival, then, autarky is counterproductive for legislators, elected or unelected.

The collective benefits to citizens and the parties in power, however, come with the costs of liberalization that are imposed on some districts $(i < a)$.[22] Thus, enacting liberalization bills presents a classic collective goods dilemma: legislators are collectively better off committing to liberalization, but the distribution of costs and benefits makes the collective action difficult. Legislators representing districts where $i < a$ bear the electoral costs of liberalization, while legislators representing districts $i > a$ reap the electoral benefits. The size of electoral costs that a legislator incurs becomes larger toward the protectionist end of the spectrum on the policy dimension, assuming that constituents' decrease in income directly translates into the decline in political support (Hillman 1982).

How do party leaders and backbenchers weigh the relative importance of maintaining individual rents (available under autarky) versus expansion of the economy and government resources (under an open economy)? Party leaders are more likely to weigh the expansion of the economy and the government's resources more heavily than maintaining individual rents because they have a longer time horizon, derived from their higher electoral security (Evans 1994; Gilligan 1997; Nielson 2003). Backbenchers, on the other hand, are more short sighted and sensitive to districts' protectionist demands, due to their higher

---

example (see Naoi and Krauss 2009). A loophole of this Japanese regulation exists, however, as discussed later in Chapter 4.

[21] The resource dissipation is not a serious concern for countries endowed with natural resources (see, e.g., Ross 1999; Dunning 2008). Also see footnote 9.

[22] i denotes the location of district on X-axis of Figure 1.6.

Building Open Economy Coalitions

level of electoral insecurity. Given these tensions, how do party leaders overcome this collective action problem and build a majority coalition?

Exit, Voice, and Loyalty of Legislators: Formal and Informal Majority Requirements

Once party leaders decide to lower the barriers to trade, legislators facing the electoral costs of liberalization (district $i < a$) have three options: exit, voice, or loyalty.[23] First, legislators can break away from the party over the policy disagreement ("exit") and either form a new party or join the opposition. This will lead to a decreased share of seats for the incumbent party. Second, legislators can vote against the legislation on the floor ("voice"). This will lead to decreased Yea votes for the bill on the floor. Finally, legislators can follow the party line and vote for the liberalization ("loyalty").

Party leaders prefer that backbenchers stay "loyal" to ensure majority support for their legislation as well as to maintain the party's seat shares. This means that with the formal majority requirements specified by state constitutions (point b, which also denotes MR, i.e., a majority requirement), the party leaders need to buy off legislators between points a and b (Figure 1.6). Moreover, even if a liberalization proposal does not formally require a majority of votes in the legislature (e.g., the executive decides whether to lift import quota restrictions), the party leaders still have incentives to mitigate the electoral costs of legislators located in the area $i < a$ to make them stay within the party. In other words, in political systems in which party switching and breakups are prevalent, the informal threat of exit by the ruling party's legislators can prompt party leaders to mitigate the electoral costs of liberalization, just as the formal majority requirements defined by state constitutions do (more detailed discussion on the nonlegislative route for liberalization in the text that follows).

Given these incentives of party leaders and backbenchers, what is the cost of effectively using the government's budget to mitigate the electoral costs to individual legislators in the area $i < a$? The most efficient use of government resources is to target side payments to fence-sitters, namely, legislators who are representing districts *between* points a and b. This is so for two reasons. First, because net income loss from liberalization is relatively small in these districts, legislators are more likely to support a liberalization bill if enticed with particularistic benefits than legislators representing districts with big net income losses (e.g., district $i < b$). In other words, the same amount of a budget can buy off a larger number of legislators in districts between points a and b than in districts $i < b$.[24] Second, the legislator- or district-specific, targeted

---

[23] Hirschman (1970); Kato (1998).

[24] Why would party leaders not buy off open economy supporters to legislate protectionist policies? Figure 1.6 suggests that the process of buying support (to the left or to the right of a dividing point a) is symmetric and thus the vote buying process can go either direction. Yet,

Optimal Use of Pork, Policy, and Institutional Reforms

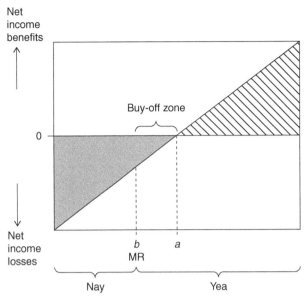

FIGURE 1.6. The GL and legislators' position-taking.
Note: MR denotes majority requirement in the legislature.

benefits, such as personnel appointments and pork barrel projects, can prevent the free-riding of legislators through monitoring, that is, legislators receive the side payments but do not vote in support of the liberalization bill. The targeted benefits also solve the similar free-riding problem among constituents. They facilitate the legislators' monitoring of constituents to ensure that voters support legislators in exchange of the material benefits. Finally, the party should target particularistic benefits to co-partisan legislators to maintain the party's seat shares in a parliament.

Particularistic benefits, such as infrastructure projects and the promotion of legislators to higher ranking positions in the party, can mitigate the losses through two distinct mechanisms: (1) income substitution effects for industries and voters; and (2) credit-claiming and rent-extraction effects for legislators. First, from the perspective of industry and workers, particularistic projects can mitigate income loss by generating new jobs and capital investment. From the perspective of legislators, these particularistic benefits give them a way to

---

party leaders are more likely to buy off support from protectionist legislators (i.e., legislators located to the left of the point *a*) because party leaders are more concerned than backbenchers with (i) improvement of citizens' welfare through an open economy and (ii) securing the government's resources for political mobilization and redistribution via economic growth in the long run. See Chapter 6 on the Thai case, where party leaders sought to buy off support for protectionist legislations.

"save face," that is, credibly claim credit in the face of losing a battle against pro-liberalization groups. The public work project or a legislator's promotion to higher and more visible position in the government can also mobilize votes and campaign donations from constituents. Thus, particularistic benefits can help both vote-seeking and rent-seeking legislators, who incur the electoral costs of liberalization, survive the next election.

The distributional implication of this optimal use of side payments is that small net losers from a global economy (e.g., electoral districts located $b < i < a$), not big net losers, will receive more particularistic benefits. Furthermore, among small net losers, organized interests (such as industries), rather than diffused interests (such as unorganized workers), will receive more side payments, as party leaders can better manage free-riding problems by legislators (i.e., receiving side payments without supporting the legislation). Finally, because party leaders are concerned about seat shares, they are more likely to target the side payment to co-partisan legislators. Legislative majorities, not minorities, will receive more side payments (Diermeier and Feddersen 1998).

In sum, from the perspective of incumbent party leaders, the optimal use of particularistic benefits to build majoritarian coalitions for an open economy is to target (1) fence-sitters of liberalization (small net losers, in terms of income losses, located between points a and b); (2) concentrated rather than diffused interests;[25] and (3) co-partisan legislators. I call this hypothesis, "Optimal Use of Pork."

The Second Puzzle: Pork or Policy?

The theory of optimal use of pork developed in the preceding text suggests that particularistic benefits are generally the most efficient way to build a majority coalition for an open economy for their targetability and ability to prevent free-riding. Yet, a government sometimes adopts policies that broadly benefit diffused losers, who are spread across many electoral districts, such as small and medium-sized firms or low-skilled workers, despite their inefficiency. Why?

This section argues that the government chooses Policy that broadly benefits diffuse losers to build majority support for liberalization when (1) the losers are vast in number and diffused across districts and/or fiscal resource is constrained; and (2) party systems are centralized (i.e., fewer parties in a government). I call this hypothesis, "Optimal Use of Policy over Pork."

The first condition makes the costs of Pork become prohibitively expensive for the government (the demand-side condition) because of a larger number of legislators to be bought off. Appeasing a vast number of losers with

---

[25] In this argument, the size of income loss from liberalization is orthogonal to whether an industry is organized or diffused. See Chapters 5 and 6 for the industry case studies.

Optimal Use of Pork, Policy, and Institutional Reforms

broad policy programs is more cost efficient even if some free-riding occurs. The second condition, centralized party systems can change the relative costs and effectiveness of Pork vs. Policy strategy to buy off legislators' support and influence party leader's choices. Party systems – especially the number of parties in the government – influence the party leader's choice between Pork vs. Policy by changing the costs of intraelite bargaining over the government resource. I elaborate on each point in the text that follows.

When Pork Becomes Too Costly

The Demand-Side Condition: Diffused Losers

Figure 1.7 describes the liberalization case where the vast number of voters who lose from liberalization is spread across electoral districts (I call these voters "diffused losers"). Diffused losers arise under three conditions: economic shocks interacting with economic characteristics of constituents (e.g., consumers who suffered from inflation during energy crises);[26] fiscal constraints; and the geographic size of the electoral district (e.g., a larger electoral district encompasses more diverse losers).[27] Point b is the majority requirement to pass the liberalization law. The party leaders must buy off much larger numbers of legislators to pass the liberalization bill (the area between points a and b). Pork, in this scenario, can become prohibitively expensive.

Even if party leaders can target Pork to legislators representing districts between points a and b by expanding the Pork budget, the expected reward in exchange (i.e., legislators' support for an open economy legislation) might not be forthcoming for two reasons. First, collective action is inherently harder for the larger number of legislators. Second, with Pork that broadly benefits many legislators, party leaders cannot effectively monitor or enforce beneficiaries of a policy to reward the party with votes.

---

[26] I do not intend to argue here that the economic characteristic of an industry is independent of politics. Industries such as steel and automobile have fewer and larger firms that are more geographically concentrated. Pork is more efficient if losers are contained in a few electoral districts. See Uriu (1996). The politics can also shape the economic characteristic of an industry – for instance, the land reform enacted by the Allied Occupation in postwar Japan vastly increased the number of farmers and decreased the average size of farmland.

[27] Cox (1987). Countries such as Japan, Italy, New Zealand, and Thailand all went through electoral reform from a MMD to a mixed system of SMDs with PR during the mid-1990s. As a result, a Lower House legislator in Japan must campaign for a district that is on average 170 percent larger in its geographic size, with more diverse constituents for each member of parliament. Furthermore, PR systems either use the nationwide electoral district or regional blocks that encompass much larger geographic areas than MMD systems. A government with a larger geographic size of electoral districts per seat, such as Japan and Thailand after their electoral reforms (1996 and 2001 respectively), is more likely to use Policy over Pork to build a majority coalition for an open economy.

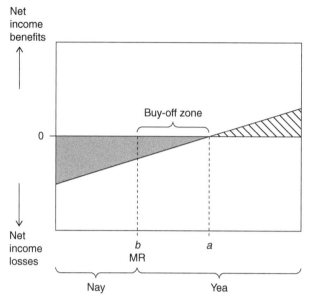

FIGURE 1.7. Pork becomes too expensive with diffused losers.
Note: MR denotes the majority requirement in legislature.

The Dilemma: Pork Is Too Costly, but Policy Is Undersupplied

While the diffused losers and large electoral districts can make Pork too costly for the party leaders, Policy favoring diffused losers is often undersupplied. Governments tend to undersupply Policy because backbenchers who have electorally benefited from Pork would oppose the government's resource shift to Policy.[28] The party leaders often lack power or disciplinary tools to whip into line the backbenchers who oppose the shift to Policy.

The undersupply of Policy for diffused losers can lead to the backrush against liberalization, as seen in Japanese consumer's organized meetings and protests on inflation during the energy crises in 1970s and Thai farmers' protests on the street after the Asian financial crisis (see Chapter 3). This presents a classic collective goods dilemma, because although the incumbent legislators are collectively better off by switching to Policy during hard times, a loss of Pork to mobilize votes and campaign contributions makes some legislators worse off. This dilemma is magnified under a candidate-centered electoral system, in which voters cast votes on individual candidates and their achievements in districts (such as their levels of constituency service), rather than on achievements of political parties and their policy platforms.

---

[28] The discussion on the trade-off between Pork vs. Policy here assumes that governments are facing a certain degree of budget constraints (Ramseyer and Rosenbluth 2009).

Optimal Use of Pork, Policy, and Institutional Reforms

A quintessential example of such a candidate-centered system is MMD system used in countries such as Italy, Japan, Thailand, and New Zealand until the mid-1990s. Under the MMD system, a district elects multiple candidates and same-party candidates often compete for seats. The intraparty competition for seats means that legislators' political survival rests on their local reputation in districts via constituency service rather than the party's national-level reputation. Candidate-centered electoral systems are thus associated with public policies favoring narrow and parochial interests over broader constituents (McCubbins and Rosenbluth 1995; Tatebayashi 2004; Hirano 2006). Under such systems, legislators have little incentives to give up their shares of Pork for Policy, or to follow party leaders' lead to enact Policy favoring diffused losers.

Moreover, unlike Pork, which comes with its ability to exclude and closely monitor its beneficiaries,[29] Policy does not prevent legislator free-riding. Legislators who voted against liberalization can also receive the policy benefits. The free-riding problem can also be prevalent among constituents – because enforcing the exchange of votes and Policy is difficult with a large number of voters, voters can receive the policy benefits without voting for the incumbent.

Given these challenges, how can party leaders shift resource allocation from Pork to Policy and make backbenchers follow the shift? A conventional answer to this question is to strengthen party discipline and punish those who oppose the shift. Yet, disciplining alone does not ensure the political survival of backbenchers whose electoral success dependent on Pork. Whipping could also backfire, leading to unhappy backbenchers leaving the party. Thus, instead of whipping, the party leaders must substitute the loss of Pork with other perks – such as a promise of high positions in the party or access to rents – to make backbenchers happily stay with the party.

I argue that centralized party systems, in which there are fewer parties in the government, are associated with the use of Policy over Pork because of its relative ease in striking an intraelite bargain over new resource allocation. This is so for two reasons. First, the costs of bargaining over resource allocation are easier with a fewer number of parties, especially in a single-party government, because the costs of bargaining over resources are internalized within the party (Bawn and Rosenbluth 2006). By contrast, party leaders in a multiparty coalition government have to strike bargains with other parties as well as within the party, which substantially raises the costs of bargaining over resources. Second, in centralized party systems, such as under a single-party government, party leaders can generate other perks (e.g., personnel promotions and rents) that could compensate for the loss of Pork and help backbenchers survive elections. These other perks can also regulate backbenchers' fights over budgets and induce their collective decisions to give up shares of Pork. Multiparty coalition

---

[29] Stokes (2005); Keefer and Vlaicu (2008).

26   *Building Open Economy Coalitions*

governments have more difficulty coming up with common sets of perks that could substitute the loss of Pork for backbenchers.[30]

This argument about party systems stands in stark contrast with the voluminous literature linking a variety of electoral systems with governments' economic policies favoring broad versus narrow constituents (Cox 1987; Rogowski and Kayser 2002). I argue that electoral systems are neither a necessary nor sufficient explanation for the party leaders' choice between Pork versus Policy to build the majority coalition. Although electoral systems can influence which constituent's interests legislators represent and the power balance between party leaders and backbenchers (i.e., the strength of party discipline), they do not account for the costs of intraelites bargaining (Bawn and Rosenbluth 2006). Party systems, defined here as the number of parties in a government, affect the costs, and ultimately account for the party leaders' coalition-building strategies.

In sum, the rise of diffused losers and the centralized party systems account for the government's use of Policy over Pork.

The Third Puzzle: Institutional Reforms

The third puzzle is why party leaders use institutional reforms to buy off backbenchers' support for an open economy. I define institutional reforms as changing the rules of the game in politics rather than changing how government resources are allocated (i.e., Pork or Policy discussed previously). In particular, I focus on institutional reforms that increase the backbenchers' probability of staying with the party even when liberalization is expected to impose political costs (i.e., loss of votes and/or money) on them.

Such reforms are ubiquitous. For instance, an electoral reform from a MMD to a SMD system might improve the chance of top two-party legislators win elections and lower such chance for small-party candidates. The political finance reform that prohibits the contribution from labor unions might help the electoral success of conservative party candidates by reducing the organized power of labor unions. Party leaders can also change internal rules within a party, such as personnel promotion and committee assignments to improve backbenchers' chance of winning elections (Pekkanen et al. 2006) or to make otherwise unhappy backbenchers stay with the party for promotions (Kawato 1996; Nemoto et al. 2008). Whatever the stated rationale for these reforms might be (e.g., campaign finance reform aims to limit corruption), these reforms can buy off legislators' support for an open economy by compensating their loss of votes and rents incurred by the liberalization.

Use of these institutional reforms is a puzzle. Institutional reforms are a much costlier and riskier strategy for party leaders to build a majority coalition

---

[30] Bawn and Rosenbluth (2006).

Optimal Use of Pork, Policy, and Institutional Reforms 27

for an open economy, because institutions are much harder to change than Pork or Policy. Pork, such as public works projects, can be given or taken away each fiscal year.[31] A policy reversal is more costly than Pork as it usually requires a majority support in parliament, yet legislators can still tailor how policy is delivered – through its budget allocation and implementation (see Chapters 3 and 6). Institutional reforms lack this flexibility precisely because the agents of reform themselves (i.e., legislators) are heavily vested in existing rules. Institutional reforms are also politically costly because they can increase the chance of electoral survival of some legislators while decreasing the chance for others.[32]

Yet, party leaders sometimes resort to institutional reforms to buy off legislator support and build the coalition for an open economy. What are conditions under which this occurs? I argue that Institutional Reforms to compensate legislators' electoral losses are chosen over Pork or Policy when (1) uncertainty regarding future resource availability is high, which increases party leaders' incentives to renege on Pork or Policy promises and (2) party systems is centralized (i.e., a fewer number of parties in the government). I call this hypothesis, "Optimal Use of Institutional Reforms" and elaborate each point below.

I first consider two distinct advantages of using institutional reforms over Pork or Policy. One is that institutional commitments are best suited when the party leader's incentives to renege on Pork or Policy promises with backbenchers are prevalent. When are party leader incentives to renege prevalent? Such incentives to renege are strong when there is high uncertainty regarding the future availability of fiscal resources for Pork or Policy. A variety of factors can generate such fiscal uncertainty, such as exogenous economic shocks (e.g., exchange rate fluctuation, energy crisis, etc.) and domestic political economy (e.g., aging society). Institutional reforms bind the party leaders' promises to backbenchers and make them stay with the party in the face of losses incurred by the liberalization.

Yet, precisely because institutional reforms aim to affect legislators' political survival, party leaders are often unable to act collectively. Centralized party systems, that is, a fewer number of parties in a government, again facilitate institutional reforms because of the lower costs of intraelite bargaining over the new rules of the game. A single-party government, for instance, can essentially create and enforce new rules with intraparty bargaining, whereas a multiparty coalition government must strike a bargain with a larger number of actors.

In sum, party leaders are more likely to choose Institutional Reform over Pork or Policy when fiscal uncertainty makes their Pork or Policy promises not

---

[31] Saito (2009) shows that legislators cannot take away pork once the construction is completed and this accounts for declining LDP votes in areas with high road/transportation densities. My point is that legislators can change allocation of public work projects every fiscal year, but institutional reforms are harder to reverse.

[32] McElwain (2008).

28   *Building Open Economy Coalitions*

credible to backbenchers, and when the costs of intraelite bargaining over new
rules are lower via the centralized party systems.

Summary and Broader Implications

This chapter developed a novel approach to the politics of globalization,
Globalization as Legislation (the GL). The GL approach views the liberalization of foreign trade as a series of "general interest legislation" in which
legislators collectively benefit from passing the legislation but the electoral
costs and benefits are distributed unevenly among individual legislators. This
approach highlights the classic collective goods dilemma, whereby the government is unable to legislate many, if not any, liberalization bills, when all
legislators take policy positions that sincerely reflect their districts' interests.
Candidate-centered electoral systems, such as MMD systems, have been understood to worsen this classic collective goods dilemma. Yet, even during economic down times, some countries with candidate-centered electoral systems,
such as Japan and Thailand, have shown little sign of protectionist backlash
and have continued to liberalize trade.

To solve this puzzle, I developed a typology of three strategies – *Pork*, *Policy*,
and *Institutional Reforms* – that illustrates how party leaders build majority coalitions supporting an open economy. These three strategies help party
leaders build an open economy coalition by mitigating the electoral costs of
liberalization that is imposed on some legislators. The primary goal of these
strategies is to help *legislators* representing losing districts to survive in subsequent elections, rather than to save declining *industries*. Thus, party leaders
distribute compensation not based on the industries' sheer economic needs,
that is, the size of their income loss from liberalization. Rather, it is based
on the political needs of party leaders and backbenchers, that is, how best to
allocate government resources to prevent defections on the floor (i.e., voting
against the liberalization bill), party breakups, and declining votes. In a nut-
shell, policy-, and seat-maximizing incentives of party leaders affect legislators'
policy-positioning on globalization through leaders' allocation of government
resources.

The three hypotheses derived from this approach – *Optimal Use of
Pork*, *Policy*, and *Institutional Reforms* – predict how some countries with
"protectionism-friendly political institutions" are able to build stable majority
support for the open economy. Furthermore, answering this question helps us
solve some additional puzzles left unexplained by the existing approaches to
legislators' position-taking: why legislator position-taking often deviates from
their districts' interests (i.e., the electoral disconnection) and why the government's compensation does not always favor the big net losers of globalization.

The approach shows that from the party leader's perspective, the marginal
utility of a coalition-building strategy (Pork, Policy, or Institutional Reforms)

Optimal Use of Pork, Policy, and Institutional Reforms 29

does not differ between developed and developing economies (or countries with different factor endowments). The instrument choice is a function of how much legislative support party leaders can buy with the fiscal resources at hand, given the costs of coordination and bargaining among elites. Accordingly, countries' differences in factor endowments (or comparative advantage) only gives rise to different profiles of liberalization losers (e.g., manufacturing vs. agriculture) and thus different constituents and legislator profiles of who gets what side payments. The logic of buying off legislator support stays the same.

The broader implications of the GL approach, beyond the politics of globalization, are twofold. First, Pork does not necessarily emerge in economically poor (or rural), or politically backward regions, contrary to the conventional wisdom (Stokes 2005; Scheiner 2006; Keefer 2007; Keefer and Vlaicu 2008) (see Chapter 2 for more details). The GL approach predicts that party leaders use Pork to convince legislators who are sitting on the fence regarding liberalization and highlights two puzzles about pork barrel politics that are left untreated by domestic theories.

The first puzzle is why pork barrel politics is prevalent in urban and industrial areas in some countries, while in others it is more common in rural and agricultural areas. The second is why we often observe a shift in how governments allocate pork barrel projects *over time* in a country without major institutional changes such as electoral reform. The Japanese government's Pork allocation shifted from an urban to a rural bias in the late 1960s, for instance, without changes in its government's partisanship or electoral systems. The Thai government had ignored rural areas for a long time until the single-party majority of the Thai Rak Thai party took hold in the 2001 (Chapter 3).

The GL approach unravels these puzzles by showing that losers of the open economy emerge in urban versus rural areas depending on the factor endowments of a given country (e.g., "losers" of globalization emerge in urban and industrial areas in developing economies while they emerge in rural and agricultural areas in developed economies). The GL also accounts for the shift in pork allocation within a country over time. As Chapter 2 demonstrates, the Japanese government exposed small net losers to trade liberalization first (i.e., urban and industrial areas) and big net losers later (i.e., rural and agricultural areas). The government's allocation of pork followed this sequence by first targeting the urban and industrial areas and then shifted to rural areas.

Second, party leader control over sufficient fiscal resources is necessary for Pork or Policy strategies to work in democracies – it is electorally too costly to undergo liberalization without distributing side payments that can offset the legislators' electoral costs. An important policy implication is that it is politically too costly for governments to simultaneously exercise strict budgetary discipline and liberalize their economies. Accordingly, the IMF and World Bank should not push for fiscal reform and economic liberalization at the same time – these neoliberal reforms, even if there is a consensus on their

30 *Building Open Economy Coalitions*

respective benefits, should be sequenced (liberalization first and fiscal discipline next) to allow party leaders to build the necessary majority coalitions for an open economy.

THE EMPIRICAL SCOPE OF THE BOOK AND ITS GENERALIZABILITY

Finally, I discuss the theoretical and empirical scope of this book and the generalizability of my argument beyond the cases addressed here. First, the GL approach is applicable to both presidential and parliamentary systems (see Evans 2004). I chose to test the GL approach with two parliamentary systems, in part to hold the political institutions relatively constant, but also because the politics of globalization has been vastly understudied in parliamentary settings compared to presidential systems (see Gilligan 1997 and Hiscox 1999 on the United States and Nielson 2003 on Latin America). Moreover, existing studies on the United States tend to focus on one institutional reform that directly changed the trade-policymaking process, that is, the Reciprocal Trade Agreement Act (RTAA). However, such direct reforms on trade policymaking are rare around the world, while trade liberalization has been ubiquitous. The GL approach closes this gulf.

Two institutional characteristics of parliamentary systems, however, merit further discussion here: the vote of no-confidence procedure and parliamentary dissolution. The vote of no-confidence procedure, where legislators can directly vote on a government's survival (Huber 1996), is believed to increase party cohesion in parliamentary systems (e.g., less defection by backbenchers) (Diermeier and Feddersen 1998). This is because, with the existence of this procedure (even without invoking it), party leaders can tie the fate of the government with the fate of legislation and raise the costs of defection by backbenchers. By voting against the ruling coalition, backbenchers will lose the incumbent benefits derived from being in the ruling coalition (e.g., electoral advantage, rents, personnel appointments, etc.). Parliamentary dissolution, where the prime minister can call for an election, can also tie the fate of the government with the fate of legislation. The implications of these procedures for building the majority coalition is that they allow party leaders to buy backbencher support for legislation at a much cheaper cost than without the presence of this procedure (Diermeier and Feddersen 1998). Moreover, with the existence of these procedures, scholars have predicted that side-payment allocation should favor legislative majorities (i.e., those who are in the ruling coalition). Empirical tests of these claims, however, are beyond the scope of this book because they would require the controlled comparison of parliamentary and presidential systems with careful attention to identification and measurement issues.

Second, the GL can be applied to other policy issues beyond globalization as long as legislating the given policy presents a collective goods dilemma for party leaders and legislators: that is, legislators are collectively better off in the

Optimal Use of Pork, Policy, and Institutional Reforms

long run by legislating the bill, but some legislators incur short-term electoral losses. This book focuses primarily on trade liberalization but includes some discussion of the liberalization of foreign direct investment (Chapter 6), which, along with trade liberalization, is one of the three pillars of globalization (the third pillar, which this book does not explore, is migration). Policy issues that are characterized by the collective goods dilemma are numerous: deregulation and regulation of producers, privatization and nationalization of public utilities, taxation, welfare, security policies, and so on.

Third, this book analyzes fiscally centralized systems, Japan and Thailand, where the key parameter that affects party leaders' bargain over fiscal resources is the party systems (i.e., the number of parties in a government, especially a single-party vs. multiparty coalition).[33] Decentralized fiscal systems, such as federalism, can introduce two additional complexities into the GL approach. First, the GL would predict that the lack of fiscal resources for the central government is likely to lead party leaders to use Institutional Reforms over Pork or Policy. Second, even when the central government has sufficient fiscal resources, federalism skews the political rewards of Pork allocation by over-representing some constituencies in the national legislature (Gibson and Calvo 2000 on Argentina). Testing these predictions, however, is beyond the scope of this book.

---

[33] Both Japan and Thailand went through fiscal decentralization reforms, Thailand in the late 1990s and Japan in the early 2000s. Yet, the effect has been moderate – for example, the proportion of fiscal revenues raised by local governments increased from 30 percent to 40 percent in Japan after the reform, yet 60 percent of revenues on average still come from the central government. See Ministry of Finance (2007), http://www.mof.go.jp/pri/research/conference/zko58/zko58b.pdf. Thailand's Decentralization Act (1999) mandates that local revenues must increase from 25 percent to 35 percent of total government revenues by the year 2006, and even if they are achieved, the proportion is still much lower than fiscally decentralized economies such as that of the United States, where local governments raise more than 60 percent of revenues.

PART II

EMPIRICAL EVIDENCE

2

Use of Pork as a Side Payment

This chapter tests the Optimal Use of Pork hypothesis developed in the previous chapter using commodity and district-level data on import liberalization in Japan and Thailand during the decade following each country's accession to General Agreement on Tariffs and Trade (GATT) (1955–1965 for Japan and 1980–1988 for Thailand).[1] Building a majority coalition for liberalization is the most difficult during the early phases, owing to the general lack of consensus among elites over the benefits of liberalization as well as the resistance from vested protectionist interests.

During the respective decades, the two countries reduced a substantial portion of trade barriers unilaterally. Although pressure from the United States and multilateral organizations (e.g., GATT and International Monetary Fund [IMF]) gave an initial impetus for domestic policymakers to liberalize trade, Japan and Thailand both exceeded their expectations and demands. After Japan's accession to GATT in 1955, its government doubled its "import liberalization ratio" – that is, percentage of total imported goods (in value terms) imported without a government license, permission, or foreign exchange allocation quota[2] – from 42 percent to 92 percent in a mere three years.[3]

---

[1] Thailand's accession to GATT was in 1982. In this chapter, I focus on the period from 1980 to 1988, when Prime Minister Prem's cabinets ruled Thailand, because it allows me to hold prime ministership and institutional settings (i.e., semidemocracy with unelected prime minister and some cabinet members and elected legislators) relatively constant and test the effects of electoral and coalitional politics on trade liberalization.

[2] I discuss foreign exchange allocation system, which served as a de facto import restriction in Japan until 1964, in detail later. See Okazaki (2010).

[3] The import liberalization ratio was calculated for 1960, when the Japanese government announced the "Trade and Exchange Liberalization Plan," and for 1963. In the context of the foreign exchange allocation system, this means that 92 percent of commodities in 1963 were under "automatic allocation" (AA system) where industries freely import without the government's permission. See Okazaki (2011).

35

36 *Empirical Evidence*

After Thailand's accession to GATT in 1982, its government also achieved a 92 percent import liberalization ratio within a decade, requiring the remaining 8 percent of commodities, such as automobiles, motorcycles, chemical manufacturing, and rice and sugar to obtain import licenses as of 1991.

The dramatic liberalization is a puzzle in light of Japan's and Thailand's electoral systems – that is, "protectionism-friendly," multimember district (MMD) electoral systems, and fluid party systems at that time. A half year preceding its accession to GATT, Japan had just experienced the unification of the left parties, which was immediately followed by the merger of two conservative parties (1955). The party mergers fueled intraparty fights among factions seeking votes, campaign donations, and ministerial appointments. Intraparty competition within the Liberal Democratic Party (LDP) and powerful left posed a challenge for majority coalition-building in the parliament. Thailand in the 1980s was also characterized by high political uncertainty, with attempted coups, party breakups, and coalitional changes in the multiparty coalition government.

Yet, the archival research discussed in detail later suggests that the liberalization faced much less opposition than expected. How did party leaders in these two countries achieve this? Conventional wisdom suggests that the insulation of trade policymaking from the special-interest groups and electorates, in the form of delegation from legislatures to bureaucracies and to executives, was a key to Japan's and Thailand's trade liberalization ("the insulation thesis").[4]

Contrary to the insulation thesis, this chapter shows, using new commodity and district-level data on import liberalization, that party leaders in Japan and Thailand had a large influence over which commodities to liberalize and when. This is surprising, because in both Japan and Thailand, the bulk of early trade liberalization went through executive routes requiring only cabinet approval, and not requiring the majority approval from legislators. Despite the lack of formal majority requirements, party leaders' calculations for the majority coalition-building with legislators – that is, securing the majority seat shares and helping backbenchers survive elections – still dictated the government's

---

[4] See Johnson (1982); Lawrence and Weinstein (2001); Pekkanen (2003); and Okazaki (2011) on Japan, and Doner and Laothamatas (1994) on Thailand. Analyzing the patterns of various governments' support to industries (subsidies and tariffs, etc.) during the same time period, Pekkanen (2003) shows that economic criteria account for the pattern of protection, but political strength of industries does not. My analysis differs from Pekkanen's (2003) in two important respects. First, because legislators are likely to respond to district demands for free trade or protectionism, I use measures of trade liberalization at prefectural levels and match them with political data, such as electoral results and percentage of the LDP seats at the prefecture. These prefectural-level measures differ from Pekkanen (2003), which measured trade protection and industry's political strength at the national level. Second, I analyze not just the cross-sectional levels of protection at a time t, but also their changes over time (i.e., how changes in electoral environment in districts as well as changes in ruling coalition at the national level affects changes in the levels of protection) (Angrist and Pischke 2008).

Use of Pork as a Side Payment   37

liberalization decisions and side-payment allocations, as predicted by the Optimal Use of Pork hypothesis developed in Chapter 1.

Second, the Japanese and Thai governments scheduled "fence-sitters" of trade liberalization for early liberalization, that is, labor-intensive manufacturing industries that would incur small net losses from liberalization, not those who would have incurred big losses. Consequently, despite their difference in comparative advantage (factor endowment) at this time, in both Japan and Thailand, industries located in more urban and industrial regions were first exposed to trade liberalization after their accession to GATT.

Third, consistent with the Optimal Use of Pork hypothesis (see Chapter 1), both governments allocated pork barrel projects to buy off support from the fence-sitting legislators representing urban and industrial areas where the manufacturing trade losers were concentrated. The urban bias in pork barreling in both Japan (developed economy) and Thailand (developing economy) challenges the conventional view that pork barrel is more prevalent in rural and poor areas. Instead, the findings suggest that urban bias in pork barreling can occur when the party leaders are policy-seeking, not necessarily vote- or office-seeking. They allocate Pork to hold the majority coalition together and to buy support from legislators for a liberalization policy.

Also consistent with the second condition for the Optimal Use of Pork (i.e., Pork is effective when losers are organized and concentrated), the Thai government did not use Pork to compensate rural legislators representing a vast number of farmers ("diffused losers"). Instead, the Thai government used broader Policy (tariffs and subsidization for agricultural commodities) to reward rural legislators who stayed with the ruling coalition, and punish those who broke away from it. This lends support to the co-partisan hypothesis in Optimal Use of Pork. I elaborate each finding in detail in the text that follows.

JAPAN'S COALITION-BUILDING FOR OPEN ECONOMY: 1955–1965

Political Economic Structure after World War II

Japan's political economy structure was highly in flux and fluid after its defeat in World War II, which made the party leaders' majority coalition-building for open economy challenging.[5] The Occupational Force, mostly led by the United States, implemented a series of domestic reforms to diffuse and decentralize the previously concentrated power structure, with an understanding that Japan's oligopolistic market structure led to its past militarism. Two noteworthy reforms were the dissolution of oligopolistic family firms (*zaibatsu*) (1945–1952) and agrarian reform (1947), which granted land ownership to tenant farmers. These reforms diffused the concentration of power from big capitalists and landowners to small

---

[5] Noguchi (1995) argued that the structures of the Japanese economy and interest groups were carried over from the wartime (i.e., 1940 system) to the postwar period.

38 Empirical Evidence

and medium-sized firms and small landowners. As a result, the sheer number of interest groups that sought to influence policymaking increased.

The Occupational Force also increased the power of interest groups in the political market. The Occupation helped the previously powerless labor unions develop enterprise-based unions and facilitated their centralization into three national centers between 1948 and 1954.[6] Five business associations, such as the Japan Society of Commerce and Industry and the National Banking Association, formed the Federation of Economic Organization (*Keidanren*) in 1946 to represent big business interests and influence public policy after the dissolution of *Zaibatsu*.[7]

The diffusion of economic power in the market occurred in tandem with the revival of the prewar MMD system. In the 1947 election, the ruling Liberal Party adopted the prewar MMD system with single nontransferable vote (SNTV).[8] The combination of an MMD system and a decentralized interest group structure in the market further fueled special-interest politics.[9] The report of the 1946 and 1947 elections under the MMD system, for instance, suggests that interest groups sought to influence politics directly by running their members for elections and by mobilizing support for the party and candidates.

The Rise of Intraparty Competition and Factional Fights

The half year preceding Japan's accession to GATT in 1955 was the historical moment of party unification and the emergence of intraparty competition. In the 1955 Lower House election, the two left parties (left vs. right Socialist Parties) won 156 of 467 seats and decided to unify into a single party.[10] The unification of the left led to the merger of the two conservative parties, the

---

[6] These were the General Council of Trade Unions (Sohyo; 1952), Industrial-level Labor Unions (Sanbetsu; 1948), and Association of National Labor Union (Zen-rou Kaigi, later Doumei; 1954). See Kume (1998).

[7] Soma (1977: 256).

[8] Initially, the Occupational Force instituted a multimember electoral system with limited voting in which the prefecture was an electoral district and voters could cast several votes for different candidates. The larger constituent size and the limited voting were intended to insulate legislators from the pressures from organized interests. Yet, the plural ballot system benefited the Japanese Communist Party, because many electorates voted for the conservative and the left. Soma (1977: 256).

[9] In other words, during the prewar era, political parties were captured by a fewer number of interest groups: *Zaibatsu* represented the centralized and concentrated business interests, big landowners represented farm interests, and voting rights were given only to men older than the age twenty-five. The MMD, which encourages special-interest politics, truly became a mirror image of the decentralized structure of economic interests in the market after the General Headquarter (GHQ)'s reforms.

[10] The rise of the left was partly due to socioeconomic changes (i.e., urbanization and industrialization) and also to highly educated voters' sympathy toward communist and socialist ideology (Soma 1977: 365–368, 378–390).

Use of Pork as a Side Payment 39

Liberal Party (*Jiyū Tō*) and the Democratic Party (*Minshu Tō*), into the Liberal Democratic Party (LDP). This marked the beginning of the thirty-eight years of LDP's one-party dominance (i.e., the 1955 system).

The party unifications that occurred under the MMD system had two implications for legislators' relationship with interest groups. First, intraparty competition under an MMD increased the costs of elections. It fueled legislators' incentives to mobilize votes and political donations from organized interests.[11] Second, the party merger gave rise to intraparty factions, that is, legislators formed groups with whom they shared ideology, policy agendas, and/or political financiers. By the late 1950s, there were ten factions within the LDP, fiercely competing for votes, campaign donations, factional membership, and cabinet posts.[12] The major cleavage was formed along the career background of legislators, that is, whether they were former technocrats (*kanryo-ha*) or professional legislators (*toujin-ha*).

In sum, the ruling LDP legislators had to fight two political wars simultaneously, one against the rise of a unified left and another against intraparty enemies. There was no established rule to regulate intraparty factional fights at this time yet, such as seniority-based and factional quota allocation rules for cabinet posts. In the face of this dual political uncertainty and the heightened interest group influence, the LDP party leaders built a majority coalition in the parliament to support trade liberalization.

1955–1958: Accession to GATT and Building a Consensus for Trade Liberalization

Japan's accession to GATT in 1955 was a much less polarizing issue in the Japanese parliament than what trade theorems would predict,[13] for three reasons. First, the Japanese government and citizens were anxious to "rejoin the international community" after the defeat in World War II. Joining GATT thus was perceived as something in Japan's national interest. Consequently, in the elites' and citizens' discourse regarding GATT at that time, there was much less focus on the distributional consequences of joining – that is, who benefits and loses from trade liberalization. Moreover, the Japanese government and exporting industries both believed that GATT would give them better and

---

[11] *Kokusei Senkyo to Seitou Seiji*. Ibid. Cox and Rosenbluth (1993); Kawato (2005).

[12] On factional politics in Japanese party systems, see Cox and Rosenbluth (1993); Kawato (1996a, 1996b); McCubbins and Thies (1997).

[13] Despite Occupational Force's encouragement for Japan to join GATT, the government postponed its decision making in an effort to avoid negotiating the accession under Occupation rule. The Japanese government understood that tariff structures negotiated through GATT accession would have a long-term impact on its economy, and thus it was best to wait until Japan regained its sovereignty in 1952. In 1951, when another defeated nation West Germany joined GATT and Japan regained its sovereignty, the time was ripe for Japanese policymakers to prepare for accession.

40   *Empirical Evidence*

fairer terms of trade through the most-favored nation principle than through bilateral trade negotiations.[14]

Second, the "biggest potential losers" predicted by the Stolper–Samuelson theorem (i.e., agriculture) were relatively shielded from the concession. The government was able to retain rights to decide tariff rates for flour, barley, and wheat for the foreseeable future and to keep ongoing tariff rates for soy, dairy, and corn.[15] As a result, agricultural interests considered the GATT tariff negotiations to be a big success. The fishery industry, by contrast, benefited the most from the accession, as a result of the tariff reduction for canned tuna, clams, oysters, and such among the GATT member states.[16] Automobile and industrial machinery manufacturers opposed trade liberalization because of their infant industry status, but the GATT tariff concession also reflected these demands. For the automobile industry, the government agreed to lower import tariffs only for large and medium-sized vehicles that did not directly compete against smaller Japanese cars. For industrial machineries, the government managed to keep the ongoing tariff rates for the time being.[17]

Finally, the lack of a protectionist lobby over the GATT concession was due to the existing foreign exchange allocation system (*gaika yosan seido*), which functioned as a de facto import quota restriction. Under the Foreign Exchange and Foreign Trade Administration Law legislated in 1949, the government centralized the foreign exchange budget and allocated this budget to private sector firms based on the balance of payment and industrial policy goals.[18] This foreign exchange allocation in essence determined the amount of imports each firm and industry could engage in. Indeed, after conducting "A survey on the effect of GATT accession" for firms and industry associations, *Keidanren* concluded that because of the existence of the foreign exchange allocation system not many industries raised serious concerns about GATT accession.[19]

After a series of tariff negotiations, GATT officially approved Japan's accession on September 10, 1955. Among 248 commodities that were discussed at the negotiation, the Japanese government lowered tariffs for 75 commodities and kept existing tariff rates in place for 173 commodities.[20] The foreign

---

[14] Akaneya (1992, chapter 3). Exporting industries, especially the textile industry, were competitive abroad and were facing discriminatory protectionism in advanced industrial nations.

[15] Ibid.

[16] Other reported beneficiaries were toy manufacturers, grove manufacturers, and pottery and optical instruments industries. Ibid, and "Gatto kanzei kousho no seika," opinion editorial by Fujino Chujiro, June 11, 1955, *Asahi Shimbun*.

[17] Ibid.

[18] Using a microlevel data on wool industry, Okazaki and Korenaga (1999) found that the allocation of foreign exchange was based on objective economic criteria, rather than on rent-seeking motives of the government.

[19] Okazaki and Korenaga (1999). This system was in place from 1949 to the early 1960s.

[20] Because Japan discussed the rates of the same commodity with multiple member states, the total number of the concession cases was 318, in which the tariff was lowered for 94 cases and kept

Joined GATT – What's Next?

Even after Japan's accession to GATT, policymakers at ministries and industries were yet still predominantly protectionist for two reasons. First, it was partly a response to the uncertainty about whether Western Europe would move forward with trade liberalization.[21] Discussing Western Europe's recovery of currency convertibility, Ministry of International Trade and Industry (MITI)'s Commerce Section reported: "It is risky to immediately associate their liberalization of foreign exchange with liberalization of trade ... as they [European countries] might rather strengthen import restrictions."[22]

Second, the Japanese government considered that "hastening" trade liberalization would hurt the Japanese economy because of insufficient foreign reserves ($862 million as of March 1958) and uncompetitive domestic industries, such as infant industries and small and medium-sized firms. Even Japanese textile industries, perceived then to be sufficiently competitive in the international market, argued that the government should postpone the liberalization of finished textile products and lower the import tariffs only for raw textile materials.[23]

1959: Sea of Change toward Trade Liberalization

A sea of change toward trade liberalization occurred just within a year, with a dramatic increase in Japan's exports to the United States as well as accumulated foreign reserves reaching $1.3 billion (a 66 percent increase from the previous year). As a result, the Japanese government faced new external and internal pressures to lower foreign exchange and trade restrictions. Externally, the U.S. government's demands to lower Japan's trade restriction soared. At the IMF's General Assembly Meeting in October 1959, member states suggested that Japan stop using the balance of payment issues as an excuse for foreign exchange restriction and move on with further liberalization. They also expressed strong dissatisfaction with Japanese Finance Minister Eisaku Sato's proposed liberalization plan, which was to liberalize thirteen more commodities and to prepare for foreign exchange liberalization.[24] At the GATT General

---

as they were for 224 cases. Seventeen GATT member states with which Japan concluded the agreement, lowered tariff for 215 commodities and kept the ongoing rates for 73 commodities. See MITI (1991, Vol. 6, chapter 4).

[21] MITI (1991, Vol. 8, chapter 2).
[22] Ibid., p. 171.
[23] Akaneya (1992: 172).
[24] MITI (1991: Vol. 8: 180).

42 *Empirical Evidence*

Assembly meeting, held in November 1959, member states further pressed Japan to make progress with liberalization.[25]

Domestically, Japan's export-oriented industries began advocating for free trade. *Keidanren* issued a "Resolution Regarding Japanese Business's Determination to Deal with the World's Trend to Liberalize Trade and Our Basic Requests" at their twentieth general meeting. The resolution advocated for deregulation and revision of existing laws that inhibited trade liberalization, such as the Foreign Exchange and Trade Control Law, Anti-monopoly Law, and Export Import Transaction Law. *Keidanren's* Special Committee to Deal with Liberalization conducted hearings with various industries, and the only industries that strongly opposed liberalization were soda and sugar. Other industries accepted that liberalization "could not be avoided."[26] Another business association, *Keizai Douyukai*, also followed the lead: "Even with temporary frictions, we should move forward with trade liberalization – otherwise, we will be left behind the majority of countries in the world. The Japanese economy has enough strength to survive liberalization."[27] Thus, industry's opposition to liberalization was fairly limited.

The LDP leaders quickly responded to the change in industry preferences for liberalization. In April of 1960, the LDP's Kishi Cabinet announced the Foreign Trade and Exchange Liberalization Plan, which aimed to liberalize more than 90 percent of commodities regulated under the foreign exchange allocation system within three years.

Although general support for liberalization emerged, this did not prevent some legislators from opposing liberalization. These oppositions cross-cut the partisan divides – some among the LDP as well as the opposition legislators backed protectionist arguments. The LDP leaders were thus left with the task of building the majority coalition to legislate trade liberalization.

Coalition-Building within the LDP

The LDP under Prime Minister Ikeda Hayato (1960–1964) held a stable, one-party dominance vis-à-vis opposition parties in the Lower House. It survived two general elections (1960 and 1963) and consistently held more than 60 percent of the Lower House seats. The factional competition within the LDP, however, was fierce: three major factions that formed Ikeda's first cabinet (July to November 1960) each held roughly 15 percent of the LDP seats.[28] The intraparty conflict between the ruling coalition of the three factions and others surfaced over personnel appointments as well as over key policy issues such

---

[25] Akaneya (1992: 184).
[26] Ibid, p. 193.
[27] Akaneya (1992: 178–179).
[28] These were Ikeda, Kishi, and Sato factions.

Use of Pork as a Side Payment

as the renewal of the Japan–U.S. Security Treaty.[29] The media described the factional alignment then as the conflict between the ruling coalition of "technocratic group" (*kanryo ha*) versus "professional legislator group" (*toujin ha*), from the career background of these LDP legislators.[30]

Within the LDP, three faction leaders from the professional legislator group explicitly opposed liberalization.[31] Although none of them argued that Japan should keep the economy closed for the long term, they made three claims about slowing down the pace of liberalization. The first argument, made by Kono Ichiro, the leader of the Shunju-kai faction,[32] was the survivability of small and medium-sized companies and farmers in the open economy. He argued that the government should not repeat its history of the 1930s that the impoverishment of farm villages led Japan to engage in a costly war.[33] The second claim, made by all three factional leaders, was that liberalization was being imposed on Japan by the United States, rather than decided voluntarily by the Japanese government and citizens. The government thus should "take liberalization cautiously and slowly" (*shincho ni*). The final claim, made specifically by Matsumura Kenzo and Miki Takeo, was that the Japanese government put too much emphasis on its trade relationship with the United States. Matsumura was especially interested in reopening Japan's trade relations with China.[34]

There were three distinct sources of these three factional leaders' protectionist positions. The first was the interests of the electoral districts each represented. These legislators who voiced the opposition represented electoral districts with industries that the government targeted for early liberalization. Kono Ichiro represented Kanagawa Prefecture's third district, which the government's trade liberalization plan between 1960 and 1964 targeted the most, counting eleven commodities (see details of this plan in the text that follows). Matsumura Kenzo represented Toyama Prefecture's second district, which produced Ferro-Alloy (liberalized in 1962). Miki Takeo represented Tokushima's

---

[29] Nonruling factions within the LDP at that time were Ohno, Kono, Ishii, Matsumura, Miki, and Ishibashi factions.

[30] Pempel (2010); "Bimyo na kankei: Kishi to Kono," August 25, 1959, *Asahi Shimbun*.

[31] "Boueki jiyuka ha shincho ni: Kono-shi 'Ikeda seisaku' wo hihan," *Asahi Shinbun*, p. 2. February 20, 1960.

[32] Kono Ichiro established Shunju-kai in 1956 and it was the largest faction until 1959. He competed against Ikeda Hayato for the LDP's presidency position (i.e., synonymous with the prime minister position under the LDP's one-party dominance) and lost in 1960. Kono then sought to break away from the LDP by establishing a new party, but failed. Kono made up with Prime Minister Ikeda Hayato and was promoted to a Minister of Agriculture and Forestry in July of 1961.

[33] Ibid.

[34] And Matsumura was instrumental in negotiating and concluding the "LT Trade Agreement" (Memorandum on Japan-China Long-Term Comprehensive Trade), which allowed Japan and China to trade through quasi-governmental agencies without normalizing their diplomatic relations. See Soeya (1999).

only MMD where the majority of voters engaged in farming and fishing. In the manufacturing field, the two major sectors of employment were food processing and chemical industries.[35]

Second, these protectionist legislators belonged to minority factions and thus lacked lucrative access to campaign donations from businesses. Because factions expand by mobilizing campaign contributions from industries and by "buying off" additional members from other factions, the largest majority faction in the LDP was usually the faction with the most financial resources (e.g., Ikeda Hayato's Kouchi-kai faction). This means that legislators who belonged to the minority factions weighted votes in their districts more heavily than campaign donations from big businesses, which led to their protectionist positions.[36]

The third source of the opposition was to extract side payments from the party leaders by threatening to break away from the party line. The Kono and Miki factions together held 18 percent of LDP seats (fifty-six seats as of the November 1960 election), which was almost sufficient to take away the LDP's majority party status if they were to break away.[37] The two factions had a track record of defying the party line over controversial legislations, such as the renewal of the Japan–U.S. Security Treaty in 1960.[38] As discussed in detail later, the two factions successfully extracted side payments from the party leaders by opposing trade liberalization and signaling their ability to organize and break away from the party.

Given these oppositions, how did the party leaders design and implement the Foreign Trade and Exchange Liberalization Plan?

Foreign Trade and Exchange Liberalization Plan, 1960

The Foreign Trade and Exchange Liberalization Plan, announced by the Kishi Cabinet in April of 1960, laid out the trade liberalization schedule of seventy-five commodities into four phases:

- Phase 1: Should liberalize as soon as possible.
- Phase 2: Liberalize within three years at the latest.

---

[35] Ministry of Agriculture, Forestry and Fisheries (1960), *Agricultural Census*, and MITI (1960), *Industrial Census*. The three factional leaders were professional legislators (*toujin ha*). They were a new and increasingly powerful group within the LDP, still led by former technocrats who tended to have more conservative policy preferences in security (i.e., reliance on the United States) and economic policy issues (i.e., small government). See Pempel (2010).

[36] Grossman and Helpman (1994).

[37] The LDP held 296 seats of the total 467 seats as of November 1960 election. Thus, the LDP would have lost the dominant party status by losing 63 seats.

[38] The conflict between Kishi and Kono over personnel appointment as well as Japan–U.S. Security Treaty was well documented in the media. See "Bimyo na kankei: Kishi to Kono," August 25, 1959, *Asahi Shimbun*.

Use of Pork as a Side Payment

- Phase 3: Would be difficult to liberalize within three years, but should try to liberalize soon.
- Phase 4: Would be difficult to liberalize for a long period of time.

The Kishi Cabinet's liberalization plan explained the government's economic rationales for categorizing commodities into the four phases as follows. First, lowering the costs of raw materials will have spillover effects on a wide range of industries, and thus the government targets liberalization of industries with a high proportion of raw material input. Second, the government then liberalizes commodities with low import substitutability, such as domestically produced commodities that differ in quality or characteristics from foreign imports, or industries that are competitive in the international market. Third, if a given industry is in the middle of structural reform or currently using policy measures to rationalize itself, the government schedules its liberalization later to allow the restructuring. Fourth, for commodities that are difficult to liberalize soon (i.e., Phase 4), the government will liberalize the commodity when the demands from trading partners are high, or will gradually expand the quantity of import while encouraging liberalization.

Because the Plan required only unanimous cabinet approval and did not require majority approval from the legislatures, scholars have considered the liberalization as an executive achievement, not a legislative triumph.[39] Yet, how the government actually implemented this Plan diverged from the original plan. Among sixty-three commodities discussed, thirty-two were liberalized later than outlined in the plan.

Contrary to the economic rationales of the Plan laid out by the Cabinet, I show that the LDP leaders' strategy for the majority coalition-building dictated both the liberalization Plan and its implementation. The party leaders first scheduled the liberalization of relatively competitive industries (i.e., small net losers) and generously paid side payments, in the form of public work projects and ministerial appointments, to opposing legislators from Miki and Kono factions. By contrast, the party leaders delayed the liberalization of commodities produced in districts where the LDP was losing votes to ensure that the party retained its share of seats in the parliament.

To show this, I leverage the results of three general Lower House elections (1958, 1960, and 1963) that overlapped with the period of liberalization planning (1958–1960) as well as its implementation (1960–1964). Because the timing of import liberalization is critical to estimate the effects of election results on the implementation, I used the official government's daily announcement of import liberalization (*yunyu kohyo*) available at the government's Official Gazette (*kanpou*) used in Okazaki (2011).[40] I matched six-digit (Harmonized Commodity Description and Coding System [HS] code) commodity-level data

---

[39] Okazaki (2010); Pekkanen (2003).
[40] I thank Professor Okazaki for generously sharing the data.

of liberalization with 1959's Industrial Census (*kogyo toukei*) and Agricultural and Forestry Census to identify the prefecture with the highest production or shipping values of a given commodity.

The higher the number of commodities that were liberalized in a prefecture during this period, the higher the electoral costs were to legislators representing a given prefecture. Thus, I call this prefectural level data on the number of commodities that were liberalized the *Liberalization Index*.

Explaining the Original Plan

Targeting the Fence-Sitters

Figure 2.1 shows that in the original Liberalization Plan, the Japanese government targeted fence-sitters of trade liberalization concentrated mostly in industrial and urban areas. The government was more likely to liberalize industries in prefectures with highly skilled labor and exporting manufacturing industries, and this relationship is statistically significant at the 5 percent level.[41] By contrast, the government shielded the biggest potential losers (e.g., agriculture) from the liberalization process. The parliamentary testimony given by the Executive Director of the Agricultural Cooperatives in 1960, during the drafting phase of the Kishi Cabinet Plan,[42] confirms that agriculture was shielded from trade liberalization then:

We, farmers, are amateur about trade liberalization so we first feared getting the hardest hit by it. Yet, as we listened to what the government had to say, we have learned that there isn't much to be afraid of – the government will consider our situation and protect us just like other countries have done (to their farmers). For instance, the government decided to liberalize soybeans – we understand that this could not be avoided. But the Ministry of Agriculture and Forestry came up with various measures to help farmers deal with this shock, and I believe that they will make farmers feel more secure. At this point, we do not have any critical and concrete objections with the government's proposed plans [for liberalization]. Obviously, the government will not liberalize rice or barley under the current food control system, and for dairy and livestock, the government told us that they intend to nurture[43] these industries. Thus, overall, I feel that we do not need to worry for the time being.[44]

---

[41] Statistical significance is from bivariate regressions. The prefectural wage data highly correlate with prefectural ranking of export values and proportion of manufacturing employees (higher wage, higher ranking of export values and percent of manufacturing employees).

[42] The government officially announced the Plan in April of 1960, a month after Ichiraku's testimony.

[43] In the Japanese policy discourse, the term "nurture" (*ikusei*) has been synonymous with "infant industry protection."

[44] Ichiraku Teruo, testimony given to the Lower-House Commerce Committee, March 2, 1960. Translation by the author.

Use of Pork as a Side Payment   47

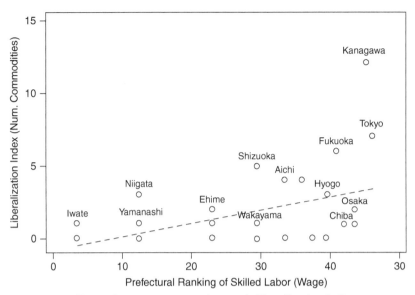

FIGURE 2.1. Fence-sitters were exposed to trade liberalization in Japan, 1960–1964.
Note: Data for skilled labor is prefectural-level wage index data in 1960 from Fukao and Yue (2000)'s *Nihon Fuken Data*, where the average wage of male workers with junior high school education is set to one. High numbers indicate prefectures with more high-skilled labor.

In sum, the government targeted fence-sitting industries for the easier coalition-building during the initial phase of trade liberalization.

The Original Plan: Liberalization Schedules in Four Phases

To what extent was the original Kishi Cabinet Plan actually consistent with the government's stated economic rationales? Did the LDP influence the original Plan and implementation? To answer this question, I analyze the scheduled timing of liberalization for the seventy-one commodities specified in the Plan. Owing to the incompatibility of the data with the Japanese government's commodity classification in the Industrial Census and Agricultural and Forestry Census 1960, I narrowed down the cases to sixty-three commodities. I use linear estimates of the phase in which a commodity i was planned to be liberalized (Y_i =1, 2, 3, and 4).[45] Key covariates are variables capturing the government's

---

[45] I chose ordinary least squares (OLS) over ordered probit because of the ease of interpreting substantive effects, but the key results do not change with ordered probit estimates.

stated economic rationales as well as the LDP's vote shares for the 1958 election as well as their vote share changes from 1958 to 1960.

For economic reasons, I used variables that matched the government's key reasons for dividing commodities into four phases: percentage of raw materials (with values in yen) used for an industry (% *Raw Materials*), the percentage of small and medium-sized firms per total number of firms in a given industry (% *SM Firms*), and value added-ness per capita labor (*Value Added PerCap*).[46] I also include variables to test Stolper–Samuelson and Ricardo–Viner models of trade, such as average wage of workers per prefecture to capture skilled versus unskilled labor endowment (*Skilled Labor*); net export (*Net Export*); and a 0–1 dummy variable for primary industry commodities in agriculture, forestry, livestock, or fishery sectors (*Primary*).

For political incentives, I matched the timing of liberalization at time t with the Lower House election results held at least a day prior to the announcement of liberalization. The variable *LDP Vote Share in 1958* is a percentage variable indicating the LDP's vote share in forty-six prefectures for the 1958 Lower House election, and the variable named *LDP Vote Change, 1958 to 1960* indicates a percentage point change in the LDP vote share in prefectures between the 1958 and 1960 Lower House elections.[47]

Table 2.1 summarizes the results comparing the Plan and its implementation. Models 1 to 5 are the linear estimates of the planned liberalization schedule (Y_i =1, 2, 3, and 4). Overall, they suggest that the Japanese government's stated reasons for the Plan were more or less consistent with the liberalization schedule and the economic characteristics of industries. Specifically, for the early liberalization, the government targeted industries with a lower proportion of small and medium-sized firms. A 12 percentage point increase in the proportion of small- to medium-sized firms in a given industry is associated with one phase delay in the planned timing of liberalization. Capital-intensive industries, measured by value added per capita, were likely to liberalize later, reflecting their comparative disadvantage in the international economy at that time. Contrary to the stated reason, however, industries with a higher dependence on raw materials were not liberalized earlier (model 4).[48]

---

[46] % *Raw Materials*, %*SM Firms*, *Value Added PerCap*, and the number of employees per industry and per office are from 1959 *Kogyo-toukei* (Industrial Census) and 1960 *Nourin-gyo Sensasu* (Agricultural and Forestry Census). *Skilled labor* is prefectural-level, relative wage index data from Fukao and Yue's (2000) Nihon Fuken Database and *Net Export* is from Shimano (1980).

[47] Lower House election data are from Leviathan Data Bank, *Sousenkyo Deeta beesu: JED-M data* (from the twenty-eighth to the fortieth elections).

[48] The results on small to medium-sized firms are consistent with Okazaki's analysis on textile industries, and the results on raw material dependence are the opposite of what Okazaki has found. See Okazaki (2011).

TABLE 2.1. *The Determinants of the Planned Liberalization in Four Phases, 1960*

	Model 1	Model 2	Model 3	Model 4	Model 5
Political Rationales	Agriculture and manufacturing	Agri and Man	Manufacturing	Manufacturing	Manufacturing
LDP vote share in 1958	0.0170 (0.0158)	−0.0022 (0.0175)	0.0081 (0.0166)		
LDP vote change, 1958 to 1960		−0.0814 (0.0363)**	−0.0723 (0.0333)**	−0.0682 (0.0291)**	−0.0739 (0.0268)***
Economic Rationales					
ln number of employees	−0.0307 (0.101)	0.0431 (0.103)	0.0146 (0.0929)	−0.0766 (0.0900)	−0.0482 (0.0862)
Net export	−0.375 (0.284)	−0.279 (0.277)	−0.0987 (0.224)	−0.0360 (0.224)	−0.0098 (0.219)
Domestic consumption	0.702 (0.366)*	0.758 (0.354)**	0.612 (0.344)*		
ln production (1,000 ton)	0.109 (0.0607)*	0.0942 (0.0589)	0.107 (0.0505)**	0.0594 (0.0518)	0.0815 (0.0488)
Value added per capita			0.305 (0.152)*		0.308* (0.153)
% Raw Materials				−0.0031 (0.0084)	
% Small to medium-sized firms			0.0772 (0.0242)***	0.0795 (0.0243)***	0.0896 (0.0235)***
Agriculture, forestry, and fisheries (0–1)	0.568 (0.344)	0.589 (0.332)*			
Constant	0.502 (1.441)	0.918 (1.401)	−6.812 (2.322)***	−4.658 (2.240)**	−6.586 (2.271)***
R^2	0.175	0.249	0.455	0.398	0.398
Obs.	59	59	39	39	39

Note: Statistically significant at *10%; **5%; ***1%. Models 1 and 2 includes both agricultural and manufacturing products and models 3 to 5 include manufacturing products only. Standard errors are in parentheses.

50   *Empirical Evidence*

Furthermore, the LDP's collective incentives to reduce future vote losses associated with trade liberalization also influenced the Plan. Liberalization was scheduled in later phases for industries whose main prefecture of production decreased LDP votes from the 1958 to 1960 Lower House elections.[49] Substantive effects were large: a 12 to 16 percentage point decrease in the LDP votes in a prefecture from 1958 to 1960 where a given industry was mainly located were associated with one phase delay in trade liberalization. By contrast, industries located in prefectures where the LDP increased votes were liberalized earlier than what the Plan had specified. The results confirm the archival evidence suggesting the LDP's intervention in the planning.[50]

In sum, the original Foreign Trade and Exchange Liberalization Plan, announced in April 1960, considered two key criteria: (1) industries' survivability under international competition and (2) the LDP legislators' survivability given the decline of votes from the 1958 to 1960 election. Thus, the Plan reflected economic reasons as well as the LDP's collective strategies to reduce further vote loss in weak districts by scheduling these commodities later in the liberalization sequence. By sequencing the liberalization to first expose industries that were likely to survive international competition (i.e., small net losers), the LDP was able to reduce the opposition and mobilize majority support for trade liberalization. The LDP also designed the liberalization sequence to minimize the vote loss associated with liberalization by delaying the liberalization of commodities produced in prefectures where the party lost votes from 1958 to 1960. The actual implementation of this Plan, discussed later, further confirms the LDP's open economy coalition-building strategy.

Explaining the Implementation of the Plan: Faster, Delayed, and as Planned

The actual implementation of the liberalization plan substantially diverged from the original schedule. Among sixty-three commodities divided into four liberalization phases, twenty-six were liberalized as scheduled, thirty-two were liberalized later than scheduled, and five were liberalized faster than scheduled. With three general Lower House elections between the drafting and implementation of the Plan (May 1958, November 1960, and November 1963), this gap between the Plan and implementation provides a wealth of information for

---

[49] The 1960 Lower House election was held in November, and the Liberalization Plan was announced in April of 1960. Thus, estimating the effect of the LDP's vote loss from 1958 to 1960 on the Plan announced in April can be problematic. Yet, I use the vote loss from 1958 to 1960 elections, rather than from the 1955 to 1958 elections because the official Diet discussion on the Plan began on October 22, 1960, just a month before the 1960 Lower House election. Moreover, the left and right party mergers after the 1955 election made the 1955 and 1958 elections not comparable.

[50] MITI (1991, Vol. 8).

Use of Pork as a Side Payment

testing how the LDP's political incentives shaped the implementation of trade liberalization.

Table 2.2 summarizes the results for the linear estimates of the government's actual decisions to liberalize or protect commodities discussed in the Plan. Models 1 and 2 estimate a dichotomous dependent variable, which takes a value of 1 if a commodity was liberalized between 1960 and 1964, and zero if it remained protected as of 1964. Models 3 to 6 summarize a linear estimates of the four phases in which a given commodity was liberalized (Y_i =1, 2, 3, and 4). Model 7 estimates a dichotomous dependent variable that takes a value of one if the liberalization of commodities was delayed past the Plan schedule, and zero otherwise. In addition to the covariates used to estimate the Plan, I included the election results of 1960 and 1963 (percentage variables, *LDP Vote Share, 1960* and *LDP Vote Share, 1963* respectively) as well as changes in the LDP's vote share in districts from between 1958 and 1960 Lower House elections (*LDP Vote Change, 58–63*), between 1960 and 1963 Lower House elections (*LDP Vote Change, 60–63*), and between 1958 and 1963 Lower House elections (*LDP Vote Change, 58–63*).[51]

Three differences between the Plan and its implementation stand out. First, some economic characteristics of industries that mattered for the planned liberalization schedule, such as the proportion of small and medium-sized firms (*% SM Firms*) in a given industry, has inconsistent effects across the models.

Second, the implementation did not favor the LDP's stronghold or weak districts – the LDP's vote share in 1958 and 1960 Lower House elections turned out to have no systematic effects on the government's implementation of the Plan.[52] What affected the implementation were *changes* in the LDP's vote shares between elections. The government was likely to liberalize a given industry when the LDP increased votes in districts where a given product or commodity was produced (i.e., positive coefficients of *LDP Vote Change, 58–63* for models 1 and 2). The government was likely to delay the Plan's liberalization when the LDP lost votes in districts where a given product or commodity was produced (i.e., negative coefficients of *LDP Vote Change, 58–63* for models 4, 5 and 7). The pattern is consistent and statistically significant when analyzed with agricultural and manufacturing commodities (models 1 to 3) or manufacturing commodities only (models 4 and 5).[53]

---

[51] See Naoi and Okazaki (2013) on how the government used two different tactics (protectionism and side payments) of trade liberalization by responding to the results of Lower House versus Upper House elections.

[52] The results for model 1 shows that, at only the 10% level of significance, agricultural commodities produced in prefectures with higher LDP vote share in the 1958 election were more likely to be liberalized between 1960 and 1964.

[53] The results for model 6 suggest that, however, the government's decisions were responsive to the changes in LDP's vote share between 1958 and 1963 elections, but not the changes between the 1960 and 1963 elections.

TABLE 2.2. *The Determinants of Actual Trade Liberalization (Implementation)*

	Model 1	Model 2	Model 3	Model 4	Model 5	Model 6	Model 7
Dependent variable	Liberalized (0–1)			Liberalized Phase (1–4)			Delayed (0–1)
Sample	Agriculture	Manufac	All	Agriculture	Manufac	All	All
Political Rationales							
LDP vote share, 1958	0.0388	0.0014		−0.076	0.0188		−0.0017
	(0.0199)*	(0.0103)		(0.0516)	(0.0249)		(0.0099)
LDP vote change, 58–63	0.0982	0.0298		−0.215	−0.0640		−0.0299
	(0.0336)**	(0.0143)**		(0.0862)**	(0.0346)*		(0.0151)*
LDP vote share, 1960						0.0194	
						(0.0244)	
LDP vote change, 60–63						−0.0378	
						(0.0356)	
Economic Rationales							
ln Number of employees	−0.114	−0.0177	0.0445	0.223	0.132	0.0922	0.078
	(0.0965)	(0.0554)	(0.114)	(0.247)	(0.134)	(0.123)	(0.0545)
Net export	0.341	0.130	−0.209	−0.832	−0.140	−0.348	0.0826
	(0.358)	(0.150)	(0.319)	(0.946)	(0.362)	(0.343)	(0.151)
ln production	−0.224		0.0567	0.473*			
	(0.0880)**		(0.0685)	(0.224)			

TABLE 2.2 (*continued*)

Dependent variable	Model 1	Model 2	Model 3	Model 4	Model 5	Model 6	Model 7
	Liberalized (0–1)			Liberalized Phase (1–4)			Delayed (0–1)
Sample	Agriculture	Manufac	All	Agriculture	Manufac	All	All
Value added per cap		0.0575			0.0371	−0.0119	−0.123
		(0.113)			(0.273)	(0.254)	(0.120)
% Small to medium-sized firms		−0.0308			0.0725	0.0605	0.0006
		(0.0154)*			(0.0372)*	(0.0368)	(0.0164)
% Raw materials		−0.0001			0.0005		0.0009
		(0.0060)			(0.0145)		(0.0060)
Domestic consumption			0.208	0.586			
			(0.404)	(0.728)			
Agriculture			0.346			0.159	−0.412
			(0.387)			(0.579)	(0.263)
Constant	1.221	3.505	1.822	1.112	−6.443	−4.694	−0.188
	(0.973)	(1.555)**	(1.175)	(2.523)	(3.757)*	(3.473)	(1.650)
R^2	0.511	0.256	0.0503	0.463	0.261	0.199	0.217
Obs.	16	40	59	16	40	47	47

Note: OLS estimates. Statistically significant at * 10%; ** 5%; *** 1%. Standard errors are in parentheses. Models 1 and 2 analyzed a dichotomous dependent variable where liberalized commodities between 1960 and 1964 take a value of one, and zero if they remained protected. Models 3 to 6 analyzed the actual phase in which a given commodity was liberalized (1 to 4) and the Model 7 analyzed the dichotomous dependent variable that takes a value of one when the government delayed liberalization of a given commodity and zero otherwise.

Substantive effects of the changes in the LDP vote shares are large. A 5 percentage point increase in the LDP vote share in a given prefecture (e.g., 50 to 55 percent) was associated with a 50 percentage point increase in the probability of liberalization for primary commodities (model 1) and a 15 percentage point increase in the probability of liberalization for manufacturing industries (model 2). Likewise, a 5 percentage point loss in the LDP vote share in a given prefecture was associated with one phase later scheduling of the liberalization of primary commodities, and 0.3 phase later scheduling of manufacturing industries.

In sum, the LDP collectively considered the electoral costs of trade liberalization: the government delayed the liberalization of industries where the LDP lost votes and implemented the liberalization on time for commodities produced in prefectures where the LDP increased votes. The pattern of implementation does not lend support to the conventional view of powerless politicians, who simply transmit districts' interests into their policy positions. Party leaders did not implement the Plan to cater to their core constituents, either. The pattern thus contradicts the established wisdom that legislators are likely to cater to the core, not swing, districts in an MMD system.[54] Instead, the LDP pursued a collective strategy to increase (or minimize the decrease of) vote and seat shares for the party, and as a result, delayed trade liberalization for the districts that decreased LDP support.

By targeting the fence-sitters of trade liberalization, such as industries with a lower proportion of small and medium-sized firms and labor-intensive industries that had a comparative advantage at that time, the LDP was able to preempt the backlash against trade liberalization. The LDP also minimized electoral costs of liberalization by delaying the liberalization of commodities that were produced where the party lost votes.

Optimal Use of Pork to Build an Open Economy Coalition

The period of drastic trade liberalization coincided with the surge in side-payment legislation, defined here as legislation that aimed to mitigate the effects of trade liberalization and deregulation. Figure 2.2 shows that the side-payment legislations peaked during early 1960s, when the Foreign Exchange and Trade Liberalization Plan was implemented. Examples include the Agricultural Basic Law (1961), Price Stabilization Law for Dairy Industry

---

[54] It is important to differentiate the core/swing voters from the core/swing districts. See Cox (2009). Most of the theoretical conjectures on distributive politics consider whether legislators target the core or swing voters or groups. Yet, empirical tests of these conjectures mostly use the district-level data on party vote shares to infer whether legislators targeted the core or swing, which is not the exact operationalization of the theoretical conjectures. The finding I discussed here strictly concerns the core versus swing districts.

Use of Pork as a Side Payment

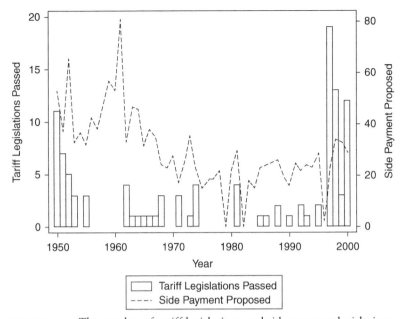

FIGURE 2.2. The number of tariff legislations and side-payment legislation.
Source: The author constructed this figure using data from Fukumoto (2000). Side-payment legislations include those related to agriculture, construction and land development, industry, and small and medium-sized firms. The government legislated a few tariff-related bills in the early 1960s, yet, as this chapter demonstrates, more drastic liberalization was implemented via the executive, not the legislative route.

(1961), Special Law for Promoting Fruit Farming (1961), Law to Promote Industrial Development of Under-developed Regions (1961), Special Law for Areas of Heavy Snowfalls (1962), Small and Medium-sized Enterprise Basic Act (1963), Forest and Forestry Basic Act (1964), Law to Consolidate and Promote Special Areas for Industrial Development (1964),[55] Industrial Law to Develop Mountain Villages (1965), and Price Adjustment Law for Sugar and Starch (1965).[56]

Some of this legislation specifically aimed to mitigate the effect of liberalization on industries, such as agriculture, dairy, and fruit farming. Other legislation

---

[55] In Japanese, this law was called *Kogyo seibi tokubetsu chiiki seibi tokushin hou*.
[56] The list of legislations was compiled using the government's official database of legislations, http://law.e-gov.go.jp/ (accessed September 19, 2011). Some of these legislations were submitted by legislators, rather than the Cabinet, and were sarcastically called "souvenir legislation" (*omiyage houan*). Almost every year since 1958, the government had to request the LDP to "restrain" submissions of legislations. The increase in souvenir legislations caused the expansion of budget and Ministry of Finance asked the LDP to regulate the number of submissions in 1958. See Kawato (2005, chapter 6).

Empirical Evidence

targeted geographic areas, such as the northeastern part of Japan with its heavy snowfall. Such side-payment legislation was passed under the balanced budget following the fiscal and monetary contraction policy of the Occupational Force called the "Dodge Line," which was named after Joseph Dodge.[57] This means that the government needed to prioritize carefully which constituents it should please in allocating the budget.

Among these side payments, geographically targetable public investment projects constituted a large portion of the government budget: 13 billion yen, which was approximately 4 percent of GDP. Between 1961 and 1970, public investment grew by 15.4 percent each year.[58] The largest public investment projects during this time period were concentrated in the urban and industrial areas, referred to as the "Asia-Pacific Industrial Belts." They were legislated under the Law to Consolidate and Promote Special Areas for Industrial Development, which was passed in 1964. More than 55 percent of the public investment budget was allocated to prefectures facing the Pacific Ocean, such as Shizuoka and Aichi Prefectures. On the contrary, public investment for rural areas declined substantially during this period from 40 percent of public investment in 1947 to less than 10 percent by 1960.[59]

Even a cursory look at the budget data during this period reveals the urban and industrial bias in the government's budget allocation, which challenges the conventional wisdom linking Japan's MMD electoral system with the prevalence of pork barreling in rural areas.[60] Under the same multimember electoral system, the LDP government's budget allocation shifted dramatically from rural bias (1947) to urban bias (1950s and early 1960s and early 1970s during energy crisis) and then back to rural bias. The pattern is consistent with the theory of optimal use of Pork to build the open economy coalition, developed in Chapter 1. The party leaders targeted side payments to small net losers – in this context, urban and industrial areas that were targeted for trade liberalization.

The next section of this chapter provides more systematic evidence suggesting that the government granted "Special Areas for Industrial Development" in 1964 to mitigate the costs of trade liberalization imposed on some prefectures.

---

[57] Joseph Dodge was an economic advisor to the Occupational Force and was a chairman of Detroit Bank.

[58] Fujii (2004, table 3-2 on p. 190). Also OECD (1999), *National Accounts of OECD Countries*. In 1960, 3.9 percent of Japan's GDP was spent on public investment, and this proportion increased to 4.7 percent in 1966.

[59] See Fujii (table 4-1 on p. 225 and table 4-3 on p. 227).

[60] Curtis and Ishikawa (1983); Scheiner (2006). See a different critique to these literature that the LDP did allocate more to rural areas but this allocation consequently weakened their vote-mobilization machines (Saito 2009).

Use of Pork as a Side Payment 57

THE LAW TO CONSOLIDATE AND PROMOTE SPECIAL AREAS FOR INDUSTRIAL DEVELOPMENT, 1964

The Law originated as "The Plan to Develop Asia-Pacific Industrial Belts" aimed to transform Japan from an agrarian to an industrial society as well as to solve the issue of factory congestion in Tokyo and its vicinity (see Chapter 6 for how the Thai government followed this model).[61] During the drafting and deliberation stages, intra-LDP disagreements arose regarding whether this program should target urban and industrial areas for export-led growth, or rural areas to reduce the widening regional inequality. The intraparty conflict corroborates TJ Pempel's observation that "the most important intra-conservative tension can best be understood as that between 'pork' and 'productivity'" (2010: 234).

Business organizations quickly backed the productivity coalition. Since 1958, *Keidanren* had advocated for more infrastructure development to facilitate industrialization: "strengthening infrastructure for industrial development is especially an urgent task...regarding the public investment, focus on priorities...and aggressively utilize it."[62] Observing the disagreements within the LDP over whether to concentrate government resources on industrial areas or diffuse them to rural areas, *Keidanren* again pushed the government in 1963: "It is not desirable to have industry locations to be diffused to rural areas; in preparing for trade liberalization, we need to strengthen our industry's competitiveness...therefore, we need to focus on areas with increasing return to scale."[63] MITI also echoed this view and stated that the aim of this Law was to manage trade and foreign exchange liberalization by strengthening the competitiveness of heavy industry, such as petrochemical and shipping.[64] Local Chambers of Commerce and Industry also lobbied the government to win the designation because they perceived that the designation could be "quick fertilizer [for industries] to prepare for trade liberalization."[65]

The LDP government in the end decided to prioritize its public investment on coastal areas facing the Pacific Ocean. The productivity coalition won over the pork coalition because of three factors. The first was that legislators in the ruling Ikeda faction, whose career backgrounds predominantly were as bureaucrats (*Kanryo-ha*), were pro-economic growth and pro-small government.[66] The major factions in the LDP also responded to strong lobbying by

---

[61] The LDP legislators, not the Cabinet, submitted the law. See Fujii (2004).
[62] Fujii (2004) p. 236.
[63] Ibid. (2004) pp. 237–238.
[64] Ibid. (2004) p. 242.
[65] Ibid. (2004) p. 291 citing the comment from Hikari Chamber of Commerce and Industry in Yamaguchi Prefecture.
[66] Ibid. (2004) p. 179.

58 Empirical Evidence

TABLE 2.3. *Prefectures that Received Side Payments, 1960–1964*

Designated Special Areas	Ministerial Positions to Kono-Miki Factions
Ibaragi	Hokkaido
Shizuoka	Chiba
Aichi	Tokyo
Hyogo	Kanagawa
Okayama	Toyama
Hiroshima	Tottori
Yamaguchi	Shimane
	Tokushima
	Kumamoto

Source: Information on designated special areas was from Fujii (2004). Information on ministerial appointments is from the Cabinet Office's website on "History of Cabinets (*Rekidai Naikaku*)" available at: http://www.kantei.go.jp/jp/rekidai/kakuryo/showa20.html (accessed September, 2011).

big businesses, the key financiers of the party and factions. Thus, the LDP party leaders were more responsive to economic winners, not losers.[67]

The second reason why the productivity coalition won was the urban representatives holding several major party and ministerial positions.[68] They wanted the Law to focus on infrastructure development for industrial growth, rather than redistribution to rural, hinterland. Finally, roughly in tandem, the LDP proposed and legislated the Law to Promote Construction of New Industrial Cities in 1962, the primary aim of which was to reduce regional inequality and create jobs in depressed areas. A package deal, one that focused on industrial growth in Asia-Pacific industrial belts and another on creating jobs in depressed areas, was able to mobilize majority support among the divided LDP legislators.

The government invited prefectural governments to apply for the designation of Special Areas, excluding Tokyo and Osaka, which were major cities with factory congestion. After intense prefectural lobbying, seven areas were designated as Special Areas for Industrial Development (see Table 2.3). Furthermore, another form of side payment, ministerial positions, was given to the Kono and Miki factions who opposed the trade liberalization. Since Ikeda's second cabinet (July of 1961), Ikeda began appointing at least two legislators

[67] Chapter 4 shows how the revision of Political Finance Law in 1975, which put ceiling on firms' and organizations' campaign contribution, shifted the locus of LDP legislators' rent-seeking activities to geographically organized, import-competing industries.

[68] Examples were Nakamura Umekichi from district in Tokyo holding the Minister of Construction (Ikeda's first two cabinets) and Kono Ichiro from Kanagawa district holding the Minister of Construction (since the second cabinet's reshuffling) and Director General of Science and Technology Agency (the third cabinet).

Use of Pork as a Side Payment

TABLE 2.4. *Side-Payment Allocations and Mean Liberalization Index*

		Ministerial Positions to Kono-Miki Factions	
		Yes	No
Special Areas	Yes	No Prefecture	2.286 (0.837)** Seven prefectures
	No	2.889 (1.378)** Nine Prefectures	0.633 (0.232) 30 Prefectures

Note: Numbers in each row indicate the mean *Liberalization Index* of prefectures. Numbers in parentheses are standard errors and **Statistically significant at the 5% level in the difference-in-means test where the lower right values (No–No side payment) are a base group.

from the Kono faction and one legislator from the Miki faction to ministerial positions.

Table 2.4 summarizes the LDP's decisions to grant two forms of side payment to forty-six prefectures[69]: (1) Special Areas and (2) ministerial positions to factional leaders representing districts in a given prefecture. The values in each box represent the mean values of *Liberalization Index* – the number of commodities that were implemented for liberalization between 1960 and 1964 in a given prefecture. Standard errors are described in the parentheses and two asterisks next to the parentheses indicate 5% statistical significance in the difference-in-means test of Liberalization Index scores, where prefectures that received neither of the two side payments (the bottom right cell) serves as a base group.

No prefecture received both forms of side payments, that is, designation of special areas for industrial development and ministerial positions, which lends support to my argument that the LDP leaders used these side payments substitutively to buy off legislators' support. To lend more systematic support, Table 2.5 shows probit estimates on prefectures' likelihood of receiving side payments given their *Liberalization Index*. Consistent with the argument developed in Chapter 1 about the optimal allocation of Pork, the LDP used pork barrel projects to co-partisan fence-sitters of globalization and to mitigate these legislators' electoral costs of liberalization. Figure 2.3 summarizes the effect of electoral costs from liberalization on the probability of a prefecture receiving particularistic benefits.

---

[69] 47th, Okinawa prefecture belonged to the United States during 1960s.

TABLE 2.5. *Liberalization Index and Side-Payment Allocations in Japanese Prefectures*

DV: Side Payment to a prefecture (0–1)	DV1: Special Industrial Region and Ministerial Positions				DV2: Ministerial Positions to Kono and Miki Factions		
	(Probit Estimates)				(Probit Estimates)		
	Model 1	Model 2	Model 3	Model 4	Model 5	Model 6	Model 7
Number of commodities liberalized ("electoral costs")	0.271 (0.113)**	0.403 (0.149)***	0.43 (0.158)***	0.422 (0.160)***	0.323 (0.140)**	0.406 (0.187)**	0.316 (0.140)**
LDP vote share in 1958		0.067 (0.039)*	0.063 (0.040)	0.071 (0.040)*	0.065 (0.044)	0.060 (0.045)	0.060 (0.045)
LDP vote change from 1958 to 1963		0.016 (0.032)	0.011 (0.034)	0.018 (0.032)	0.062 (0.040)	0.058 (0.041)	0.061 (0.040)
Ranking of skilled labor			−0.011 (0.020)			−0.021 (0.024)	
% of employees in net exporting sector				0.003 (0.007)			−0.006 (0.008)
Obs.	46	46	46	46	46	46	46
LR Chi²(3)	7.94	11.43	13.17	11.59	7.44	8.23	8.03
Prob > Chi²	0.0048	0.0096	0.0105	0.0207	0.0592	0.0836	0.0906
Pseudo R^2	0.1336	0.1923	0.2215	0.195	0.1636	0.1809	0.1765

Note: Statistically significant at *10%; **5%; ***1%. The dependent variable for models 1 to 4 is a dichotomous variable one if a prefecture received one of the two forms of side payments and zero otherwise. The dependent variable for models 5 to 7 is a dichotomous variable one if a prefecture received a ministerial position for legislators in Kono–Miki factions and zero otherwise.

Use of Pork as a Side Payment 61

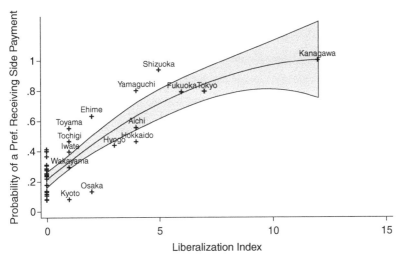

FIGURE 2.3. Trade liberalization and predicted probability of pork allocations.
Note: Predicted probability is calculated based on model 3 in Table 2.5. Estimation included prefectures with no commodity targeted for liberalization during this period, but they are not shown because of space constraints.

In sum, party leaders in Japan designed trade liberalization to ensure majority coalition-building for liberalization on the floor as well as political survival of co-partisan legislators. They did so by first exposing fence-sitters (small net losers) to liberalization. Legislators representing districts that were exposed to early trade liberalization did voice opposition, and some, such as the Kono and Miki factions, issued credible threats of party breakaway. In the end, however, these legislators supported the liberalization with generous side-payment Pork projects, in the form of the designation of Special Industrial Areas and ministerial positions. The government used protectionism for the biggest potential losers, agriculture, as the use of Pork would have been prohibitively expensive. These findings lend strong support to the Optimal Use of Pork hypothesis developed in Chapter 1 and challenge the conventional wisdom, which has credited the bureaucracy and executives for achieving the liberalization.

Finally, the findings challenge the conventional wisdom that pork barrel politics are prevalent in rural areas because of the cheaper costs for legislators to buy support from voters and better collective action capacity among voters. In contrast, this chapter has shown that urban and industrial bias in pork barreling can occur as a result of party leaders' policy-seeking incentives. In advanced industrial nations, urban and industrial areas tend to incur smaller income losses from trade liberalization than rural and agricultural regions. Accordingly, it is cheaper for party leaders to buy support for liberalization from legislators representing urban and industrial areas than in rural and agricultural areas. As a result, small net losers, rather than big net losers, received particularistic benefits.

62   *Empirical Evidence*

THAILAND'S COALITION-BUILDING FOR AN OPEN ECONOMY, 1980–1988

Economic and Political Landscape of Thailand in the Early 1980s

After World War II, Thailand continued to preserve the structure of oligopolistic firms, mostly run by families from the prewar era.[70] Suehiro and Wailerdsak documented that 220 family- or state-owned business groups in Thailand controlled 62 percent of nominal GDP in 1997 and they accounted for 58 percent of total sales of the 1,000 largest firms in Thailand.[71] This concentrated market structure contrasts with the Japanese case, where the postwar Occupation reforms decentralized the oligopolistic power structures in the economy (e.g., see earlier discussion in this chapter).

Most of these oligopolistic businesses were located in Bangkok, and as a result, the relationship between legislators and local businesses in their districts remained weak until the late 1980s.[72] Interest groups captured legislators at the center, not at the local districts, which contradicts the established argument that an MMD system should encourage legislators' capture by local special interests.

Although Thailand was never colonized or occupied by Allied forces, the postwar U.S. effort to deter the spread of communism in Asia nonetheless shaped the political economy of Thailand. First, with the assistance from the United States and the World Bank, the Thai government heavily invested in transportation and infrastructural development in rural areas (Bowie and Unger 1997: 131; Pasuk and Baker 2002).[73] The infrastructural development contributed to the subsequent rise of "local bosses" (*Chao Po*) in rural areas, who owned trading businesses between Bangkok and hinterlands and became powerful political actors leveraging their wealth.[74] Foreign aid from the Japanese government took over the U.S. aid in the late 1970s, and focused on the infrastructural development and export for manufacturing industries in urban areas.[75]

Despite the influence of these external financiers of development, Thai policymakers pursued an import-substitution strategy and had little interest in trade liberalization until the early 1980s. The manufacturing sector enjoyed substantially higher levels of trade protection compared to agriculture (Jongwanich and Kohpaiboon 2007: 281), reflecting the government's goal of industrialization and Thailand's comparative advantage in agriculture.[76] By

---

[70] Suehiro (1989).

[71] Suehiro and Wailerdsak (2004: 83).

[72] See Laothamatas's (1992) survey results.

[73] Between 1966 and 1971, World Bank and U.S. military aid constituted one-third of public capital spending in Thailand. (Bowie and Unger 1997: 135).

[74] McVey (2004).

[75] Doner and Laothamatas (1994); Ariga and Kijima 2000.

[76] Even if we consider only tariff levels, the manufacturing tariff was higher than agricultural tariff until the mid-1990s. Farmers suffered from an additional tax burden, in the form of price and tax support for consumers.

Use of Pork as a Side Payment 63

contrast, agriculture had been taxed heavily (e.g., the government suppressed the price of agricultural produce to one that was lower than the world market value) to support urban consumers and industrialization. Such urban bias in trade protection is common among developing economies, owing to stronger collective action by industrial interests and urban consumers over a vast number of farmers (Bates 1981).

The elites' lack of interests in trade liberalization was due to the continuous expansion of domestic market and the importance of tariffs as the government's revenue sources. The maturation of the domestic market, in conjunction with export-led growth of Thai's neighboring economies, such as Japan and South Korea, had spurred policymakers' interests in liberalization. To fuel the momentum, agricultural export experienced a 19 percent growth in volume (Punyaratabandhu-Bhakdi 1983), while imports and domestic consumptions declined as a result of the worldwide recession after the 1979 energy crisis (Sucharithanarugse 1983: 284). The worldwide recession also raised tariff and non-tariff barriers that the Thai government faced abroad (Sucharithanarugse 1983: 283). These global market changes provided preconditions for the Thai government's shift from import-substitution to open economy.

Prem Tinsulanonda's Cabinets (1980–1988): Policy Shift toward an Open Economy

Although the economic condition was ripe for trade liberalization, intraelite disagreements over economic policies persisted in the early 1980s. One group followed the Japanese development model and advocated for heavy government intervention and infant industry protection using industrial policy and macroeconomic stimulus. Another group advocated for minimal state intervention to ensure stable prices and external balances.[77] Ultimately, the latter, neoliberal group won.[78]

The Thai government initiated drastic, unilateral import liberalization a month preceding Thailand's official accession to GATT (October, 1982). Tariffs for finished manufacturing goods were reduced by 6 percentage points, and

---

[77] Bowie and Unger (1997: 129).
[78] The literature has provided reasons for why the neoliberal group won over the "infant industry protection" group: the expansion of Thai agricultural and manufacturing export, relocation of Japanese manufacturing industries to Thailand after the Plaza Accord (1985), and the military-backed, Prime Minister Prem's alignment with neoliberal technocrats (see Chapter 6). This chapter does not refute the first two points – i.e., economic conditions were important in explaining the policy shift. Regarding Prem's alignment with technocrats, this chapter argues that Prem's coalition-building involved much broader segment of elites and market actors than it has been portrayed. Warr (1996); Bowie and Unger (1997); and Hicken's (2004) discussion on "reserve domain."

64 *Empirical Evidence*

their effective rate of protection[79] declined by 12 percentage points.[80] On the other hand, the government reduced the tax burden for agricultural produce and granted subsidies and tax incentives to promote their export. Liberalizing long-protected manufacturing industries while reducing the tax burden for agriculture marked the turning point for Thai trade policy.

The conventional wisdom about this shift to an open economy under Prem is that the semidemocratic system where legislators were elected, but the prime minister was appointed by the military, facilitated the coalition-building for the policy shift. The prime minister and technocrats were insulated from the business lobby and controlled macroeconomic policymaking, while elected legislators engaged in pork barrel politics through line ministers, which Hicken (2004) has called "pork-policy compromise." Bowie and Unger (1997:155) also argue: "A supportive political coalition facilitated moves toward greater economic openness. This coalition, however, was not a broad, formal one. Narrower, informal coalitions were important, particularly those among state technocrats and military leaders who provided the former with policymaking autonomy." Furthermore, an emergency decree (*Phrarachakamnot*) was often used for tariff-related policy changes. The decree required no majority approval from the parliament, simply an approval by the King (Imaizumi 2009).[81]

Yet, what this insulation argument misses is the fact that in a semidemocratic system, Prime Minister Prem was vulnerable to the parliamentary procedure of a nonconfidence vote and thus needed to buy off support from legislators (see Chapter 1 for more details). The military backing during Prem's term, moreover, was increasingly fragmented. The military themselves perceived that they could not rule alone (Prasirtsuk 2007: 875). For instance, in 1987, 41 members of Prem's multiparty coalition government defected on the land transportation bill (regarding the gasoline and diesel vehicle tax), which forced Prem to reshuffle his cabinet members (Neher 1987). In 1988, military staged the nonconfidence vote against Prem, yet the coup failed because one faction in

---

[79] Effective rate of protection is the level of trade protection estimated with tariffs on manufacturing finished goods as well as on intermediate and capital input, while nominal rate of protection is the tariff imposed on a given produce when it enters the country. Like many newly industrializing countries, Thailand has high tariffs on intermediate manufacturing goods (called "tariff cascade").

[80] Economists have debated whether the effective rate of protection and nominal rate of protection are suitable measures to analyze why a government favors some industries over others. Jongwanich and Kohpaiboon (2007) have shown that a political bargain was struck over effective rate of protection in Thailand, due to rent-seeking incentives. Of note, however, is that the correlations between nominal versus effective rates are often high. For example, Urata and Yokota's (1994) estimations on 1982 Thai trade protection data show the correlations at 79 percent for 1975 and 75 percent for 1982.

[81] An emergency decree can become a law later if the parliament approves with a majority and expires without the approval. See Imaizumi (2009: 6).

Use of Pork as a Side Payment

Khon Kaen province switched its alliance at the last minute from the military to Prem (Ockey 2000:89).[82] In sum, Prime Minister Prem was not electorally accountable to citizens, but he had to respond to the demands from legislators for legislating policies and surviving the nonconfidence vote. Prem cabinet's design of trade liberalization should then reflect the concerns for majority coalition-building with legislators.

Explaining Manufacturing Liberalization: Rewarding Voter Mobilization

To analyze the determinants of manufacturing liberalization, I use Nominal Rates of Protection (NRP) for eight manufacturing industries (two digits in HS code) that are calculated from *Input-Output Table of Thailand for Analytical Uses*, 1975 (pre-liberalization) and 1982 (Urata and Yokota 1994: 447, table 2).[83] Nominal Rates of Protection (NRP) are tariff rates imposed on a given good when it enters the country and ranges from zero (no protection, market price) to a value larger than zero.[84] Table 2.6 describes the pattern of liberalization. It shows that the government steadily liberalized industries such as foods and chemicals from 1975 to 1982, and it applied the higher levels of protection over time for other industries such as machinery and wood.[85]

---

[82] Khon Kaen Province was the fifth most populous province as of 1991 (which is important for vote mobilization), and 20 percent of its gross provincial product came from agriculture and 18 percent from industry. Khon Kaen is located in the poorest northeastern region, yet has been a regional trading hub for Bangkok, Cambodia, Laos, and Vietnam. During this time period, commerce with neighboring countries increased and the nonagricultural sector experienced 7 percent annual growth. See Hewison and Thongyou (2000: 201–208).

[83] These are foods, textiles, wood/wood products, pulp/paper, chemicals, ceramics, steel/nonferrous metals and machinery and transportation equipment.

[84] I also analyzed the determinants of effective rates of protection (ERP), which is the level of trade protection estimated with tariffs on finished goods as well as tariffs on intermediate and capital input. NRP and ERP measures correlate highly at 79 percent (for 1975 data) and 75 percent (for 1982 data) and the main results hold similarly. Thus I report the results for NRP here.

[85] Using estimates of NRP and ERP on manufacturing industries from 2003, Jongwanich and Kohpaiboon (2007) show that political strength of industries (measured by industry concentration and employment at the national level) account for the levels of effective rates of protection, but not nominal rates of protection. Thus they conclude that "political bargains in Thailand are struck over ERP rather than NRP" (p. 276). In addition to the time period of analysis and the inclusion of agricultural sector, my analysis differs from theirs in two important respects. First, because legislators are likely to respond to district demands for free trade or protectionism, I use measures of industry's political strength at provincial or prefectural levels and match them with political data, such as electoral results and percentage of seats at the province occupied by the parties in ruling coalition. Second, I analyze not just the cross-sectional levels of protection at a time t, but also their changes over time (i.e., how changes in electoral environment in districts as well as the stability of ruling coalition at the national level affects changes in the levels of protection) (Angrist and Pischke 2008).

TABLE 2.6. *Nominal Rates of Protection for Manufacturing Industries*

Commodity	1975	1982	1985
Total manufacturing	20.4	14.8	14.1
Foods	22.6	14.5	17.3
Textiles	25.7	24.4	8.6
Wood	11.6	12.7	25.1
Pulp/paper	13.4	9.9	11.4
Chemicals	22.3	14.4	12
Ceramics	15.3	15.3	15.1
Steel/metals	7.7	7.1	8.4
Machinery	16.7	11.5	17.5
Other manufacturing	12	2.9	6

Source: Table II in Urata and Yokota (1994: 447).

I weigh these industry-level protection data with the industry composition of labor force among eight industries in each province, using data from the pre-liberalization, 1980 Thailand's *Housing and Population Census*. The weighting method is described in Appendix Table A2.1 and follows a work of Topalova (2007).[86] After calculating weighted Nominal Rates of Protection for province i in year j, I calculated *Change Province NRP* for each province i, which is the change in weighted NRP for province i between 1975 and 1988. I then match these data on provincial-level reduction in trade barriers with district-level election data aggregated into provincial levels. Election data cover House of Representative elections held in 1979, 1983, 1986, and 1988, and come from the Kollman et al. (2012) Constituency-level Election Archive (CLEA).[87]

Ruling Vote Share (%) is the percentage of votes casted for political parties in Prem's ruling coalition (1980–1988) in a given province during a given House of Representative election. This variable and other variables below reflect yearly changes in party exit from and entries to Prem coalition between elections.

Ruling Vote Share Change is the change in Ruling Vote Share (%) from year t to year $t + 1$. Unit is a percentage point. *Ruling Vote Share Change* occurs due to House of Representative elections from 1980 to 1988 (1983, 1986, and 1988).

---

[86] The data are available from University of Minnesota's Minnesota Population Center. Ideally, I would have liked to use the Labor Force Survey or Industrial Census, which reports provincial-level workforce composition in a much finer industry classifications. Yet, there was no Labor Force Survey or Industrial Census data available by province during this time. Personal communications with an officer at Ministry of Industry, June 2012 and an officer at National Statistics Office in Thailand, June 2013.

[87] See www.electiondataarchive.org. The version used here is the one from December 17, 2012.

Ruling Seat Share (%) is the percentage of total House of Representative Seats in a province occupied by political parties in Prem's ruling coalition (1980–1988).

Ruling Seat Share Change is the change in Ruling Seat Share (%) from year t to year $t + 1$. Unit is a percentage point. *Ruling Seat Share Change* occurs as a result of two conditions: House of Representative elections from 1980 to 1988 (1983, 1986, and 1988) and party breakaway and realignment of ruling coalition.

Swing Party Vote Share (%) is the percentage of votes in House of Representative elections cast for the three political parties that exit and rejoin the Prem's ruling coalition at least twice during his term: Chart Thai, Social Action, and Prachakon Thai Party. Because of their track record in breaking away from and rejoining the coalition, we can consider these three parties' threat of coalition exit to be credible in the eyes of Prem's coalition leaders.

Same Party Share (%) is the percentage of votes in House of Representative elections cast for the same party in a given provice. It aims to measure the collective action capacity of voters to converge their support around the same party.

To understand how the government liberalized productive or unproductive industries more, I also calculate province's total factor productivity before the 1982 trade liberalization by using the national-level, industry-level data on total factor productivity calculated by Yokota and Urata (1982). Just like the trade barrier reduction data, I calculate the provincial-level total factor productivity by weighting the industry-level total factor productivity data with the provincial-level data on the proportion of industry-level employment recorded in 1980 Thailand's *Housing and Population Census* (a variable name, *Total Factor Productivity,* 76–82).[88]

Table 2.7 summarizes the results for the determinants of trade liberalization in manufacturing industries during Prem (the changes in Nominal Rate of Protection between 1975 and 1985). Contrary to the conventional wisdom that trade liberalization in 1980s was an executive decision insulated from electoral politics, the liberalization decisions were highly responsive to the changes in electoral support. Yet, the pattern of trade liberalization did not favor Prem coalition's stronghold ("core") or weak districts ("swing"), as predicted by electoral system arguments (Cox and McCubbins 1986; Cox 2009). It was *changes* in the Prem coalition's vote shares between elections that dictated the patterns of manufacturing liberalization. The government rewarded protection for industries located in provinces

---

[88] I used the individual-level 1980 census data available through University of Minnesota's Minnesota Population Center (see https://international.ipums.org/international/). I have communicated with Thailand's National Statistics Office (NSO) to cross-check the validity of the data, yet NSO told me that they did not own these data or any reports on 1980 Housing and Population Census categorized by provinces (Changwat). Personal communication with NSO officer, June 2013.

68   *Empirical Evidence*

TABLE 2.7. *The Determinants of Manufacturing Trade Liberalization in Thailand, 1975–1985*

	Model 1	Model 2	Model 3	Model 4
Change in coalition vote share 1980–1983	0.0162 (0.0092)*	0.0202 (0.0118)*	0.0273 (0.0119)**	0.0387 (0.0158)**
Change in swing party's vote shares	−0.0093 (0.0128)	−0.0115 (0.0135)		
Change in total factor productivity 1976–1982	−1.631 (0.156)***	−1.626 (0.157)***	−1.265 (0.204)***	−1.267 (0.206)***
Coalition vote share in 1983		−0.0077 (0.0136)		−0.0123 (0.0170)
Change in coalition seat share 1982–1985				−0.869 (0.945)
Constant	−6.503 (0.339)***	−6.054 (0.869)***	−2.982 (0.367)***	−2.239 (0.999)**
R^2	0.628	0.629	0.379	0.392
Obs.	70	70	70	70

Note: OLS estimates. Standard errors in parentheses. Statistically significant at *10%; **5%; ***1%.

that increased support for the ruling coalition between 1980 and 1983 elections,[89] and liberalized industries located in provinces that decreased the support.[90] The pattern is the opposite from the Japanese trade liberalization in the 1960s, in which the government liberalized industries located in districts that increased the support for the LDP, and protected industries located in districts that decreased the support. I explore the sources of this divergence later.

[89] House of Representative election before 1983 was held in 1979. I match these 1979 election data with Prem's coalitional parties as of 1980, when Prem assumed prime ministership and established the coalition, and calculate the changes in vote share by province between 1980 and 1983.

[90] Voters' support for Prem coalition increased more among provinces with the lower level of support in the previous election, which suggests that the increase was due to the additional mobilization in the swing districts, rather than in the core districts. Bivariate linear regression estimating the increase in vote share for the Prem coalition between 1980 and 1983 elections during this period (Change Ruling Vote Share, 1980–1983) suggests that the additional vote mobilization for the ruling coalition was more prevalent in the swing districts, i.e., the lower ruling coalition's ruling vote share in 1980 had reductive effects on increase, and the effect and the relationship is significant at the 1% level (coefficients −0.678 and standard errors 0.114).

Use of Pork as a Side Payment 69

Substantive effects of additional vote mobilization in support for the ruling coalition on liberalization were modest: a 20 percentage point increase in vote share for the ruling coalition between the two elections (1980 and 1983) was associated with 0.3 to 0.8 additional nominal rates of protection, which is about a quarter of one standard deviation.[91] The association between increase in Prem's coalition vote share and protection is robust and consistent across different specifications.[92]

The initial level of voters' support for the ruling coalition in 1980 did not turn out to have systematic effects on liberalization decisions, which challenges the established argument that politicians reward the core supporters under an MMD. Instead, the government's trade policy was responsive to the changes in support for the ruling coalition, where it rewarded protection to increased voter mobilization in provinces. Control variables show expected results. Just like the Japanese case, the government was more likely to liberalize productive industries (i.e., high total factor productivity growth between 1976 and 1982).

In sum, the Prem government liberalized manufacturing industries where the ruling coalition experienced declining voter support and provided trade protection to industries where the ruling coalitions experienced increased voter mobilization. The results are consistent with the Globalization as Legislation approach that Thai party leaders' concerns for keeping the majority seat shares on the floor affected the liberalization process even when trade liberalization went through an executive, not legislative, route (Imaizumi 2011). The prime minister's coalition building with legislators dictated a trade liberalization process even under a semidemocratic Thailand during this time period, where the prime minister and some technocrats were appointed rather than elected.[93]

Why Thai Prime Minister use trade protection for districts with increasing voter support, while Japanese Prime Minister used protection to declining support, however, requires a further discussion. Electoral systems do not account for this divergence because both countries adopted an MMD system with single nontransferable vote, which predicts that parties should reward higher vote mobilization ("the core voter"), consistent with the pattern for manufacturing liberalization in Thailand.

Party system difference explains this divergence. The LDP was one-party dominant in the 1960s, which allowed the party leaders to have a centralized control over trade liberalization as well as over the flows of particularistic benefits such as public work projects and ministerial appointments. The threat of

---

[91] Descriptive statistics for the change in NRP in 1985 are: 2.99 (mean), 3.82 (standard deviation), −15.8 (minimum), and 9.25 (maximum).

[92] The results do not change when using the effective rates of protection as the dependent variable.

[93] In addition to Prime Minister Prem, 74 percent (in 1980) to 44 percent (in 1985–1986) of Prem's cabinet ministers were appointed as opposed to elected, according to the author's data.

70 *Empirical Evidence*

legislator breakaway came from within the party, which facilitated negotiating the side-payment deals with co-partisan legislators.

By contrast, multiparty coalitions under Prem were unstable and fragile. The pattern of vote mobilization was unpredictable as a result of fluid party systems with rampant party switching, party realignment, and vote buying. With the high level of uncertainty regarding where vote gains and losses for the ruling coalition would occur in the future, it made more sense for party leaders to reward protection to organized vote mobilization (for manufacturing).

Explaining Agricultural Liberalization: Rewarding Loyal Legislators, Not Voters

The pattern of agricultural liberalization, however, is strikingly different from that of manufacturing industries. Table 2.8 summarizes the results for agricultural liberalization during the Prem cabinets (1980 to 1988) with similar sets of covariates as the models estimating manufacturing liberalization.[94] As a measure of agricultural protection, I use Nominal Rates of Assistance (NRA), which is defined as the percentage by which a bundle of government agricultural policies (e.g., price support, subsidies, tariffs, and taxation) have raised or lowered gross returns to farmers above what they would be in the free market without the government's intervention. NRA is expressed as a percentage of the undistorted price (NRA = 0), and positive values (NRA > 0) indicate that a commodity is subsidized or protected, and negative values (NRA < 0) indicate that a commodity is taxed (i.e., farmers sell their produce lower than the market price).

I use World Bank's *Database of Global Distortions to Agricultural Incentives, 1955 to 2010* (Anderson and Valenzuela, 2011), which estimated nominal rates of assistance for eight commodities in Thailand from 1970 to 2010: rice, cassava, maize, sugar, palm oil, rubber, pig meat, and poultry.[95] The production values of the eight commodities together constitute 60 to 71 percent of total agricultural production in Thailand, depending on year. Figure 2.4 summarizes changes in NRA for four representative commodities between 1981 and 1988, the period under Prime Minister Prem's cabinet.[96] I then weigh the change in

---

[94] To be precise, Thai agricultural liberalization went back and forth in three phases between 1980 and 1988. I used the progress in agricultural liberalization between 1981 and 1988 as the main dependent variable (Change in NRA, 81–88), as it highly correlates with the major liberalization that occurred between 1981 and 1982 at 0.99. The government vastly reduced the taxation (NRA < 0) for farmers during the first phase (1980–1982), which amounted on average to a 14 percentage point increase in nominal rates of assistance (i.e., less taxation and more closer to the undistorted market price, where NRA = 0).

[95] The NRA data for soybeans are available only since 1984, and hence not used in my analysis in this chapter.

[96] The October 1982 liberalization reduced the tariff levels across manufacturing industries in a short period of time. In contrast, government agricultural policies went back and forth among

TABLE 2.8. *The Determinants of Agricultural Trade Liberalization in Thailand, 1981–1988*

	Model 1	Model 2	Model 3	Model 4	Model 5
Change in coalition seat shares	−0.148 (0.0703)**	−0.152 (0.0717)**	−0.127 (0.0703)*	−0.127 (0.0697)*	−0.148 (0.0712)**
Coalition seat share, 1980					0.0028 (0.0327)
Change in coalition vote share, 1980–1983	0.0001 (0.0004)	0.0002 (0.0004)	0.0002 (0.0004)	0.0002 (0.0004)	0.0001 (0.0004)
Coalition vote share, 1980	0.0002 (0.0004)	0.0002 (0.0004)	0.0003 (0.0004)	0.0002 (0.0004)	0.0002 (0.0005)
Total number of seats					0.0036 (0.0051)
% Same party in ruling coalition		0.0118 (0.0283)	0.0206 (0.0286)	0.0175 (0.0256)	
% Rice (area)	0.251 (0.0513)***	0.256 (0.0532)***	0.248 (0.0537)***	0.240 (0.0435)***	0.260 (0.0537)***
ln agricultural population	−0.0006 (0.0119)	−0.0027 (0.0130)	−0.0037 (0.0149)		−0.0120 (0.0203)
% Literate	0.184 (0.123)	0.172 (0.127)			0.170 (0.126)
% Education > 9 years			−0.0122 (0.210)	0.0122 (0.184)	
Constant	−0.146 (0.119)	−0.131 (0.126)	0.0067 (0.102)	−0.0157 (0.0478)	−0.0737 (0.160)
R^2	0.413	0.414	0.397	0.396	0.418
Obs.	70	70	70	70	70

Note: OLS estimates. Standard errors in parentheses. Statistically significant at *10%; **5%; ***1%.

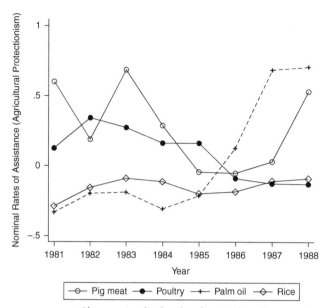

FIGURE 2.4. Changes in the levels of agricultural protection (nominal rates of assistance) in Thailand, selected commodities, 1981–1988.
Source: Anderson and Valenzuela (2011), *Database of Global Distortions to Agricultural Incentives, 1955 to 2010*. Available at World Bank.
Note: Positive values indicate that a given commodity is protected and/or subsidized, and negative values indicate that a given commodity is taxed. A value of zero indicates no market distortion (i.e., no subsidy or taxation).

commodity-level NRA from 1981 to 1988 with provincial data on the composition of labor force by agricultural commodities before the liberalization, available in seventy-two provincial reports from 1978 *Thailand Agricultural Census*.[97] Change Province NRA *i* is the dependent variable for province *i*, which indicates the provincial-level agricultural trade liberalization (or taxation), weighted by the composition of agricultural labor force by commodities. Positive values for

protectionism (NRA > 0), liberalization (NRA converging to zero), and taxation (NRA < 0), and the liberalization patterns differed among different commodities as well. Figure 2.6 shows the diversity of government policy shifts across commodities and over time: while taxation on rice (solid black line with black marker) had been reduced over time (i.e., policy shift from taxing rice farmers to allowing them to sell rice at closer to the market price, where NRA = 0), poultry (solid black line with a cross marker) experienced the opposite.

[97] In 1978 *Agricultural Census*, the labor force for rubber industry is reported missing for all the provinces, and thus the rubber industry is dropped from the analysis. Furthermore, provincial reports use inconsistent units (land area vs. the number of holdings) for cassava and sugar cane producers. I dropped cassava and sugar cane industries from the analysis. This leaves me with rice, poultry, and pork, which constitute on average 73 percent, 75 percent, and 29 percent of total farm holdings across provinces, respectively. The sugar cane industry constitutes 6 percent of total farm holdings.

Use of Pork as a Side Payment 73

Change Province NRA indicate an increase in the government's support for a given commodity, and negative values indicate a decline in support.

THE RESULTS

Overall, the results suggest that the party leaders' incentive to maintain the majority seat shares on the floor dictated the agricultural liberalization process. In particular, three results stand out. First, the government's liberalization decisions responded to legislators' decisions to stay or breakaway from the Prem coalition, but not electorates' voting behaviors in districts. The results are contrary to the manufacturing liberalization. The government rewarded more protection to commodities located in provinces represented by Social Action Party legislators who broke away from the Prem coalition and returned a few months before the major trade liberalization (1982).[98] By contrast, the government liberalized commodities located in provinces represented by legislators who had committed to stay with the Prem coalition. The substantive impact of legislators' defection from the coalition on trade liberalization is large. The defection and return of one Social Action Party legislator in a province with five House of Representative seats is associated with a 0.25 to 0.34 percentage point increase in trade barriers on a given commodity. This liberalization amounted to four standard deviations of changes in NRA at seventy-one provinces, where the NRA ranged from −0.002 to 0.302 in 1982.

By contrast, electorates' voting behaviors did not have any systematic effects on the Prem government's liberalization decisions. Liberalization equally hit Prem's strong hold and weak hold, contrary to the debates regarding whether a government favors core or swing districts (i.e., the lack of statistical significance of Ruling Coalition Vote Share). Unlike the Japanese case, the government liberalization decisions were not related to the changes in vote shares in support for the coalition between elections, either (i.e., the lack of statistical significance of Ruling Coalition Vote Share Change).

Control variables are mostly insignificant except for the percentage of total farm holdings in a province that engaged in rice farming (% Rice Holding). The higher the proportion of rice farmers among a province's farm holdings, the higher level of protection they received. This lends support to the expectation that it is easier for a vast number of farmers to overcome the collective action problem if they can organize their interests around the single crop, rather than spreading across multiple commodities.

---

[98] Social Action Party's coalition exit and return both occurred in 1981 (exit in March, return in December), which was before the major trade liberalization in 1982. The Social Action Party exited from Prem's coalition in March of 1981, owing to its disagreement over Arab oil deals with another coalition partner, Chart Thai Party. The disagreement was about the distribution of oil rents, not over policy disagreements over trade liberalization or major economic policy issues. See Sirikrai (1982). Thus, we can eliminate the possibility of reverse causality that the 1982 trade liberalization led to legislator defections, not vice versa.

74 *Empirical Evidence*

DISCUSSION: COMPARING MANUFACTURING AND AGRICULTURAL
LIBERALIZATION

For manufacturing industries, Prem's liberalization decisions appeared to be vote-seeking, that is, rewarding voter mobilization. For agriculture, the Prem's liberalization decisions seemed seat-seeking, rewarding parties that entered the coalition. These results are paradoxical at first glance, because manufacturing workforce seemed too small to matter as a voting block (i.e., average 0.6 percent of the total workforce), whereas farmers constituted on average 73 percent of the workforce in provinces then (Population and Housing Census of Thailand, 1980).

The key to understanding this divergence is the logic of collection action for organized versus diffused interests (Olson 1965). Urban legislators had easier time organizing and mobilizing votes from industries and their workers, as they constituted small and organized groups in districts. Indeed, Prem's coalition drew higher and more organized support from provinces with manufacturing workforce than farmers. As of the 1983 election, a 1 percent higher proportion of manufacturing workforce in a province was associated with a 3.9 percent higher vote share for Prem's coalition.[99] By contrast, rural legislators had difficulty organizing and mobilizing votes from the vast number of farmers, often scattered across different commodities and crops. Vote-buying (i.e., legislators distributing goods and money to buy votes during elections) has also been rampant, especially in rural areas, making rural votes volatile and unreliable for party leaders to count on (Limmanee 1999).

Yet, party leaders could not ignore rural *representatives*, because they constituted the majority of Prem's coalition, outnumbering urban representatives. Thus, instead of rewarding rural voters for their mobilization, Prem's coalition rewarded trade protection to rural legislators for rejoining their coalition. For party leaders, it was easier to enforce the exchange of coalition loyalty and trade protection with legislators rather than with a vast number of rural voters.

Optimal Use of Pork to Build an Open Economy Coalition

The period of drastic trade liberalization in Thailand in the early 1980s coincided with the tight fiscal condition in the aftermath of the second energy crisis. Thus, the Thai government leveraged public work projects funded by the World Bank and the Japanese official development aid and ministerial appointments

---

[99] The bivariate regression estimating the Prem's coalition vote shares with the percentage manufacturing workforce per total workforce in 71 provinces in 1983 is significant at the 5% level. The percentage of agricultural workforce was not systematically associated with Prem's coalition vote shares, which is consistent with my interpretation of farmers' difficulty in organizing around the same party.

Use of Pork as a Side Payment 75

as Pork to buy off legislator support. In particular, the Thai government developed "Eastern Seaboard Development Program," which designated three coastal provinces on the gulf of Thailand for the development of infrastructure and manufacturing industries. The program was a pillar of Thailand's Fifth National Development Plan (1982–1986) under the Prem government, which marked the shift from a closed to an open economy (Doner 1998; Ariga and Ejima 2000).

The stated aim of this program was to transform Thailand from an agrarian to an industrial economy with the inflow of foreign capital, and to solve the congestion of factories in Bangkok by creating more manufacturing and trading hubs in eastern seaboard provinces. It is no surprise that the two goals of this program were identical to Japan's Law to Consolidate and Promote Special Areas for Industrial Development (*Kogyo Seibi Tokubetsu Chiiki Seibi Hou*) enacted in 1964, because the Thai government explicitly followed Japan's development strategy in formulating the program (see earlier discussion in this chapter and Chapter 5; Doner 1998: 143–145).

The total estimated public investment for the master plan of this project was $US4.5 billion (in 1981 constant price), which promised to put severe fiscal burdens on Thai government, even with external funding from the World Bank and the Japanese government. The initial financier of the program, the World Bank, recommended against developing new trading hubs, and instead suggested using existing port facilities around Bangkok to ease the fiscal burden.[100] Thai policymakers were also split over using existing port facilities (the World Bank's position) or developing new trading hubs around the eastern seaboard provinces. This disagreement within the Thai government emerged between elected legislators and appointed technocrats, similar to the pork vs. productivity conflicts that emerged within the Japanese LDP over the Industrial Development Law (see earlier discussion in this chapter; Pempel 2010). For example, fiscally conservative Snoh Unakl, the Secretary General of the National Economic and Social Development Board (NESDB) and a prominent economist, supported the World Bank's position to use the existing port facilities, which led to the 45 days of freezing of the program in 1985 (Shimomura 2003: 175–177).

Ultimately, however, elected legislators supported the program with an anticipation of construction booms and economic growth and the Prem government needed the majority legislator support to survive the nonconfidence votes. After reevaluation, the cabinet overturned the technocrats' and World Bank's opposition, and went ahead with the Eastern Seaboard Development Program. The Japanese aid amounted to 20 percent of the estimated costs in the master plan, and allowed the Thai government to implement the plan without the World Bank's support (Shimomura 2003).

---

[100] Shimomura (2003: 175–177).

Empirical Evidence

With the appreciation of yen after the Plaza Accord (1985), the Eastern Seaboard Development Program attracted many Japanese and other foreign investment projects in industries such as automobiles, petrochemicals, and steel, and estimated to have generated 460,000 new jobs (Shatkin 2003: 22). The Thai government continued to put one of the highest priorities on this program during the sixth development plan (1987–1991), and favorably allocated the government's budget to the three provinces.

In addition to the Eastern Seaboard Development Program, the Prem government distributed another form of Pork, ministerial positions, to legislators who were hit by trade liberalization. During his term (1980–1988), Prem formed three cabinets with five major reshufflings of ministers, which resulted in a total of sixty-four ministerial positions granted, of which 31 positions were given to elected legislators representing MMD constituencies in provinces.[101] Table 2.9 summarizes Prem's decisions to grant two forms of Pork to seventy-one provinces during his term[102]: (1) designations to the Eastern Seaboard Development Program and (2) ministerial positions to legislators representing districts in a given province. The values in each box represent the mean values of manufacturing liberalization in each province, that is, changes in nominal rate of protection (NRP) between 1975 and 1982. Standard errors are in the parentheses below and one asterisk next to the parentheses indicates a 10% statistical significance in the difference-in-means test of changes in NRP, where provinces that received neither of the two side payments (the bottom right cell) serve as a base group.

No province received both forms of side payments, that is, designation of the Eastern Seaboard Development Program and ministerial positions, which lends support to my argument that the Prem cabinet used these side payments substitutively to buy off legislators' support. Furthermore, Pork was given to provinces that experienced a much deeper than average reduction of trade barriers. The three provinces designated for the Eastern Seaboard Development Program were on average hit by a 1.8 percentage point additional reduction in NRP for manufacturing industries than provinces that did not receive either side

---

[101] To identify constituency information for elected ministers, I matched the individual names of all the ministers at the official website of the Secretariat of the Cabinet (http://www.cabinet.thaigov.go.th/eng/) with Constituency-Level Election Archive (CLEA) data at University of Michigan (2012 version). When there was no matching name in the CLEA dataset, I reason that these ministers were appointed, nonelected ministers. I thank Allen Hicken and his research assistant for making individual names of candidates available to me and Chayathorn Termariyabuit and Krantarat Krongsiriwat for excellent research assistance. Deputy ministerial positions can also be used as a side payment, but this analysis focuses only on ministerial positions. Thirty-one positions were cumulative totals, including repeated appointments of the same legislators.

[102] Bangkok is dropped from the analysis because its labor composition data is missing in 1980 Housing and Population Census.

Use of Pork as a Side Payment

TABLE 2.9. *Side-Payment Allocations and the Depth of Manufacturing Liberalization*

		Ministerial Positions	
		Yes	No
Eastern Seaboard Development Program	Yes	No Province	−5.41 (0.837)* 3 Provinces
	No	−4.319 (0.315) 6 Provinces	−3.539 (0.213) 61 Provinces

Note: Numbers in each row indicate mean values in *Changes in NRP 1975–1982* of provinces. Negative values indicate trade liberalization (i.e., the reduction in tariff barriers) and positive values indicate increase in trade protection during the time period. Numbers in parentheses are standard errors and * indicates a 10% level of statistical significance in difference-in-means test where the lower right values (No–No side payment) are a base group ($Pr(|T| > |t|) = 0.0627$).

payment.[103] This difference was larger than one standard deviation in changes in NRP between 1975 and 1982, which ranged from −7.91 to +0.13, and statistically significant at the 10% level.[104] By contrast, provinces that received ministerial positions did not differ in their extent of trade liberalization from the base group (i.e., no side-payment group in the lower right column).

To lend more systematic support, Table 2.10 shows probit estimates (marginal effects) on provinces' likelihood of receiving either form of side payments given the extent of their liberalization. Models 1 to 3 present the results on the effect of trade liberalization in manufacturing, and models 4 and 5 present the

[103] Although the three provinces were initially chosen in the government's master plan developed as early as late 1970s (Ariga and Ejima 2000; Shimomura 2003), the final decision regarding the designation of Eastern Seaboard provinces occurred in 1985 after a substantial back and forth among the World Bank, Thai government, and the Japanese government over the plan regarding the priority of public investment. Moreover, before the 1982 liberalization, the three Eastern Seaboard provinces had on average 0.2 percent of their workforce in manufacturing sector, while other provinces had 0.6 percent (source: 1980 Housing and Population Census). This means that the causality between trade liberalization and the designation of these provinces was not reversed (i.e., the designation in the master plan during the 1970s attracted manufacturing investment and this was why the Eastern Seaboard provinces were hit by a deeper liberalization).

[104] When controlled for covariates, the effect of manufacturing liberalization (Changes in NRP) on the probability of receiving a side payment (probit estimates) is significant at 5%. See Table 2.10.

78   Empirical Evidence

TABLE 2.10. *Trade Liberalization and Pork Allocations in Thai Provinces (Marginal Effects of Probit Estimates)*

	Model 1	Model 2	Model 3	Model 4	Model 5
Manufacturing liberalization (Change in NRP 75–82)	−0.061 (0.0243)**	−0.066 (0.028)**	−0.068 (0.0291)**		
Agricultural liberalization (Change in NRA 81–82)				0.0266 (0.553)	0.0751 (0.575)
Ruling vote share, 1980	0.0022 (0.001)	0.0022 (0.001)	0.0021 (0.002)	0.0016 (0.002)	0.0018 (0.002)
Ruling coalition seats, 1980	−0.0128 (0.025)	−0.0127 (0.025)	−0.01 (0.027)	−0.017 (0.026)	−0.0199 (0.028)
Total factor productivity 1976–1982		−0.0098 (0.028)	−0.0112 (0.029)		
Change in ruling seat share 1980–1981			−0.0667 (0.286)		0.0986 (0.332)
N	70	70	70	70	70

Note: Reported here are marginal effects from probit estimation and standard errors are in parentheses. Statistical significance at $*p < 0.10$, $**p < 0.05$, and $***p < 0.01$. The dependent variable is a dichotomous variable one if a province received one of the two forms of side payments and zero otherwise.

results on the effect of agricultural liberalization. A province that was hit by the deeper reduction in manufacturing trade barriers (i.e., the larger negative values of Changes in NRP 75–82) was more likely to receive Pork. The effect of additional liberalization on the likelihood of receiving the side payment was large: one standard deviation-worth of additional manufacturing liberalization in a province would bring a 10 percentage point increased likelihood of legislators receiving either Eastern Seaboard designation or ministerial positions. By contrast, the government did not use side payment to mitigate the liberalization effects for agriculture (i.e., the lack of statistical significance of Change in NRA, 1981–1982, in models 4 and 5).

The results are consistent with the Optimal Use of Pork hypothesis developed in Chapter 1. The government used Pork to buy off support from organized groups (i.e., manufacturing industries), but did not use Pork for diffused losers that were vast in numbers and spread across electoral districts (i.e., agriculture). Instead, the government used protectionism (i.e., a loser-friendly

Policy) for agricultural commodities in districts where legislators defected and rejoined the Prem coalition, and liberalized commodities without side payments in districts where legislators who stayed loyal to the coalition.

The Prem government's use of both Pork and Policy strategies allowed the majority coalition building. Pork mitigated the electoral costs of trade liberalization and help co-partisan legislators mobilize more support in districts. When Pork was prohibitively expensive with diffused losers, such as farmers, protectionism was used to reward legislators who broke away and rejoined the coalition. The patterns of electoral competition (e.g., core or swing) did not have any systematic influence over the allocation of Pork (i.e., the lack of statistical significance of Ruling Vote Share), contrary to the literature that considers pork barreling as legislators' vote-seeking endeavor. Instead, incentives for majority coalition-building dictated the Pork allocation.

Overall, the Thai government employed coalition-building strategies for an open economy similar to Japan's. It exposed fence-sitters for deeper trade liberalization (e.g., competitive manufacturing industries, measured by total factor productivity), and compensated them with generous Pork to help co-partisans survive elections. Prem government bought loyalty of rural representatives by granting protectionism to agricultural commodities. As a result, Pork was allocated more heavily to urban and industrial areas. Despite the difference in factor endowment in the two economies (i.e., Japan as a developed economy as of 1964, Thailand as a developing economy), both governments used Pork to convince urban and industrial representatives to support an open economy.

CONCLUSION

This chapter has shown that party leaders and their incentives for majority-coalition building had substantial influence over the patterns of trade liberalization in Japan and Thailand, even when trade liberalization did not require a majority support in the parliaments. The findings challenge a widely believed insulation thesis that East Asian governments were able to liberalize their economies because of their insulation from special- interest politics.

Second, the electoral disconnection, where legislators take policy positions that deviate from their districts' interests, is prevalent, partially because of the party leaders' effort (and success) to "buy off" back-benchers' support for an open economy. This forces us to reconsider the dominant approach in the literature that links districts' economic characteristics with legislators' policy positions. Indeed, despite the massive electoral costs of liberalization, this period witnessed remarkably restrained and pro-liberalization Japanese and Thai legislators.

Finally, this chapter has further shown that policy-seeking party leaders can use pork barrel projects to buy off legislator support for the open economy. Pork can facilitate, rather than inhibit, the government's provision of collective goods, such as trade liberalization. Precisely because party leaders allocate Pork to build the majority coalition and to help co-partisan legislators survive elections, however, Pork allocation favored fence-sitting legislators, whose districts incurred small net losses from liberalization, not those who incurred the largest income losses from liberalization. Party leaders' and legislators' needs for policymaking and political survival, not industries' sheer needs for compensation, dictated the government's resource allocation. Furthermore, Pork allocation was highly responsive to legislators' collective action capacity, especially their ability to issue a credible threat of party or coalition exit, not necessarily industry's collective action capacity. These findings call us to revisit the literature linking globalization and the rise of compensation programs for losers (such as social welfare), which assumes that the organizational capacity of losers (such as centralized labor union and left party strength) translates into the size of compensation programs. The finding also challenges the conventional wisdom linking rural and poor districts with the prevalence of pork barrel politics (Stokes 2005). Both in Japan and Thailand, two economies with different factor endowment, pork allocation favored urban and industrial areas during their early phase of trade liberalization.

APPENDIX: CALCULATING THE DEPTH OF TRADE LIBERALIZATION ACROSS ELECTORAL DISTRICTS

To understand how party leaders build coalition for liberalization with legislators, we need to first identify variations in reduction in trade barriers across electoral districts (geographic units). I follow Topalova's work on India (2007), and calculate the province or prefecture's additional exposure to imports by weighting the reduction in trade barriers in each industry by the proportion of localities' labor force employed by these industries (also see Kovak 2013).

Table A2.1 provides an example. Consider three industries – Rice, Chemicals, and Machinery – which experienced the reduction in trade barriers (here expressed in tariff levels) by 15, 13, and 7 percentage points respectively. To calculate the effect of these tariff reductions on the labor force in a given province, I weight the industry-level tariff reduction proportionally to the percentage of the labor force employed in a given province in each of these industries. This is the same weighting strategy employed in numerous studies on constituents' influence on trade policy (Bailey, Goldstein, and Weingast 1997; Irwin and Kroszner 1999; Ladewig 2006), except that I use data on prefectural/provincial composition of *labor force*, not the

Use of Pork as a Side Payment

TABLE A2.1. *Provincial-Level Tariff Reduction, Weighted by Labor Force Composition*

Industry	Tariff Reduction	Province A (% Industry Employment)	Province B (% Industry Employment)
Rice	−15	10	33
Chemical	−13	25	25
Machinery	−7	33	5
Provincial-level reduction, weighted by % industry employment		=(−15*0.1) + (−13*0.25) + (−7*0.33) =−7.06%	=(−15*0.33) + (−13*0.25) + (−7*0.05) =−8.55%

composition of industry's production or shipping values. Because my theory concerns how party leaders seek to compensate the income effects of trade liberalization felt by the constituents and legislators who represent them, use of labor force composition data from the pre-liberalization period is more appropriate.

Although this example uses tariff reduction as the measure of trade liberalization, this weighting strategy can be used for any measures of trade barriers, such as Nominal Rate of Assistance (NRA) for agricultural commodities.

3

Pro-Loser Policy during Hard Times

In Chapter 2 I showed that party leaders targeted Pork to legislators fence-sitting on liberalization, in the form of public work projects and personnel appointments, to build a majority coalition for an open economy. Pork is the preferred instrument for coalition-building for party leaders, precisely because leaders can target Pork to specific legislators to buy off their support and exclude others.

Despite the efficiency and political benefits of Pork, however, even governments in candidate-centered electoral systems sometimes use policy programs that benefit diffused losers (i.e., liberalization losers that are spread across many electoral districts) to build a coalition for an open economy. Examples of such initiatives include Japan's Basic Law for Small-Medium Size Firms (1953) in preparation for the accession to General Agreement on Tariffs and Trade (GATT); Japan's Large-scale Retail Store Law passed to protect domestic mom-and-pop shops from retail investment liberalization (1973);[1] and price stabilization programs to help inflation-suffering consumers and the expansion of welfare expenditures in the 1970s in Japan and of government healthcare programs and debt-relief programs for farmers in Thailand (2001–2005).[2]

Interestingly, moreover, these initiatives occurred under the multimember district (MMD) system in Japan (which should encourage legislators' responsiveness to organized interests), and under a mixed electoral system combining

---

[1] Aramaki (2004). The retail market liberalization was implemented gradually by first allowing the investment of 50 percent foreign ownership in 1969 and then increasing the ratio to 100 percent by 1975.

[2] Note that Thailand's healthcare and debt-relief programs were initiated under the Thaksin cabinet, which had a combination of a single-member district system with a closed list, proportional representation system, which is considered less personalistic than the multimember district system. It is important to note that farmers were diffused losers after the 1997 financial crisis in Thailand – they constituted more than a half of the labor force.

Pro-Loser Policy during Hard Times 83

TABLE 3.1. *Predictions for Pork versus Policy*

	Japan	Thailand		
	Energy Crises	Energy Recession	Financial Crisis	Financial Crisis
Time period	1973–1980	1983–1986	1997–2000	2001–2005
Cabinets	Tanaka, Miki and Fukuda	Prem	Chuan	Thaksin
Demand-side	Diffused losers and Resource constraints			
Supply-side: party systems	Centralized (one-party)	Decentralized (multiparty)	Decentralized (multiparty)	Centralized (one-party)
Electoral system prediction	Pork	Pork	Pork	Policy
Optimal use of policy prediction	Policy	Pork	Pork	Policy
Outcome	Policy	Pork	Pork	Policy

single-member districts (SMDs) with proportional representation (PR) systems in Thailand (which should encourage legislators' responsiveness to diffused losers) (Selway 2011). The Japanese case especially poses a puzzle for the conventional argument linking candidate-centered electoral systems with public policies that benefit narrow and organized interests (Myerson 1993; Cox 1990; Tatebayashi 2004; Hirano 2006; Scheiner 2006).

The theory of *Optimal Use of Policy* developed in Chapter 1 suggests two conditions under which governments are likely to rely on Policy over Pork: (1) the losers are vast in number and diffused across districts and/or fiscal resource is constrained (the demand-side condition); (2) party systems are centralized, that is, a fewer number of parties in a government (the supply-side condition). Contrary to the conventional electoral system argument, this chapter shows that party systems have substantial effects on the party leaders' use of Policy over Pork by changing the costs of intraelite bargaining over the government resource. The centralized party systems, in which the fewer number of parties is in the government, are associated with the use of Policy over Pork due to its relative ease in striking an intraelite bargain over new resource allocation.

To test this argument, I focus on periods during and immediately after major economic crises in Japan and Thailand, because they hold the demand-side conditions (the rise of diffused losers and fiscal constraints) relatively constant,[3] and provide sufficient variations on the Condition 2 (centralized vs. decentralized party systems) as summarized in Table 3.1. This chapter shows that a more centralized party system under the one-party dominance of the

---

[3] For the definition of diffused losers and the two conditions in which they arise, see Chapter 1.

84　　　　　　　　　　　　　　　　　　　　　　　　　　*Empirical Evidence*

Liberal Democratic Party (LDP) and establishment of intraparty organizations allowed party leaders in Japan to shift from Pork to Policy strategy during the 1970s when two energy crises (1973 and 1978) hit the economy.

Under a similar electoral system (i.e., MMDs with a block vote system), Thai party leaders faced similar challenges during the recession (1983–1986) caused by the two energy crises and by the 1997 Asian financial crisis. Yet, owing to a multiparty coalition government, Thai party leaders continued to use a Pork strategy to buy off legislators' support for an open economy. The shift from Pork to Policy then occurred after 2001 when the Thai Rak Thai Party achieved the one-party majority for the first time in Thai democratic history. Table 3.1 summarizes the predictions derived from the Optimal Use of Policy and compares them with the conventional, electoral system arguments.

OPTIMAL USE OF POLICY UNDER ONE-PARTY MAJORITY: POST-ENERGY CRISIS, JAPAN

The Rise of Diffused Losers and Fiscal Constraints: Macroeconomic Conditions

After experiencing double-digit economic growth in the 1960s, two major macroeconomic changes exposed the Japanese economy to volatility in the global market in the 1970s. The first was the end of the Bretton Woods system and the Japanese government's decision to transition from a fixed to a floating exchange rate system (February of 1973). The shift appreciated the yen to the U.S. dollar by 35 percent, which led to export-oriented industries' decline in competitiveness. The volatility of exchange rates in the global market also directly affected consumers and industries.

Second, the two energy crises during the 1970s (1973 and 1979) hit economies around the world. The rise of energy costs generated new economic losers in Japan: consumers who suffered inflation and primary material industries (steel and chemical, etc.), whose production depended heavily on energy input. The energy crises also led to fiscal contraction, and the government was faced with the dual challenge of buying off vast numbers of losers with a limited budget.

Despite the volatile macroeconomic conditions, the Japanese government kept its commitment to open economy and further liberalized trade and investment in the 1970s. Unlike the liberalization in the 1960s, which was heavily targeted at relatively competitive industries in manufacturing (see Chapter 2), moreover, the liberalization in the 1970s was more comprehensive, including uncompetitive manufacturing industries, agriculture, and service sectors. For manufacturing, the government further removed import restriction for twenty-seven of remaining thirty-two industries within five years (1970–1975). The removal of restrictions included industries that the government had previously justified for infant industry protection, such as high-tech industries and

Pro-Loser Policy during Hard Times

airplanes. For agriculture, the government unilaterally removed the import restriction for fifty out of seventy-three agricultural commodities within two years (1970–1972).[4] These trade liberalizations created a vast number of new losers, such as farmers, who constituted 18 percent of the total work force in 1970. Small and medium-sized manufacturing firms, which constituted more than 99 percent of manufacturing companies, were also exposed to the international competition and the volatility of macroeconomy in the 1970s.

The government also adopted drastic liberalization of foreign direct investment between 1967 and 1973. With the exceptions of five industries (e.g., agriculture, mining, and automobile),[5] all the major manufacturing sectors were liberalized for 100 percent foreign ownership by 1973. The government removed foreign ownership restriction on key service sectors as well, such as construction and banking.[6] Following the market opening, net inflows of foreign direct investment to Japan increased by threefold (in U.S. dollars), although foreign direct investment constituted a very tiny fraction of Japan's gross domestic product (GDP) at less than 0.1 percent in the 1970s (United Nations Center for Transnational Corporations 1991).[7] The most politically controversial was liberalization of retail industries in 1975. Around 10 percent of the labor force then engaged in retail and wholesale industry, and the retail sector's partisan support was still in flux, where the left party was increasingly popular among them (Tatebayashi 2004). In addition, a series of trade conflicts erupted with the United States during the 1970s: textiles (1972), steel, and color TVs (1977). With the U.S. threat of retaliation, backsliding to protectionism was not a reasonable option for the LDP.

In sum, owing to macroeconomic changes and energy crises, the government needed to buy off vast numbers of losers from liberalization with the fiscal constraints.

The Supply-Side Conditions: The LDP's One-Party Dominance and Centralization within the LDP

During the hard economic times, the LDP was dominant in both Lower House and Upper House legislatures, holding 49 percent (in the late 1970s) to 55 percent (in the early 1970s) of Lower House seat share. Yet the LDP faced increasingly popular left parties, such as the Japan Socialist Party and Japan

---

[4] These were pork, bacon, apple, refined sugar, etc.

[5] The five exceptions were agriculture, oil, leather, and mining industries and retail stores with more than eleven branches. (Ministry of International Trade and Industry 1968).

[6] Protected service sectors were media, transportation, healthcare, and waste management. See World Bank (2010), *Investing Across Borders Report*, p. 119.

[7] Net inflow of foreign direct investment still remains 5 percent of GDP as of 2010. See JETRO (2011). Report available at: https://www.jetro.go.jp/world/statistics/data/data/wir11instock_gdp.pdf.

86   *Empirical Evidence*

Communist Party.[8] These left parties mobilized support from urban workers by developing programmatic appeals in issues such as social welfare, environmental protection, child support, and protection of low-skilled workers.[9] Left parties were also increasingly popular among workers in small to medium-sized firms in manufacturing and retail sectors, which were heavily affected by trade and investment liberalization in the 1970s (Tatebayashi 2004). These programmatic appeals to diffused losers were not only consistent with the left parties' ideological commitment to redistribution. The platform to help diffused losers also made tactical sense for left parties, as the LDP relied mostly on support from organized interests, yet had not tapped into unorganized voters.[10] The LDP backbenchers, especially those who faced the rising competition from the left in urban districts, voiced concerns for their political survival and opposed liberalization.[11] The LDP leaders needed to buy off their support for liberalization and to help them survive elections.

Yet the use of Pork would have been prohibitively costly, as the volatility of the global economy generated a vast number of losers nationwide. Moreover, the fiscal contraction did not allow the government to expand Pork expenditures. Even Prime Minister Kakuei Tanaka (1972–1974) gave up his popular plan to develop hinterlands with transportation and public work projects (i.e., "A Plan for Building New Japan" [*nihon rettou kaizou keikaku*]), due to the fiscal constraints and the necessity to ease income losses of urban workers. Thus, the LDP leaders needed to shift the resource from Pork (see Chapter 2) to Policies that broadly benefit diffused losers.

In a long run, the shift from Pork to Policy would collectively help the LDP legislators survive the competition with the left parties, especially urban legislators. Yet, the shift would generate short-term losers within the party, that is, rural legislators whose survival was dependent on Pork, such as public work projects brought to their districts. In essence, the shift from Pork to Policy posed a classic collective goods dilemma for the LDP.

---

[8] Another direct factor that contributed to the rise of left parties was urban voters' backlash against environmental pollution caused by industries in urban areas. See Muramatsu (1988). Voter's awareness of environmental issues also coincided with energy crises and the Club of Rome's 1972 publication of *Limits of Growth*, which warned the future shortage of natural resources.

[9] Tatebayashi (2004); Estevez-Abe (2008); Miyamoto (2008).

[10] Small and medium-sized firm and small retail store owners have been known as traditional supporters to the LDP, but they were not yet in the 1960s and the early 1970s. Tatebayashi (2004) documents that the partisan support among these occupations at that time was quite split between leftist parties, such as the Japan Socialist Party and Japan Communist Party. Calder (1993: 232) also documented that the Communist Party increased its popularity in these sectors through local branches of the Democratic Commercial Associations *(minshu shokou-kai)*, which boasted 175,000 members, one-sixth of all Japanese small businesses.

[11] See, for instance, Diet Testimony by Koyama Osanori (the LDP), January 23, 1974, at the Plenary Session of the Lower House.

Pro-Loser Policy during Hard Times 87

The pork-to-policy shift also meant that the LDP legislators' credit claiming strategies needed to adjust from the one focusing on district-specific services (e.g., "I built this highway") to issue-specific ones ("We legislated the health-care bill"), and from individual credit-claiming to collective credit-claiming as a party. Both of these adjustments, moreover, had to be consistent with legislators' incentives to differentiate from one another under the MMD system, which encourages intraparty competition. Hence, the issue-specific, collective credit claiming required grouping of legislators with different policy/issue specializations within the LDP.

The Solutions to the Dilemma: Policy Tribes and Personnel Appointment Rules

Two changes in intraparty organizations within the LDP that occurred in the early to mid-1970s helped legislators solve the two problems discussed earlier. First, the LDP legislators increasingly voiced their policy demands through issue-specific groups formed within the party called "policy tribes" (*zoku*). Policy tribe legislators specialized in certain policy issues through accumulation of committee experience in the Diet and within the LDP, and developed close working relationship with relevant bureaucracies (Sato and Matsuzaki 1986; Inoguchi and Iwai 1987; Krauss and Pekkanen 2010). Although legislators' policy specialization was hardly a new phenomenon in Japanese politics,[12] policy tribes became more powerful and institutionalized in the LDP's policy-making since the early 1970s in response to the fiscal contractions caused by the energy crises (Inoguchi and Iwai 1987: 21).

Although scholars and pundits have often viewed these policy tribe politicians as an obstacle to achieving collective goods (such as trade liberalization), policy tribes in fact provided a better organized channel in which legislators voice broader *sectoral* interests, as opposed to district-specific interests such as pork barrel projects (Inoguchi and Iwai 1987: 253–257, Tatebayashi 2004).[13] This new channel to voice broader policy demands also allowed backbenchers' issue-specific, collective credit claiming, and substituted their loss of credit-claiming opportunities over Pork. The policy tribe system also reduced the costs of intraparty bargaining over the budget, by lowering the number of

---

[12] Asahi Shimbun (the major national newspaper), for instance, reported the influence of *ikei giin* (medical tribe legislators) during the revision of National Health Insurance Law (*kokumin kenkou hoken hou*) in 1958. "Ishikai he hiraki naotta ikei giin," February 9, 1958, *Asahi Shimbun*. The transcripts of parliamentary discussions also document that the opposition party legislators mentioned *koukuu zoku* (aviation tribe) in the context of the Lockheed corruption scandal. Tabuchi Tetsuya, Testimony for the Special Committee on Lockheed Issue, Upper House, August 17, 1976.

[13] Krauss and Pekkanen (2004) also consider one of the functions of policy tribes as enforcing party discipline and coordination of interests via PARC system.

88   *Empirical Evidence*

LDP groups battling for their shares of the budget. This reorganization helped the LDP's shift from Pork (geographically targetable benefits) to Policy.

In addition to the specific timing in which policy tribes became influential in policymaking (in response to the energy crisis), two further pieces of evidence corroborate my argument that the policy tribe system facilitated the LDP's shift from Pork to Policy. First, scholars and bureaucrats agreed that the most influential tribe in policymaking in the 1970s and 1980s was the welfare tribe (*kousei zoku*) (Inoguchi and Iwai 1987: 194–198). Welfare tribes derived their influence from three sources: (1) coherence of legislators' policy preferences within the tribe ensured by the lack of intratribe distributive conflicts; (2) small size due to the limits placed on new entries into the tribe;[14] and (3) the rise of left parties, which made the tribe's demand for welfare programs credible and necessary for LDP survival (Inoguchi and Iwai 1987: 196). In essence, the policy tribe system empowered the voice of legislators representing sectorally organized interests over those representing geographically organized interests.

The second piece of evidence is that, starting in the 1970s, even tribes that were conventionally thought of as Pork-oriented, such as agriculture, commerce, and construction tribes,[15] needed to coordinate and propose projects that benefit broader geographic areas or sectors to win a budget. For instance, between the two big public work projects conceived around 1970, construction tribes were less enthusiastic about building Tokyo Bay Crossing Road ("Tokyo Bay Aqua Line") than the National Network of Bullet Trains, because the former benefited only representatives from the Tokyo bay area, whereas the latter benefited broader geographic regions (Inoguchi and Iwai 1987: 193–194). Unified support within construction tribes made the National Network of Bullet Train launch its construction within a few years after the legislation, and the divided support delayed the launch of the Tokyo Bay Crossing Road project by sixteen years.[16]

The coordination of interests among legislators is indeed harder for these "Pork-oriented" tribes precisely because of the geographic and distributive nature of their policy benefits, such as where to build the road (for the construction tribes) and whether to increase price support for rice (for the agricultural tribes).[17] The policy tribe system thus functioned as a coordination device

---

[14] How the welfare-and-labor tribe limited new entries was not clear. Inoguchi and Iwai (1987) attributed this to the technicality of the policy issue.

[15] The three pork-oriented tribes were the most popular choice for legislators, yet, they did not possess the level of influence that welfare and labor tribe enjoyed. See Inoguchi and Iwai (1987: 132–134).

[16] Minesaki (2003).

[17] Inoguchi and Iwai (1987: 186) documented how the "south–north war" (*nanboku sensou*) among rice farmers weakened their demands for price support in the early 1980s. The north–south cleavage emerged among rice farmers as a result of the diverging qualities of rice (high in north; low in south) produced.

Pro-Loser Policy during Hard Times 89

for even Pork-oriented legislators to voice broader policy interests, and thus assisted the LDP's shift from Pork to Policy.

Second, the LDP institutionalized two new rules over the allocation of cabinet posts between 1970 and 1976 (the end of Eisaku Sato cabinet to Takeo Fukuda cabinet)(Sato and Matsuzaki 1986; Kawato 1996 a, 1996 b), both of which helped the party leaders' shift from Pork to Policy. The first is seniority-based allocation of cabinet posts where legislators who were reelected for the higher number of terms obtained high-rank cabinet and party positions (e.g., a legislator needed to be reelected more than five times to obtain a ministerial position). The second new rule is the quota-based allocation of cabinet posts to factions, where all factions – whether they had a majority or a minority status in the LDP – receive cabinet posts proportional to their size of membership. Before the institutionalization of this rule, the majority factions monopolized the cabinet positions (e.g., Sato Eisaku cabinet from 1964 to 1972). In essence, this quota-based post allocation system shifted the LDP's cabinet allocation from the minimum winning coalition principle (Riker 1962, i.e., the smallest number of legislators necessary to stay as a majority coalition share the spoils of victory) to the oversize coalition.

Both the seniority and quota-based rules constrained the party leaders' use of personnel appointments at their discretion to buy off fence-sitting legislators during the liberalization process (see Chapter 2). These new rules, however, increased legislators' payoff for staying with the LDP even during hard times in the 1970s (Kawato 1996a, 1996b; Nemoto et al. 2008). They also reduced the costs of intraparty bargaining over resources, by regulating interfactional fights. The seniority-based appointments made the LDP legislators stay with the party even during the time of austerity for future gains via high-rank party and ministerial positions. With the quota allocation rule, even minority factions enjoyed their access to budget, which reduced their incentives to break away from the LDP. Institutionalization of these personnel appointment rules in effect allowed the LDP's collective shift from Pork to Policy.

By restraining Pork, the LDP leaders were able to package open economy legislations with compensation bills that addressed the income losses of diffused losers from liberalization, such as small to medium-sized retail businesses and consumers.[18] These compensation policies encompassed a vast number of losers across the nation and differed from those in 1960s, which tended to target specific commodities, localities, or legislators (cf. Chapter 2).

---

[18] The two bills concerning the small and medium-sized retail stores were legislated just before the eruption of the first energy crisis (September and October of 1973, respectively) and were put into force in 1974.

The Controlled Comparison: Pre- and Post-Energy Crises Budget Allocation for Losers

I provide two forms of evidence for my argument regarding how the policy tribe system and personnel appointment rules within the LDP facilitated the use of Policies for diffused losers: (1) structured comparison of budget allocation to diffused versus organized interests in pre- and post-energy crises (i.e., the energy crises as the exogenous shocks) and (2) multivariate analysis on the determinants of budget allocation to diffused (Policy) versus geographically organized interests (Pork) from 1955 to 2012.

The first evidence is the comparison of budget allocations for organized versus diffused losers across four time periods: pre-first energy crisis (fiscal years 1972 and 1973), post-first energy crisis (fiscal years 1974 and 1975), and pre-second energy crisis (1977 and 1978) and post-second energy crisis (fiscal years 1979 and 1980). Note that the electoral system and the party in power during this time stayed the same, that is, MMD system with LDP dominance, both of which are believed to encourage legislators favoring geographically organized interests. What emerged between the first and second energy crises was the LDP's centralization via policy specialization and personnel appointment rules, both of which took place between 1970 and 1976 (i.e., the supply-side condition).[19]

Consistent with the Optimal Use of Policy hypothesis, I expect that the proportion of the budget allocated to diffused losers increased after the first energy crisis as a result of the increase in diffused losers and fiscal constraints (the demand-side condition 1). Further, I expect that after the LDP's centralization and with the second energy crisis, the government continued to commit the budget allocation to diffused losers over organized losers (the supply-side condition 2) even after the economy recovered from the two waves of energy crises (1973–1974 and 1979–1980) and left parties lost their stream (late 1970s).[20] The government's fiscal commitment to diffused losers was not a short-term, symptomatic response to the demand-side conditions, such as the energy crises and/or the rise of left parties, as often portrayed in the literature. The structural change within the LDP allowed continuing allocation to diffused interests, which facilitated the open economy coalition building.

Table 3.2 documents the changes in the budget allocation by items, focusing on the dramatic shift that occurred during the 1970s. The first and second

---

[19] Here, I do not claim that the centralization was exogenous to the energy crises and the rise of left. The LDP's centralization was an adaptation to the rise of left and the fiscal contractions caused by the energy crises.

[20] The government's continuing commitment to diffused losers does not mean that Japanese welfare provision was sufficient, nor that the provision was larger than other Organisation for Economic Co-operation and Development (OECD) countries. My point here is simply that the magnitudes of pork barrel politics seen in the 1960s did not come back even after the recovery from the energy crises and the left parties' decline.

TABLE 3.2. *Government's Budget Allocation before and after the Energy Crises*

Budget Items	Pre-crisis I	Response I	% Change I	Pre-crisis II	Response II	% Change II	% Change
	1972/1973	1974/1975	Pre- vs. Post-	1977/1978	1979/1980	Pre- vs. Post-	Responses I vs. II
Diffused							
Price stabilization	23,950	33,081	38	61,558	85,000	38	157
Social welfare	37,559	68,177	82	124,730	158,390	27	132
SM enterprises	1,485	2,299	55	4,752	4,752	0	107
Diffused Total	62,994	103,557	64	191,040	248,142	30	140
Geo-Organized							
Infrastructure	6,201	7,071	14	12,636	17,944	42	154
Food control	13,368	16,218	21	17,618	19,374	10	19
Public investment	49,893	57,466	15	97,312	130,802	34	128
Organized Total	69,462	80,755	16	127,566	168,120	32	108

Unit: 100 million yen.

Source: Financial Statistics, Ministry of Finance, Various Years, and Ministry of Finance, *Zaisei Kin-yu Toukei Geppou* [Monthly Report of Fiscal and Finance Statistics], various years.

Note: The budget allocated for price stabilization programs was available only from 1972 to 2000 (when the program was abandoned) in Ministry of Finance's "Explanation of Budget" (*Yosan no Setsumei*) memorandum circulated for the Diet discussion, available in Zaisei Kin-yu Toukei Geppou, various years. Energy crises erupted during October–November of 1973 (crisis I) and November–December of 1978 (crisis II).

columns compare the budget allocation to diffused versus geographically organized interests before and after the eruption of the first energy crisis, and the third column summarizes the percentage point change in the budget allocation to each item between pre- versus post-first energy crisis.

Columns 1 to 3 show that, first, the government's support for diffused losers, such as urban consumers who suffered from inflation and workers with meager welfare provisions, increased by 64 percent from the pre-1973 energy crisis, in contrast to a 16 percent increase for the budget for geographically organized interests. As a result, the proportion of spending for diffused interests exceeded the spending for geographically organized interests for the first time in postwar Japan (also see Figure 3.1).

Although the bulk of the expanded welfare spending during this period aimed to help retirees (e.g., free medical care for those older than age seventy and improved national pension annuity), not workers directly affected by globalization, the LDP also designed the welfare programs to address the volatility of the economy brought by Japan's transition to a floating exchange system. The government introduced consumer price indexation of pensions to address inflation, which substantially increased the government expenses on the welfare programs. For instance, the government raised the monthly pension benefit by 50 percent, from 5,000 yen to 7,500 yen from 1973 to 1974.[21]

Furthermore, the government committed 8 to 9 percent of the overall budget to price stabilization programs, aimed to ease the inflation burden on consumers throughout 1970s and 1980s. The government also established the Employment Adjustment Benefits program in 1975,[22] which compensated small to medium-sized firms in certain sectors for their use of temporary leave systems for workers instead of layoffs.[23] By contrast, public works spending and subsidies for farmers increased only by 14 to 21 percentage points respectively after the first energy crisis.

Columns 4 to 6 show the government's responses to the second energy crisis. In response to the second crisis, the government expanded its allocation to both diffused interests and geographically organized interests similarly by 30 percent or so from the pre-second energy crisis, despite the tight overall budget.[24] The government continued to allocate more spending to relieve consumers from inflation (38 percent increase from the pre-crisis), and increased the spending welfare programs by 27 percent in the face of the further rise

---

[21] Ministry of Finance, *Zaisei Kinyu Toukei Geppou*, 1974.

[22] The program is called *koyou chosei kyu-fu seido*.

[23] The highest budget allocated for this Employment Adjustment Benefit program during 1970s was around six million yen, half of the budget allocation to small to medium-sized firms.

[24] It is important to note that the LDP legislated the expansion of welfare programs (via the Elderly Welfare Law, legislated in July, 1973) a few months before the eruption of the first energy crisis. Thus, the initial expansion of welfare spending was more in response to the rise of left parties rather than to energy crises or volatility of global economy.

Pro-Loser Policy during Hard Times

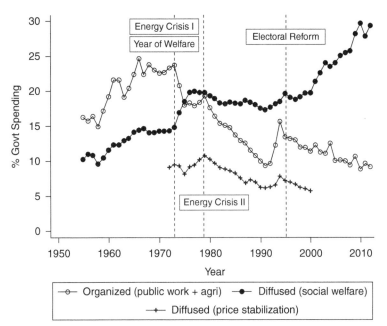

FIGURE 3.1. Japanese government's budget allocation to diffused versus organized interests, 1955–2012.
Source: Financial Statistics, Ministry of Finance, Various Years.
Note: Budget data on price stabilization was available from 1972 to 2000, in "Report Explaining the Budget" (*Yosan no setsumei*) in Ministry of Finance, *Zaisei Kin-yu Toukei Geppou* [Monthly Reports on Fiscal and Finance Statistics], Various Years.

of left parties.[25] Furthermore, the LDP legislated a series of temporary measures to provide leave and unemployment insurance and training to workers in depressed industries in 1978.[26] These measures aimed to increase the mobility of labor across sectors and regions, and by doing so, facilitate the economic adjustment of depressed industries.

By contrast, the government increased its spending for the food control system (price support and subsidies for rice farmers) only by 10 percent, and enacted a major deregulation of rice distribution in 1981. The revision of the Staple Food Control Act in 1981 changed the state ration system to a market-based

---

[25] The LDP won 44 percent of votes for the 1979 Lower House election and needed to add independent candidates, who won the election without the LDP's endorsement, to secure the majority seat shares in the Lower House.
[26] These relief measures are the Temporary Measure to Assist Unemployed in Depressed Industries and the Temporary Measure to Assist Unemployed in Depressed Regions, both of which are enacted in 1978.

94 *Empirical Evidence*

distribution system of rice. Although the spending for infrastructural development and public investment had increased by 42 percent and 34 percent respectively from the pre-second energy crisis (column 6), the investment projects tended to encompass broader geographic regions than those in the 1960s, exemplified by the construction of the National Network of Bullet Trains (see earlier discussion in this chapter).

Finally, when we compare the government's responses to the first and second energy crises (column 7), within a short, five-year window, the spending allocation to diffused interests increased by 140 percent, while allocation to geographically organized interests increased by 108%. The LDP's centralization, achieved by 1976, contributed to this shift from Pork to Policy.

Spending Allocation after the Post-Energy Crises: Demise of Left but Pork Continued to Decline

A conventional wisdom on this shift in the 1970s is that the LDP sought to win support from urban voters by implementing popular welfare programs that left-party governors adopted in prefectures (Nishio 1977; Muramatsu 1988; Estevez-Abe 2008). To lend support to this conventional wisdom, Figure 3.1 shows that after the LDP won its popularity back in 1980 Upper and Lower House elections, welfare programs retrenched. The LDP government canceled free medical care for elderly, and required the elderly to contribute 10 percent of health expenses beginning 1983 (Ministry of Health, Welfare and Labor 2011).

The explanation that the LDP expanded welfare spending to appease urban voters, however, fails to account for what happened after the LDP regained its popularity (1980). Although both the welfare and price stabilization programs were retrenched in 1980s by 5 percent and 30 percent respectively, this retrenchment was much more modest compared to the government's spending cut on items targeting geographically organized interests, such as public work projects and agriculture. Within a decade after 1980, the government cut spending on these geographically organized interests by half.[27] This suggests that

---

[27] One caveat to this observation is that during 1980s, transfers from the central to local governments (via tax revenue allocation system; *chihou koufu zei*) increased by 7 percentage points (from 15 percent in 1979 to 22 percent in 1989). See Calder's discussion on the 1985 budget (1988: 161). The tax revenue allocation system aimed to equalize the disparity in revenue-raising capacities of local governments, and no strings are attached by the central government. During the 1980s, prefectural governments on average spent 11 percent of their spending on social welfare (*minsei-hi*) and 20 percent of their spending on infrastructural development (*doboku-hi*). This means that, on average, the prefectural governments allocated 1.4 percentage points more public works spending for their citizens, while the national government allocated 10 percentage points less from 1979 to 1989. Thus, the increase in the local transfers was not sufficient enough to substitute the decline in public works spending in the national budget. See Ministry of Internal Affairs and Communications, White Paper on Local Finance [*Chihou Zaisei Hakusyo*], 1985 and 1995.

welfare retrenchment in the 1980s was not synonymous with the comeback of pork barrel politics observed in the 1960s, and that the shift from Pork to Policy was more of a structural than a symptomatic response to the rise of left or energy crises (i.e., the demand-side condition). And this structural shift occurred under the same electoral system and the LDP's ruling status, which challenges the conventional argument linking the multimember electoral system and one-party dominance with pork barrel politics (Curtis and Ishikawa 1983; Scheiner 2006).

The remaining question then is: What allowed the LDP to fend off the pressures to revert back to big pork spending, after Japan's recovery from the energy crises and the LDP's regaining its popularity? Consistent with the Optimal Use of Policy developed in Chapter 1, I show in the text that follows that the LDP's centralization via policy tribe and cabinet allocation rules allowed the LDP to continue to commit the bulk of spending for diffused interests, controlling for demographic and economic conditions.

A Systematic Test of the Optimal Use of Policy over Pork: 1955–2012

To test the Optimal Use of Policy hypothesis more systematically, I examine the determinants of the government's budget allocation to diffused losers versus geographically organized losers over the past six decades. I calculated the relative proportion (percent) of the government's total budget allocated for diffused interests vs. geographically targetable, organized interests during the past six decades in Japan, documented in Figure 3.1 using the itemized National Account Expenditure information (Ministry of Finance, various years). For spending on diffused interests, I included social welfare spending[28] and price stabilization programs, which constituted a pro-consumer policy adopted after the first energy crisis (1972–1974) to control consumer price. For spending on geographically targetable, organized interests, I include public work and agricultural spending. Although these measures do not exactly tell us whether these expenditures benefit liberalization winners or losers, they are best available proxies of the shift of government's attention to diffused versus organized interests (Policy vs. Pork).

The dependent variable is the proportion of spending for diffused interests (welfare plus price stabilization programs) over total government expenditures (in percentage) in each fiscal year t. To estimate the impact of centralization within the LDP on government spending is not an exact task, because the institutionalization occurred over a period of six years: scholars noted the emerging power of policy tribe politicians in the early 1970s and seniority and quota-based allocation of cabinet posts were institutionalized sometime between 1972 and 1976. Thus, I tried each of the three dummy variables

---

[28] Social welfare spending includes health spending and excludes education spending.

interchangeably, *Centralization 1970*, *Centralization 1972*, and *Centralization 1976*, which takes a value of 1 after a given year (1970, 1972 and 1976 respectively) and zero otherwise.

Electoral Reform is a dummy variable one for the post-electoral reform period (1996–2012)[29] and zero otherwise. It tests whether electoral reform from MMD to a mixed-member electoral system (SMD/PR) made the use of Pork too expensive for legislators and increased legislators' responsiveness to diffused interests.[30] The *LDP Seat Share t − 1* is the percentage of seats taken by the LDP in the Lower House in the year before, which measures the degree of competition the LDP faced with the oppositions.[31]

I also included three dummy variables that capture important changes in the party systems. *LDP-Komei Coalition* indicates one for years under the LDP-Clean Government Party coalition government (1999–2012), and zero otherwise. *The Optimal Use of Policy* predicts that the coalition government decreases the spending for diffused interests to finance the transaction costs necessary for the bargaining between the two coalition parties. This is so despite that the LDP's coalition-partner, the Clean Government Party, represents the interests of urban workers. *Koizumi Cabinet* indicates one for years under Prime Minister Koizumi's cabinet (2001–2006) and zero otherwise, because Prime Minister Koizumi was known to break the seniority and quota-based allocation of cabinet posts, making the personal appointment more discretional. A dummy variable *DPJ Rule* indicates one for the government ruled by the Democratic Party of Japan (DPJ) between 2009 and 2012 and zero otherwise, to address that the DPJ had a very different intraparty organization than the LDP.

Finally, I address three alternative hypotheses that commonly account for the changes in government spending: the collective action capacity of labor unions, demographic changes, and the macroeconomic environment. *Labor Union t − 1* is the organization rate of labor unions at year *t − 1*. *% Dependent Population* is percentage of the population older than age sixty-five.[32] I also included the degree of trade openness (*Trade t − 1*; sum of export and import per GDP), the GDP growth rate (*GDP Growth t − 1*), and unemployment rates

---

[29] The year 1996 is chosen (as opposed to 1994 when the electoral reform was legislated) as the first fiscal year under the new electoral system, because the 1996 election was the first Lower House election conducted under the new electoral system.

[30] Rogowski (1987b).

[31] Alternatively, I calculate the margin of victory for the LDP (percentage of votes for the LDP minus the percentage of votes for the JSP) in general elections between 1955 and 2000 and include the variable in the model. The results do not change.

[32] Thies (1998) has shown that urbanization accounts for the decline in Ministry of Agriculture, Forestry and Fisheries' budget starting in late 1970s. I included only the percentage of the dependent population as a demographic control because percentage of the urban population (from World Bank's World Development Indicators) is highly correlated with percentage of the dependent population, at 93.8 percent.

Pro-Loser Policy during Hard Times

(*Unemployment t −1*) to address the possibility that macroeconomic conditions affected the spending allocation.

Table 3.3 summarizes the results of linear regressions on the proportion of government's budget allocated to diffused interests (the sum of spending on welfare and social programs and inflation control) from 1955 to 2012.[33] Models 1 and 2 are estimated with ordinary least squares (OLS) without a lagged dependent variable. Models 3 to 5 included the lagged dependent variable (*Diffused t − 1*) to address serial correlation found in model 2.[34] Models 6 and 7 present the OLS with Newey–West standard errors without a lagged dependent variable, following Achen's (2000) concern that there might be a common factor in the data-generating process.

Overall, the LDP's intraparty centralization that occurred in the early 1970s via policy specialization system ("zoku") and the personnel appointment system, had substantial effects on the government's budget allocation to diffused interests. The LDP's centralization was associated with about a 7 to 13 percentage point increase in the allocation of spending to diffused interests. Contrary to the conventional wisdom, electoral reform of 1994 did not change the government's allocation to diffused versus organized interests in a systematic way. These results are robust after controlling for a host of economic and political conditions and addressing serial correlations with different specifications. I discuss each result in detail in the text that follows.

[33] I report the results using a dummy variable *Centralization 1972* here, because the inclusion of *Centralization 1970* instead of *Centralization 1972* produced very similar results. Models using *Centralization 1976* were not statistically significant when including the lagged dependent variable (DV), but found support in models without the lagged DV. What the inconsistent effect of *Centralization 1976* suggests is unclear. It could be that the policy specialization, which occurred earlier than 1976, had more impact on the government's shift from Pork to Policy than the institutionalization of seniority system had (although the two systems eventually became mutually dependent – i.e., seniority scores were used to assign high-rank positions in committees). Alternatively, the institutionalization of the personnel appointment system might have occurred closer to 1972, as argued by Sato and Matsuzaki (1986) and Kohno (1997).

[34] I conducted two tests for serial correlation in model 2, which includes both economic and political covariates. The Durbin–Watson d-test rejects the null hypothesis of no serial correlation (i.e., lends support to the existence of autocorrelation), where the d-statistic is 0.9927 (nine covariates, fifty-seven observations) and critical values range from 1.272 to 1.903. Breusch–Godfrey tests with a small sample with a first-order process (AR1) also lend support to the existence of serial correlation at the 1% significance level (Prob> χ^2 are 0.0003 respectively). Following Keele and Kelly (2006), I chose to include the lagged DV as opposed to generalized least squares (GLS; Prais–Winston or Cochrane–Orcutt transformation) for three reasons. First, the process underlying my model is at least weakly dynamic, which makes the use of GLS inappropriate. Second, even if the process is not dynamic, with my data with fifty-seven observations, OLS with the lagged DV produces a very small bias. Third, after including the lagged DV (model 3), the Breusch–Godfrey Lagrange multiplier test supports the null hypothesis of no serial correlation (Prob > χ^2 are 0.493, 0.408, and 0.422 for a lag of one, two, and three respectively), which suggests that the inclusion of the lagged DV addresses the serial correlation well.

TABLE 3.3. *The Japanese Government's Spending Allocation to Diffused Interests (%), 1955–2012*

	Model 1	Model 2	Model 3	Model 4	Model 5	Model 6	Model 7
	OLS	OLS	OLS/Lag DV	OLS/Lag DV	OLS/Lag DV	Newey/Lag1	Newey/Lag1
Party System Centralization							
LDP Centralization 1972		13.23 (0.722)***	7.416 (0.927)***	7.205 (0.930)***	7.333 (0.895)***	11.71 (1.239)***	11.58 (1.481)***
LDP Lower House seat share		−0.122 (0.0322)***	−0.0359 (0.0250)	−0.0321 (0.0256)	−0.0570 (0.0395)	−0.175 (0.0643)***	−0.201 (0.0875)**
Electoral Reform 94		0.188 (1.123)	0.626 (0.772)				−1.780 (1.615)
Electoral Reform 96				−0.674 (0.854)	−1.168 (0.895)	−2.095 (0.989)**	
LDP Komei coalition					−0.913 (0.757)	−1.169 (0.474)**	−1.388 (0.523)**
Koizumi cabinet					−1.445 (0.710)**	−2.427 (0.894)***	−2.424 (0.964)**
DPJ rule					−3.123 (1.679)*	−6.537 (2.265)***	−7.338 (3.312)**

TABLE 3.3 (*continued*)

	Model 1	Model 2	Model 3	Model 4	Model 5	Model 6	Model 7
	OLS	OLS	OLS/Lag DV	OLS/Lag DV	OLS/Lag DV	Newey/Lag1	Newey/Lag1
Economic Controls							
L1. Age older than 65 (%)	0.913 (0.562)	0.362 (0.213)*	0.405 (0.146)***	0.523 (0.159)***	0.784 (0.186)***	0.975 (0.232)***	0.945 (0.249)***
L1. GDP growth	−0.668 (0.229)***	0.0136 (0.0794)	0.0502 (0.0547)	0.0335 (0.0537)	0.0678 (0.0540)	0.0781 (0.0701)	0.0781 (0.0699)
L1. Labor union rate (%)	0.380 (0.489)	0.327 (0.165)*	0.360 (0.114)***	0.408 (0.121)***	0.583 (0.131)***	0.690 (0.200)***	0.633 (0.201)***
L1. Trade per GDP	0.0794 (0.172)	0.155 (0.0593)**	0.0611 (0.0426)	0.0425 (0.0411)	0.0412 (0.0431)	0.139 (0.0676)**	0.132 (0.0654)**
L1. Unemployment rate	−1.024 (1.321)	−1.002 (0.434)**	−0.697 (0.301)**	−0.474 (0.338)	0.130 (0.383)	0.202 (0.554)	0.0050 (0.504)
L1. Diffused spending (Lagged dependent variable [DV])			0.487 (0.0656)***	0.481 (0.0655)***	0.424 (0.0660)***		
Constant	4.870 (19.06)	5.064 (7.565)	−6.582 (5.421)	−8.917 (5.923)	−15.50 (6.107)**	−9.979 (9.358)	−5.826 (9.774)
R^2	0.452	0.952	0.978	0.978	0.982		
Obs	57	57	57	57	57	57	57

Note: Standard errors are in parentheses. Significance levels: * $p < 0.10$, ** $p < 0.05$, *** $p < 0.01$.

Economic Needs

Among economic needs or collective action capacity of the diffused interests, only the proportion of the dependent population and the organizational rates of labor unions have systematic effects in nine out of ten models. A 10 percentage point increase in the share of the dependent population is associated with a 5 percentage point increase in the government's spending allocation to diffused interests. Similarly, a 10 percentage point increase in the organizational rate of labor unions is associated with a 3 to 6 percentage point increase in the government's spending allocation to diffused interests. Other economic needs of diffused losers, measured by unemployment rate and the GDP growth rate, do not have systematic effects on the allocation. Citizens' increased exposure to international trade, measured by the proportion of exports and imports per GDP, is associated with the expansion of spending on diffused losers, yet this effect is inconsistent across different specifications. The finding lends only partial support to the well-established literature linking globalization with the welfare state expansion.

Party Systems

In contrast to the weak and inconsistent effects of economic factors, party systems have substantial and consistent effects on the pattern of allocation across all the models. First, the LDP's centralization via policy specialization and personnel appointment systems was associated with the expansion of spending for diffused losers; after centralization, the government allocated on average a 7 percentage point greater share of budget for the diffused interests over organized interests, controlling for a host of macroeconomic conditions and political factors.

The LDP's attention shift to diffused losers, moreover, was not a short-term, symptomatic response to the rise of left parties or the energy crises. Instead, consistent and powerful effects of party centralization, after controlling for GDP growth rates and the strength of opposition parties, suggest that the LDP's increase in spending allocation to diffused losers was induced by a structural change in how legislators organized their interests in broader sectoral groups within the party.

Indeed, models 2, 6, and 7 suggest that the weaker the LDP was over the opposition parties (i.e., lower seat share in the Lower House), the greater the share of the budget allocated to diffused losers, yet this effect is significant only in the three models without lagged dependent variables. The substantive impact is also modest; a 3 percentage point decrease in the LDP's seat share in the Lower House (e.g., from 59 to 56 percent) is associated with a 0.3 to 0.6 percentage point increase in the budget allocated to diffused interests. The finding lends limited support to the conventional wisdom that the LDP expanded the welfare programs to appeal to urban voters and to counteract the rise of left parties in the 1970s.

Furthermore, the LDP's coalition with the urban-based Clean Government (Kōmei) Party, which started in the 1999 election, was not systematically

Pro-Loser Policy during Hard Times

associated with the increase in the government spending favoring diffused losers. The LDP's Koizumi Junichiro's cabinet (2001–2006), which enacted "structural reform without sanctuary" to fight against the special interest politics, was associated with the increase in the spending allocation to organized interests ("Pork") over diffused interests ("Policy"), as expected from the Optimal Use of Policy. Koizumi weakened both the power of policy tribe legislators and the faction and seniority-based personnel appointment systems. The weakening of intraparty organizations increased the costs of bargains that Koizumi had to strike with individual legislators over resource allocation. Indeed, many of Koizumi's structural reforms were unevenly implemented geographically as "Special Zones for Structural Reforms" (*kouzo kaikaku tokku*). The geographic implementation of structural reforms can essentially function like Pork through the distribution of subsidies and tax breaks. Moreover, with more discretional power over appointments, Koizumi's used ministerial positions as Pork to buy off support (e.g., Chapter 5).[35]

Similarly, during its rule (2009–2012), the DPJ government increased its spending allocation to geographically organized interests, contrary to its pledge to shift the government's attentions from organized interests to ordinary citizens.[36] These results suggest that left versus right orientation of ruling parties did not directly translate into public policies favoring diffused vs. organized interests thus far in Japan. Rather, the extent to which the ruling party or the coalition of parties is centralized and institutionalized mattered more.

Finally, contrary to the powerful effects of the party system variables, the electoral reform of 1994,[37] which was believed to shift legislators' attention from organized to diffused interests, does not turn out to have had systematic effects on the budget allocation for diffused vs. organized interests. The findings challenge the conventional wisdom that a majoritarian electoral system, such as the SMD system, empowers the diffused interests over organized interests (Rogowski and Kayser 2002). The findings are consistent with the view that Japan's mixed electoral system, which combines the SMD system with the PR system, might wash out each other's effects (i.e., the SMD empowers

---

[35] Although Koizumi exercised strong party discipline over backbenchers who rebelled against the postal reform bill ("stick") and centralized the policymaking process to the Council on Economic and Fiscal Policy, these measures do not help backbenchers survive electorally when they face the electoral costs of open economy. Side-payments, such as public work projects and personnel appointments, can. See Chapter 1.

[36] The jury is still out regarding how we should evaluate the DPJ policies, partly because of the Great East Japan earthquake and tsunami that hit the DPJ government in 2011, and increased the need for public works projects.

[37] To test for the effect of electoral reform, I used two dummy variables interchangeably. *Electoral Reform 94* indicates one since the year 1994, when the reform bill was legislated, and zero otherwise and *Electoral Reform 96* indicates one since the year 1996, when the first Lower House election under the new electoral system was held, and zero otherwise.

102   *Empirical Evidence*

diffused interests, while the PR portion strengthens the power of organized interests)(McKean and Scheiner 2000; Bawn and Thies 2003).

The broader implication of these findings is that Optimal Use of Policy over Pork required the reorganization and centralization within the LDP, such as the shift to sectorally organized groups via the policy tribe system and personnel appointment rules that regulated the factional fights. This centralization had substantial and long-lasting effects on how the government bought off support for the open economy from diffused and unorganized interests in an increasingly volatile world economy since the 1970s.

THAILAND'S CONTINUING RELIANCE ON PORK DURING HARD TIMES

The Rise of Diffused Losers and Fiscal Constraints: Energy Crises

Like Japan, the Thai economy was hit by the two energy crises in the 1970s. The rise of the price of oil was damaging to the Thai government's fiscal health, as high-priced crude oil consumed 30 percent of the government budget.[38] The initial responses by the Thai government were expansionary economic policies, adopted by a democratic government (1973–1976) and then an authoritarian one (1976–1979).[39] After its return to a semidemocracy, where legislators were elected but Prime Minister Prem and half of the cabinet members were not (see Chapter 2), all the parties campaigned for a more expansionary budget to ease the income shock during the 1983 electoral campaigns (Doner and Laothamatas 1994).

The expansionary policies during the energy crises eventually caused a deep recession in Thailand, which took place from 1983 to 1986. Among domestic constituents, the most severely hit by the crises were (1) financial institutions, one-third of which were affected – fifteen companies collapsed and thirty-two companies received liquidity injections;[40] (2) exporters, especially farmers and textile industries; and (3) urban consumers, who incurred a 19.9 percent rise in prices in 1980 and another 12 to 15 percent rise in 1981.[41] These losers of the energy crises organized to lobby the government to mitigate the shocks. Indeed, this period had seen one of the highest levels of lobbying activities of interest groups and labor protests in postwar Thai history.[42]

---

[38] Sirikrai (1982: 1103).

[39] Under the democratic government led by the rural-based Social Action Party, public investment for rural areas increased, and under the authoritarian government, public expenditures on urban areas, such as transportation and industries, rose (Doner and Laothamatas 1994: 413–414).

[40] Lauridsen (1998: 1578).

[41] Sirikrai (1982: 1103).

[42] Laothamatas (1992: 458). Using the interest group testimony given by the business associations in the House of Representatives, Laothamatas found that the monthly frequency of interest

Pro-Loser Policy during Hard Times

Despite the rise of protectionist demands and declining terms of trade, the Thai government kept its overall commitment to an open economy,[43] while adopting a zero-growth fiscal policy.[44] Just like in the Japanese case, large-scale development projects were frozen or delayed (Doner and Laothamatas 1994: 421).

With the rise of competing demands from diffused losers under tight fiscal discipline, how did Prem's coalition of parties keep the open economy commitment and survive politically? Unlike in Japan, the two crises did not lead to the use of Policies for diffused losers or Institutional Reforms to empower the losers of the open economy. Instead, the ruling coalition of political parties continued their use of targeted side payments, that is, pork projects, to mitigate the shock for their core, organized supporters (details in the text that follows). Consistent with the Optimal Use of Pork, Policy, and Institutional Reforms developed in Chapter 1, I show that the multiparty coalition government in Thailand encouraged the party leaders' continuing use of Pork even during hard times.

Thai Government's Responses to the 1983–1986 Crisis

The Thai government took no drastic measure to mitigate diffused losers' (e.g., urban workers and farmers) hardship during the crises, and instead, concentrated the effort to please organized losers (such as financial institutions and landowners). Figure 3.2 describes the changes in the proportion of government's spending allocated for social protection programs, which included compensation for a reduction in income, medical treatments, and dependent care, using International Monetary Fund (IMF)'s Government Finance Statistics (various years).[45]

---

group testimony increased from 0.13 during 1975 to 1976 (the democratic years) and 0.14 during the subsequent military rule to an average of 4.45 between 1984 and 1987.

[43] The only exception was the tariff on industrial goods, which were raised temporarily in the mid-1980s in an effort to increase the government's revenues. See Urata and Yokota (1994).

[44] This section focuses mostly on the Thai government's responses to the energy crisis between the recessions of 1983 and 1986. The energy crises in the 1970s did not immediately cause the recession or the government's responses in Thailand, unlike in Japan. It was not until the 1983–1986 recession when the residues of the energy crises caused the severe recession and capital flight that the Thai government responded with various measures. The delayed effects and the government's responses were due to the still relatively closed nature of Thai economy in the 1970s: the economy was vastly agricultural, still pursuing the import-substitution strategy, and domestic capitalists had little interest in exporting owing to a rapidly growing domestic market (Pasuk and Baker 1995: 149).

[45] See IMF's Government Finance Statistics Manual (2001), Annex to chapter 2. "Social Protection," pp. 18–22. Another commonly used measure for the government's spending on diffused losers is social spending, which includes welfare, health, and education spending in IMF's Government Finance Statistics. The two measures for Thailand (welfare vs. social spending)

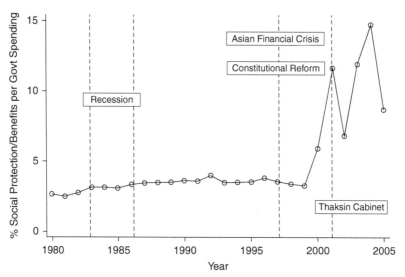

FIGURE 3.2. Thai government's budget allocation to diffused losers, 1980–2005.
Source: IMF's Government Finance Statistics Yearbook, various years. Welfare spending is defined by "social protection" spending in the Yearbook and includes compensation for a reduction in income, dependent care, medical care, etc. Percentage is calculated over the total government's outlays.

Two differences from the Japanese government's response to the energy crises are striking. First, the Thai government did not expand fiscal commitment to urban workers and the retirees in the form of welfare expansion and price stabilization programs in response to energy crises. Instead, the Thai government made the company owners (i.e., capitalists) and farmers shoulder the costs of adjustment via minimum wage increase and temporary price suppression of agricultural goods.[46] The meager fiscal commitment to welfare programs continued even after the Asian Financial Crisis, which erupted in 1997, and Constitutional Reform of 1997, which aimed to centralize political parties and empower voters. It was not until 2001, when Thai Rak Thai Party won the one-party majority in the House of Representatives under a new electoral system, that the government nearly doubled the welfare spending from 5.9 percent in 2000 to 11.6 percent in 2001.

correlate highly at 0.87, with the main results being unchanged with the use of social spending as a dependent variable.

[46] In addition to the difference in party systems between Japan and Thailand, the lack of strong left parties and weak labor unions in Thailand had contributed to the lack of government expansion of welfare programs to maintain the open economy coalition ("policy"). In addition, the continuous supply of rural migrant workers in urban factories (Doner and Laothamatas 1994: 434–444) weakened the collective action by labor to demand more compensation.

Pro-Loser Policy during Hard Times

Second, the Thai government implemented sector-specific measures to ease the income loss of exporting sectors, such as textiles and rice. Yet their sector-specific measures differed from the Japan's use of Policy after energy crises. Elected ministers implemented these relief policies unevenly across regions and farms for rent-seeking (Christensen 1992: 24, Doner and Laothamatas 1994). The uneven implementation of Policy across regions essentially functioned like Pork.[47] The Minister of Commerce's rice policies during this time period illustrate the use of Pork.

After the 1983 election, the post of Minister of Commerce, who oversaw the rice policies, was given to the Social Action Party's (SAP) Kosol Krairerk, whose electoral support came from a rural Kohn Kaen province.[48] Kosol initially implemented the price support for rice farmers, yet the actual levels of price support differed substantially among farmers (Christiansen 1991: 24). After the failure of the price support system, Kosol implemented a quota system of distributing export licenses, which was selectively granted to some rice farmers but not others (Doner and Laothamatas 1994). Although rice farmers were "diffused losers" in Thailand, as they constituted 75 percent of farming household at that time, the party leaders used Pork (i.e., the targeted and selective benefits), not Policy or Institutional Reforms, to maintain the open economy coalition.

In addition, under Prem's coalition government formed with four or five parties, each party or faction in the ruling coalition obtains cabinet posts roughly proportional to its party or faction size (i.e., a quota system discussed in Chapter 4). Such a multiparty government leads to interministerial fights over the budget, because each minister seeks control over a greater share of the budget to further his party or factional interests.[49] The battles among ministers over the budget fragmented the government's policies to mitigate the economic shocks. For instance, the Finance Minister Sommai Hoontrakul kept the rural development funds despite the zero-growth policy (Doner and Laothamatas 1994: 444), while reducing the funding for the Ministry of Public Health's community hospital construction projects.[50] The multiparty coalition raised the costs of intraelite bargain over budget, and inhibited elite coordination to use Policy for diffused losers.

---

[47] Hicken (2004) called this Prem's Pork-Policy compromise, in which Prem gave sectoral policy-making power to elected legislators, and in exchange, allowed technocrats to enjoy autonomy over macroeconomic policies. This time period, indeed, saw increasing appointment of elected officials for ministerial positions.

[48] During Prem's first cabinet (1980–1982), the Minister of Commerce position was given to non-elected appointees. Author's dataset used in Chapter 2.

[49] Niskanen (1975); Campbell (1980); Hallerberg and Marier (2004); Bawn and Rosenbluth (2006).

[50] Chapter 8 of a report by the Ministry of Public Health available at: http://eng.moph.go.th/profile97-98/CHAPTER83.htm (accessed October 14, 2011). Sommai was an unelected minister, while the Minister of Public Health (Marut Bunnag) was an elected legislator from Bangkok.

106   *Empirical Evidence*

In sum, Thailand's multiparty coalition government's responses to the 1983–1986 recession were consistent with the Optimal Use of Pork hypothesis. The government used targeted and selective benefits (i.e., Pork) to buy off support from legislators. The government continued to commit a meager 3 percent of its spending on welfare programs throughout the two major crises (post-energy crises recession in the mid-1980s and the Asian financial crisis of 1997). Even when the unelected prime minister was able to initiate trade liberalization, he was responsive to legislators' threat of coalition breakaway in implementing trade liberalization and side-payment allocations (see Chapter 2). Only macroeconomic policies, such as exchange rate policies, were relatively shielded from the political pressures from the elected legislators and the prime minister used them to help diffused losers survive the recession.[51]

The Politics of the 1997 Financial Crisis in Thailand: The Multiparty Government Neglected Diffused Losers, Again

After its recovery from the 1983–1986 recession, Thailand experienced a decade-long period of on average 9 percent economic growth, until the Asian financial crisis hit the economy hard in 1997. Unemployment increased from 0.9 percent in 1997 to 5.3 percent in 1998, and nearly one million jobs were lost between 1997 and 1998.[52] Organized lobbying demonstrations on the streets and violence ensued, demanding that the government relieve the income losses of various groups. Major economic losers in this crisis were diverse, including farmers with accumulating debt in northeastern regions, the financial sector with nonperforming loans, urban workers in the private sector (especially in construction and manufacturing), small and medium-sized firm owners, and land developers.[53]

Despite the severity of the recession, the Thai government maintained an overall commitment to an open economy.[54] The World Trade Organization

---

[51] In 1981 and 1984, the Prem government adopted several waves of currency devaluation to increase exports and reduce trade deficits. The government also switched from a fixed exchange system pegged to the U.S. dollar to a managed floating exchange rate system, which allowed exporting industries to cope flexibly with the changes in the international market. See Pasuk and Baker (2002: 150). In 1986, Prem also abolished the agricultural taxation for rice and began subsidizing rice exports to help farmers mitigate the income loss.

[52] See Australian Government (1999), "The Impact of the Asian Financial Crisis on the Health Sector in Thailand," available at http://www.ausaid.gov.au/publications/pdf/health_thailand.pdf (accessed September 28, 2011); Lee (1998); OcKey (2004: 40).

[53] Haggard (2000:98).

[54] The crisis erupted under the Chavalit Yongchaiyudh's government (1996–1997), and urban legislators and elites accused rural politicians of being responsible for mismanaged economic policy before and during the financial crisis. To address this criticism, the Chavalit government (1996–1997) engaged in populist bailout programs for bankers while committing to the IMF program and the WTO to liberalize economic policies further, including in the agricultural sector. This approach was unpopular among the public and led it to resign only a few months after the eruption of the crisis.

Pro-Loser Policy during Hard Times 107

(WTO)'s first policy reviews after the 1997 crisis praised the government for resisting protectionist temptations despite the fact that real GDP dropped 12 percent in 1997–1998: "One of the most striking aspects of the Government's policy response to the crisis … is its liberalization of several aspects of its trade and foreign investment regime in order to speed up structural adjustment" (WTO 1999). Moreover, the government kept this commitment to the open economy, despite the tight budget constraints imposed by the capital flight and IMF conditionality.[55]

The ways in two post-crisis administrations (Chuan Leekpai cabinet[56] from 1997 to 2001 and Thaksin Shinawatra cabinets from 2001 to 2006) achieved this commitment to an open economy, however, differed considerably and the difference was due to Chuan's multiparty coalition government and Thaksin's one party dominance. Table 3.4 summarizes policy responses by the post-crisis Chuan Administration to compensate economic losers (1997–2001), compared with policies under Thaksin's one-party majority (2001–2006). The Chuan government spent little of the budget for social relief policies for diffused losers, such as farmers and urban workers, despite the fact that the Chuan government signed a Letter of Intent with the IMF to support job creation, expansion of unemployment insurance coverage, and continuation of social insurance programs for those who lost jobs.[57] By contrast, the Thaksin administration shifted its resource allocation to diffused losers.

The multiparty coalition government of Chuan committed a negligible amount of the budget to relieve the income loss of diffused losers. The government spent only the 3 percent of fiscal surplus that it had promised the IMF it would spend on social relief programs.[58] These social relief policies reached only approximately 7 percent of the unemployed.[59] The rural industrial development fund was also estimated to have created a mere 3,000 jobs in rural Thailand, where the crisis hit most severely.[60]

By contrast, the Chuan's relief programs distributed benefits to organized interests such as state-owned enterprises, construction workers, and landowners. Infrastructure development projects (allotted 1.25 billion baht; $U.S. 23.8 million per the exchange rate as of June 1998), for instance, required that the government use state-owned enterprises.

---

[55] The Thai government initially agreed to IMF programs with a commitment to keep a fiscal surplus of one percent of GDP. In May of 1998, the IMF approved Thailand to run a targeted fiscal deficit of 3 percent of GDP in the face of the rise in unemployment and social instability. Lee (1998: 53).

[56] I refer to this Chuan's cabinet as "post-crisis Chuan cabinet" as Chuan was also a prime minister between 1992 and 1995.

[57] Lee (1998: 55).

[58] The Asian Development Bank also encouraged the Thai government to spend more on social relief through social relief loans. See Lee, ibid., 1998.

[59] Lee ibid., p. 55.

[60] Ibid.

TABLE 3.4. *Policies to Support Economic Losers during and post-1997 Financial Crisis in Thailand*

	Post-Asian Financial Crisis I (1997–2001)		Post-Asian Financial Crisis II (2001–2005)	
Party systems	Multiparty coalition government		One-party majority of Thai Rak Thai	
Administration	Chuan government (1997–2001)		Thaksin government (2001–2006)	
Diffused		Billion baht		Billion baht
Farmers	Rural industrial employment program	0.003	Agrarian debt relief	9.3
			Rural development fund	8.2
			One-village, one-product plan	0.8
Urban workers	Unemployment and social insurance	N/A		
	Urban development fund	0.06		
Small to medium-sized firm owners	N/A		New entrepreneur promotion and credit	52
All citizens	N/A		Universal 30-baht per visit healthcare scheme	53
Diffused Total		0.063		123.3
Organized				
State-owned enterprises and landowners	Infrastructural development	1.25		
Financial sectors	Bail-out program and state fund injection	N/A	Bail-out program and state fund injection	N/A

Sources: Lee (1998), Table 3.2, p. 56 and Warr and Sarntisart (2005) in Weiss, eds. Table 5.11, p. 203.

Note: Although the 1997 Constitution was in effect, Chuan was elected under the old multimember district system with block vote (voters cast as many votes as the district's seats) and Thaksin was elected under the mixed electoral system, which combines a single-member district system and a closed-list, proportional representation.

Pro-Loser Policy during Hard Times   109

The government's neglect of diffused losers spurred dissatisfaction among farmers. In 1998, 30,000 farmers from the northeast marched to the capital to meet with Prime Minister Chuan about agrarian debt relief.[61] In 1999, the New Aspiration Party, whose leader Chavalit had strong backing from farmers, proposed to relieve farmers from their debts in an effort to mobilize rural voters, yet the promise was not delivered because of the party's election loss.[62]

Why, despite that the majority of eligible voters in Thailand were diffused losers after the 1997 crisis (Condition 1), Thai parties could not develop policy programs to reach them and mobilize votes? Consistent with the Optimal Use of Pork over Policy hypothesis developed in Chapter 1, I show that multiparty coalition governments in which many parties must bargain over resource allocation (Condition 2) shaped party leaders' incentives to use Pork over Policy.

Budget Fights under Multiparty Coalition Governments

The Chuan cabinet's compensation policies, targeting mostly organized interests rather than diffused losers, were due to the fragile multiparty coalition governments. As was the case for Prem's multiparty coalition government after the energy crises, ministers representing different parties fought over the allocation of the budget.[63] While inter-ministerial fight over budget is common even under one-party dominance (Campbell 1980), the budgetary process under multi-party coalitions differs from the single-party one. With the single-party dominance such as Japan's LDP, the government can allocate budget to pursue a collective goal of a single, ruling party, such as maximizing seat share and minimizing electoral losses. With the unstable, multi-party coalition government, such as Thailand's Chuan government, each party pursues its own political goal with the ministerial budget, rather than collectively pursuing the coalition's political survival. For instance, the Minister of Health from the Social Action Party, a coalition partner of the Chuan government, demanded more budget resources for health care, claiming that the Chuan government biased the budget allocation to cater to wealthy interests such as financial institutions.

---

[61] *The Nation,* February 9, 1998. A similar protest was organized in June of 1998 as well. See *Deutsche Presse-Agentur,* June 22, 1998.

[62] *The Nation,* April 29, 1999.

[63] Campbell (1980) documents the budgetary fights among ministries in Japan under the LDP dominance. The budgetary process under one-party dominance differs from that of multiparty coalitions in that the former can use budget to pursue collective goals of a single-party, while the latter, each party pursues its own political goal with the resource available through ministerial positions.

Empirical Evidence

Theoretically, interministerial fights do not necessarily hinder the government's use of Policy if each minister (i.e., factional or party leader) advances the interests of broader constituents. Such examples are Thai's Social Action Party representing farmers' interests and the LDP's welfare tribe legislators representing the interests of pensioners.[64] Indeed, existing studies on cabinet post allocation have shown that posts are usually assigned to legislators to strengthen their representation of constituents' interests and hence legislators' reelection prospects, lending support to the electoral connection (e.g., a rural representative obtaining a ministerial position at the Ministry of Agriculture and Cooperatives) (Mayhew 1974; Weingast and Marshall 1988).

Despite this theory, cabinet post allocation in Thailand does not reflect constituents' interests. Between 1982 and 2005, only two of the past seventeen Ministers at the Ministry of Agriculture and Cooperatives, which oversees rural development and farm policies, were elected from rural provinces (i.e., the bottom one-third of total provinces ranked by population density), Nakhon Rachasima and Udon Thani. The majority of past agricultural ministers were elected from urban provinces (i.e., top one-third of total provinces ranked by population density).[65] All of these Ministers of Agriculture and Cooperatives, moreover, had diverse past career experience in other ministerial positions unrelated to rural interests, such as the Ministry of Industry, Finance, and Justice.

Instead of advocating for broader constituents' interests as a minister, Thai legislators' main motivation for seeking ministerial positions was to expand their factions through greater access to government resources. OcKey (2004) documents three ways in which legislators translate cabinet ministerial positions into larger factional membership. First, a minister can allocate budgetary resources to entice nonfactional members to join the faction or deter the current factional members from defecting.[66] Second, access to the ministerial budget is also critical for legislators to reward local vote canvassers (called *Hua khanean*), who mobilize votes in villages on a legislator's behalf during

---

[64] I say here "at least in a short run" because ministerial fighting over budget resources can lead to budget deficits and loose fiscal discipline in the long run, resembling a common pool resource situation.

[65] Calculated by the author using the information on cabinet ministers available at the official website of the Secretariat of the Cabinet (http://www.cabinet.thaigov.go.th/eng/) and data on the provincial population divided by land size as a measure of urbanization. I counted Shucheep Hansaward twice, as he held the ministerial positions for two terms. Niphon Promphan, Minister of Agriculture and Cooperatives under the Chuan Leekpai government (1992–1995), was the only minister who was elected from the northeastern provinces, where the majority of farmers resided (Nakhon Rachasima Province). Nakhon Rachasima, moreover, is the political and economic center of the northeastern region and is one of the more urban and wealthier provinces among northeastern provinces.

[66] OcKey (2004: 39). Another, cheaper way to expand the faction was to recruit family members to run from the same province. Chonburi and Suphan Buri Provinces had all the seats occupied by the members of the Kamnan Po and Banharn families, respectively.

Pro-Loser Policy during Hard Times

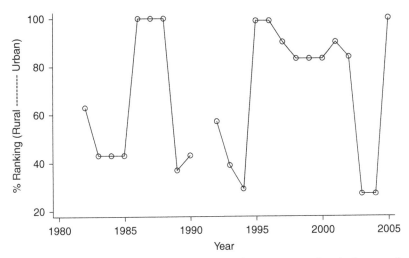

FIGURE 3.3. Percentile urban constituencies for ministers of agriculture and cooperatives in Thailand, 1982–2005.
Source: The *x*-axis indicates the year, and the *y*-axis indicates standardized ranking ($0 < n < 100$) of degrees of urbanness of a province from which a minister was elected, measured by population density. The higher the ranking (*y*-axis toward 100), the more urban a given province from which a minister was elected. The data are treated as missing (e.g., years 1991 and 1992) when ministers were appointed rather than elected. Ministers' information is from the official parliamentary website available at: www.parliament.go.th. Constituency information of ministers was matched from University of Michigan's CLEA dataset (2012).

elections (see Chapter 2).[67] In exchange for organized votes, a minister rewards canvassers' efforts with material benefits such as public works projects, money, and prestigious positions as "consultants" for the ministry.[68] Finally, through government contracts and regulations, the minister can also extract rent from organized interest groups via legal and illegal donations. The rents allow further expansion of factions by financing campaigns.[69]

In sum, unlike the Japanese legislators, Thai legislators chose ministerial positions that do not necessarily fit with their constituents' interests. They did not build their careers by specializing in particular policy issues, either. This contrasts with the policy specialization ("policy tribe") seen among Japanese legislators through committee systems and the Policy Affairs Research

---

[67] Local vote canvassers can be village heads or local capitalists such as factory owners and gambling business owners. It resembles the Japanese case, where village and town chiefs acted as local vote canvassers for the LDP.
[68] For an objection to this "exchange" argument, see Callahan (2005).
[69] OcKey (2004: 40).

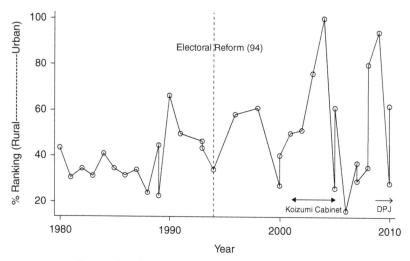

FIGURE 3.4. Percentile urban constituencies for ministers of agriculture in Japan.
Note: The higher percentile ranking on the *y*-axis suggests a district was more urban. The urbanness of multimember districts (1980–1993) is calculated by population density using Mizusaki's Densely Inhabited District (DID) data available from Mizusaki's Japan Election Day by Mizusaki (JED-M) data at Leviathan's data bank. The urbanness of single-member districts is calculated from municipality-level DID data using the 2000 National Census available at Ministry of Internal Affairs and Communication's "Toukei de miru shikuchoson no sugata" (Statistical Outlook of Municipalities).

Committee System within the LDP, in response to the tight budget brought by the energy crises (see earlier discussion in this chapter).[70] Instead, Thai ministers use ministerial budget to buy new factional members and to mobilize core votes, which accounts for the persistence of Pork strategy during hard times. Inter-ministerial fights over the budget under from multi-party coalition inhibited Thai government's shift from Pork to Policy during the recession, despite the rise of diffused losers and fiscal constraints.

To locate Thai ministers' data in a comparative perspective, Figure 3.4 summarizes the constituents' urbanness for Japanese ministers of Agriculture, Forestry and Fisheries in Japan since 1980. Except for Prime Minister Koizumi's second cabinet (2003–2005) and the first DPJ cabinet (2009), Agricultural ministers were elected from more rural districts lending support for the electoral connection in ministerial assignment to legislators.

In sum, the multiparty coalition government in Thailand made legislators' collective action to shift the resources from the geographically organized interests to diffused losers difficult. Coalition leaders used targeted benefits, in forms of budgets for geographically organized interest groups and ministerial

[70] Inoguchi and Iwai (1987); Epstein et al. (1997).

Pro-Loser Policy during Hard Times 113

positions for parties in the coalition, to hold the majority coalition together. In the absence of the centralized party system in Thailand, Pork prevailed over Policy.

THE RISE OF POLICY INITIATIVES FOR DIFFUSED LOSERS UNDER ONE-PARTY MAJORITY OF THE THAI RAK THAI PARTY 2001–2005

Electoral politics in Thailand went through dramatic shifts after the 1997 Asian Financial Crisis. The new constitution, which was approved in 1997, shaped legislators' survival strategies in three ways. The first was the change in the electoral system from MMD to a mixed-member electoral system, under which 400 seats are allocated to SMDs and 100 seats to a closed-list PR.[71] This electoral reform is parallel to Japan's electoral reform in 1994.

For cabinet ministerial appointments, the Constitution privileges the party-list candidates elected from the PR portion (Ockey 2003: 667). The new electoral system aims to strengthen party leadership through the closed-list PR portion and reduce the number of factions and parties through the SMD portion.[72] Second, the reform also aimed to empower diffused and unorganized interests through SMD's majoritarian electoral system as well as compulsory voting mandated for all citizens. In addition to the establishment of an independent anticorruption agency and the revision of the Political Finance Law, both changes were meant to increase the costs of vote buying and decrease the benefits of rent extraction from organized interest groups. Finally, the Constitution prohibits postelection party switching for the first ninety days, which increases legislators' incentives to bandwagon to a clear winner before the election.

Thaksin Shinawatra, a former business owner and telecommunications tycoon, emerged as a vastly popular party leader in the first parliamentary election held under the new electoral system in 2001.[73] Leveraging the unparalleled personal wealth he built through his telecommunication and other businesses before entering politics, he formed a new party, Thai Rak Thai. As the election date approached, more than 100 incumbent legislators as well as political parties such as the Social Action Party merged into Thai Rak Thai. Thai Rak Thai won a landslide victory, winning 248 seats of the total 500 seats in Parliament.

---

[71] A closed list PR means that parties choose candidates and their ranking on the ballot, and voters cast votes on political parties, not on individual candidates.

[72] Hicken (2006, 2009).

[73] Although telecommunication sector was severely hit by the crisis, Thaksin's company, Shin Corp, had the least damage. See McCargo and Pathmanand (2005). Thaksin entered politics in 1994 and established the Palang Tham Party. In 1998, he established the Thai Rak Thai Party under the new Constitution.

Two factors had contributed to the emergence of one-party dominance. One was Constitutional reform, which prohibited postelection party switching. Second, Thaksin was able to finance costly election campaign with his personal wealth, while many other factional leaders lost their assets during the financial crisis. Facing this resource asymmetry, faction leaders bandwagoned to the rising winner by switching parties before election.

With one-party dominance and decreasing financial power of factional leaders, Thaksin Shinawatra established a more centralized control over the party and policymaking process.[74] The one-party dominance facilitated the government's shift from Pork to Policy. Table 3.4 summarizes major legislations to compensate economic losers enacted by the Thaksin administration between 2001 and 2006.

What differentiated these policies from the policies implemented under Chuan's multiparty coalition government is twofold. First, Thai Rak Thai clearly targeted the three constituencies that were relatively neglected by the previous government led by Democrats: small and medium-sized business owners,[75] the rural poor, and urban workers. The government passed legislation for a rural development fund, an agrarian debt moratorium for rural farmers, and a 30-baht per hospital visit healthcare scheme for every Thai citizen. Furthermore, it promoted financial institutions to loan more money to small and medium-sized businesses through a New Entrepreneurs Program. Second, the Thai Rak Thai party used the principle of universalism, rather than parochialism, to implement these policies. No income ceiling or geographic criteria was set for implementing these policies. It differed from the implementation of policies under multiparty systems where targeting parochial interests, such as the interests of particular regions or firms, was used to extract rent from organized interests.

In sum, the Thai Rak Thai Party used policies for diffused losers to keep its open economy coalition. Compared to Chuan's multiparty government, ministers' fight over limited government resources was relatively moderate owing to the centralization of resources and policymaking power from faction leaders (ministers) to the prime minister.

---

[74] There is a debate concerning whether the 1997 constitutional reform and electoral reform to a mixed-member electoral system (400 SMD seats with 100 PR seats with the party list) allowed the emergence of one-party dominance of Thai Rak Thai and its centralized policymaking process. See Hicken (2006) and Nelson (2007). The case of Thailand is overidentified regarding the effect of electoral and party systems, because the two changed in tandem.

[75] In contrast to small and medium-sized firms in Japan, which enjoyed the LDP's protection and subsidies, Thai small and medium-sized firms received scant attention from the government until the Thaksin administration. The importance of small and medium-sized firms in the Thai economy is not negligible, as they represent 90 percent of the country's manufacturers and the source of 40 percent of gross domestic product. They are the country's largest employer group as well. See "SMEs in the spot light: Mid-Year Economic Review," *Bangkok Post.* 2004.

A Systematic Test of How the Multiparty Coalition Government Suppressed Welfare Spending

To systematically test how the multiparty coalition government suppressed resource allocation to diffused losers and favored organized interests, I estimate the proportion of government expenditures for social protection documented in Figure 3.2 (IMF, Various Years), which includes various compensations for a reduction in income and welfare and healthcare programs from 1980 to 2005. Two main covariates that capture the degree of centralization within the ruling coalition are the effective number of parties and factions in the cabinet. Following Laakso and Taagepera (1979), the effective number of parties and factions in the cabinet are defined by the sum of squares of each party's or factional seat shares in the cabinet, and ranges from close to zero (i.e., parties have one seat each) to one (one party monopolizes all seats). I used data reported in Table c in the Appendix from Chambers (2008) and added my own calculation for Thaksin cabinet using the cabinet portfolio information available at the Thai government's official website.[76]

To address whether economic needs of diffused losers translate into the government's policies, I include a battery of economic controls: the annual GDP growth rate, proportion of the dependent population (i.e., older than 65 years of age), and trade openness (values of export plus import divided by GDP). Economic data are from World Bank's *World Development Indicators* from various years.

Table 3.5 summarizes the results. Models 1 and 2 are the baseline models estimated with OLS. Models 3 to 5 address potential serial correlation with the inclusion of lagged dependent variable (model 3), Prais–Winsten transformation (model 4) and OLS with Newey–West standard errors with one-year lag (model 5).[77]

Overall, the results from models 2 to 5 suggest that the more centralized party system, that is, a fewer effective number of parties in a ruling coalition, the government allocated the higher proportion of spending to diffused losers. When the party system was decentralized, that is, the higher effective number of parties in a ruling coalition, the government allocated less spending for diffused losers via welfare programs. The results are robust to different specifications and controls. The substantive effects of party systems on the government's spending allocation are large. A one standard deviation decrease in the effective number of parties in a ruling coalition (e.g., from three to 2.21) is

---

[76] Party and cabinet information are available at http://www.cabinet.thaigov.go.th/eng/pm_his.htm (accessed May 20, 2014).

[77] The Durbin–Watson test of serial correlation for model 3 suggests that the d-statistic falls under a zone of indecision; i.e., the test was indeterminate regarding the existence of serial correlations, while the Breusch–Godfrey test for small samples lends support to the absence of a serial correlation.

TABLE 3.5. *Multiparty Coalition Suppresses Social Spending (%) – Thailand, 1980–2005*

	Model 1	Model 2	Model 3	Model 4	Model 5	Model 6	Model 7	Model 8	Model 9
	OLS	OLS	OLS/Lagged DV	Prais-Winsten	Newey/Lag 1	OLS	OLS/Lagged DV	Prais-Winsten	Newey/Lag 1
Party System Centralization									
Effective number of parties in ruling		−0.0345 (0.0192)*	−0.0275 (0.0116)**	−0.0210 (0.0063)***	−0.0166 (0.0067)**				
Constitutional reform (post-1997)						0.0265 (0.0178)	0.0160 (0.0158)	0.0338 (0.0138)**	0.0265 (0.0138)*
Thaksin (2001–2005)						0.0475 (0.0139)***	0.0684 (0.0142)***	0.0357 (0.0094)***	0.0475 (0.0118)***
Polity IV (0–21)		−0.0110 (0.0094)	−0.0097 (0.0056)			−0.0004 (0.0014)	−0.0014 (0.0012)	−0.0010 (0.0010)	−0.0004 (0.0011)
Authoritarian rule				0.0141 (0.0193)	0.0122 (0.0109)				
ENP ruling * Polity IV		0.0022 (0.0028)	0.0020 (0.0017)						

TABLE 3.5 (*continued*)

	Model 1	Model 2	Model 3	Model 4	Model 5	Model 6	Model 7	Model 8	Model 9
	OLS	OLS	OLS/Lagged DV	Prais-Winsten	Newey/Lag 1	OLS	OLS/Lagged DV	Prais-Winsten	Newey/Lag 1
Economic Controls									
L1. % Age older than 65	0.0281 (0.0125)**	0.0206 (0.0185)	0.0228 (0.0111)*	0.0203 (0.0114)*	0.0216 (0.0137)	0.0152 (0.0106)	0.0257 (0.0098)**	0.0217 (0.0070)***	0.0152 (0.0117)
L1.% GDP growth	0.0023 (0.0010)**	0.0024 (0.0013)*	0.0015 (0.0008)*	0.0028 (0.0008)***	0.0027 (0.0008)***	0.0024 (0.0010)**	0.0025 (0.0008)***	0.0031 (0.0008)***	0.0024 (0.0011)**
L1. % Trade per GDP	−0.0004 (0.0006)	0.0005 (0.0008)	−0.0002 (0.0005)	−0.0003 (0.0005)	−0.0003 (0.0007)	−0.0006 (0.0004)	−0.0007 (0.0004)*	−0.0008 (0.0003)**	−0.0006 (0.0005)
L1. Welfare spending			1.990 (0.392)***				−0.465 (0.170)**		
Constant	−0.153 (0.0540)**	−0.0313 (0.121)	−0.0868 (0.0737)	−0.0440 (0.0612)	−0.0649 (0.0497)	−0.0477 (0.0547)	−0.0967 (0.0502)*	−0.0867 (0.0373)**	−0.0477 (0.0597)
R^2	0.700	0.704	0.901	0.857		0.876	0.914	0.966	
Obs	25	21	21	25	25	25	25	25	25

Note: Standard errors are in parentheses. Significance levels: *$p < 0.10$; **$p < 0.05$; ***$p < 0.01$.

Source: The dependent variable is from International Monetary Fund, *Government Finance Statistics*, various years. The economic covariates are from World Bank's *World Development Indicators* and National Statistics Office of Thailand, *Population and Housing Census*.

118   *Empirical Evidence*

associated with a 1 to 2.5 percentage point increase in the government's spending allocation to welfare programs.

Instead of the continuous variables that measure the party system centralization (i.e., effective numbers of parties and factions in cabinet), models 6 to 9 used two dummy variables that indicate the structural changes in electoral rules. *Constitutional Reform* is one after the 1997 Constitutional reform (1998–2005) and zero otherwise. Thaksin Cabinet is one after Thai Rak Thai Party's one-party majority in 2001 (2001–2005) and zero otherwise. These models do not include the effective number of parties, because both of the two dummy variables correlate highly with the effective number of parties at −0.73 (Constitutional Reform) and −0.76 (Thaksin cabinet) respectively. Models 7 to 9 use different estimators to address potential serial correlation;[78] Model 7 includes the lagged dependent variable, model 8 uses Prais–Winsten transformation and model 9 uses Newey–West standard errors with a lag of one year.

Consistently, Thaksin's one-party majority cabinet was associated with the higher proportion of government's spending allocated for diffused losers. The substantive effects are large: controlling for economic environment and the constitutional reform, the Thaksin cabinet was associated with a 3.6 to 6.8 percentage point increase in the proportion of spending allocated for welfare programs. The results are robust to different specifications and inclusion of various controls. Constitutional reform in 1997 has had some effects on the expansion of welfare programs (models 8 and 9), but the effect is less consistent than the effect of one-party majority under Prime Minister Thaksin.[79]

The results for the control variables are also worth some discussion. Economic needs of citizens, measured by the percentage of the dependent population and the annual GDP growth rate, have expected results. The higher proportion of the dependent population was associated with higher welfare spending, although the effect is not significant in half of the nine models. Economic growth was associated with the increase in welfare spending, which is the opposite of the pattern of Japan. A country's exposure to international trade had no systematic effects on welfare spending, which challenges the literature linking globalization and welfare state expansion or retrenchment. Finally, whether Thailand was a democracy or authoritarian rule did not turn out to have systematic effects on the government's spending allocation. Rather, whether the party systems were centralized or decentralized have had profound

---

[78] The Durbin–Watson test of serial correlation for the model 7 lends support to the absence of serial correlation. The d-statistic (7, 25) was 2.587. The Breusch-Godfrey test for small samples indicates the existence of serial correlation at lag 1. Prob> F was 0.0238.

[79] Alternatively, I ran models seven to ten with the Constitutional Reform dummy, but without the Thaksin cabinet dummy. The results suggest that the Reform dummy is significant only at the 5% level for model 9 (Prais–Winsten transformation), and in other models, the Reform dummy is not statistically significant even at the 10% level.

effects on the government's allocation of resources to organized versus diffused losers, lending support to the Optimal Use of Pork over Policy.

CONCLUSION

Although both Japan and Thailand under multimember district systems showed stable commitment to an open economy during economic crises, their choices of coalition-building strategies differed substantially. The Japanese government expanded its budget allocation to diffused losers during the hard times of the 1970s, while the Thai government kept favoring organized and wealthy interests until the Thai Rak Thai Party's one-party dominance in 2001. The diverging choices of coalition-building strategies, in turn, had shaped the citizens' welfare. The Japanese government's price stabilization and welfare programs helped urban residents ease the hardship caused by the energy crises, and the LDP continued to commit a substantial fraction of budget to diffused losers after 1970s. By contrast, the Thai government's coalition-building strategy to reward organized interests for their political support had continued to widen economic and political inequality between organized versus diffused interests.

What accounts for this divergence was the centralization versus decentralization of party systems. The centralization of Japan's LDP, achieved by reorganization and personnel appointment rules within the party, allowed the expansion of government's budget for diffused losers since the 1970s without major resistance from backbenchers, whose political survival was dependent on Pork. The decentralized, multiparty coalition government of Thailand continued to use Pork for a majority coalition-building. Party system variations are a key to understand how party leaders strike bargains with backbenchers over resource allocation, because they shape the costs of intraelite bargains and negotiations.

This chapter has further shown that an electoral reform is not sufficient or necessary condition for the government's shift from Pork to Policy. Evidence from the Japanese case suggests that, without an electoral reform or partisan change, a ruling party's centralization generated a substantial shift from Pork to Policy. The Thai case also lends support to the importance of one-party dominance in shifting the government's spending allocation to social welfare programs. Yet, owing to the simultaneous timing in which the electoral reform and one-party majority of Thai Rak Thai occurred in 2001, the evidence from the Thai case is still inconclusive regarding the relative weight of party versus electoral systems in shaping the government's choice of the coalition-building strategy.

4

Helping Co-Partisan Legislators Survive Elections

Use of Institutional Reforms

Chapter 3 showed that diffused losers pose a threat to open economy coalition-building during hard times by making party leaders' use of pork prohibitively expensive. I argued that party leaders were more likely to use Policy to favor diffused losers over Pork when the party system is centralized with a fewer number of parties in the government and intraparty organizations.

This chapter addresses the third puzzle about governments' coalition-building strategies, namely, when party leaders adopt institutional reforms – changing the rules of the game – that help backbenchers survive elections as a way to build the open economy coalitions. The theory of Optimal Use of Institutional Reforms developed in Chapter 1 suggests that precisely because of their relative irreversibility, the ruling party leaders use institutional reforms to tie their hands to help their backbenchers survive elections when leaders' incentives to renege on Pork or Policy promise are strong. The leaders' incentives to renege are strong when the future availability of fiscal resources is uncertain.[1]

When Pork or Policy promises of party leaders are not credible to backbenchers, party leaders must come up with an alternative instrument to help backbenchers, who will incur electoral costs of liberalization, to survive future elections. Institutional reform, such as changing the rules of campaign finance and personnel promotion, can increase the backbenchers' survivability of future elections without straining the budget. It also allows party leaders to commit to backbenchers for a longer term than Pork or Policy in the face of economic and political volatility.

---

[1] Economic volatility, such as oil and commodity price volatility and exchange rates fluctuation, can change the availability of fiscal resources dramatically. Such economic volatility was inherent after the end of the Bretton Woods system and shift to the floating exchange rate system in the early 1970s.

Helping Losers Survive Elections

Yet, the demand-side condition described here is not sufficient to account for the supply of institutional reforms by party leaders. Reaching intraparty consensus on such institutional reform is difficult, precisely because a reform gives electoral advantage to some but not others. The centralized party system with a fewer number of parties in the government facilitates the institutional reform because of the lower costs of intraelite bargaining over the new rules.

I test this argument by analyzing when governments initiate institutional reforms that help co-partisan backbenchers survive elections in Japan and Thailand. I focus on institutions that govern how money translates into legislators' political survival: political finance regulations. When elections are costly, which is the case for candidate-centered electoral systems such as those in Japan and Thailand, political finance reform can make or break incumbent legislators by changing their access to campaign contributions.

Despite their similarity in the electoral systems, the prevalence of factions within parties, and the importance of money in elections, political finance regulation in Japan and Thailand differs substantially. In particular, the Japanese government enacted the political finance reform of 1975, which put a ceiling on corporate and associational donations. This new regulation weakened the power of the left by limiting contributions from labor unions, and in effect, helped urban Liberal Democratic Party (LDP) legislators survive the electoral competition with left parties. In addition, the loopholes embedded in the revision allowed legislators' rent-seeking in individual districts, which helped rural LDP legislators survive elections in the face of diminishing Pork in the 1970s (Chapter 3). In essence, party leaders used the revision of the political finance law to give a leg-up to co-partisan legislators in urban districts vis-à-vis left parties and to substitute the declining Pork resource for legislators in rural districts.

The demand-side conditions in Thailand were similar to the Japanese case: the energy crises of in the 1970s caused the rise of consumer prices, fiscal contraction, recession, and export-oriented industries' difficulties, especially between 1983 and 1986.[2] The economic condition lowered the credibility of party leaders' promises to deliver Pork or Policy to buy off backbenchers' support. Yet, Thailand's fragile multiparty coalition system inhibited party leaders' collective action to enact an institutional reform to help co-partisan backbenchers win elections.

Political finance regulation in Thailand allowed individual firms to make unlimited political donations to legislators, while prohibiting lobbying by industrial associations and labor unions. The structure of the regulation shaped

---

[2] The effect of energy crises on the Thai economy was more benign than in the Japanese case, owing to its smaller manufacturing sector and lower dependence on oil. The fiscal contraction in response to the energy crises also occurred with some time lag (i.e., 1983–1986 period), unlike the Japanese case, where the government tightened expenditures immediately after the first crisis in 1973. See Pasuk and Baker (1995: 149–151).

122   *Empirical Evidence*

the legislators' rent-seeking incentives to target the highest bidder in the market, that is, wealthy and oligopolistic firms over small and medium-sized firms. Accordingly, the locus of this rent-seeking was at the national, rather than the local, district level. The coalition leaders had incentives to keep this status quo rather than to change it, owing to their short time horizon under short-lived, multiparty coalition governments.

Why the divergence in the use of institutional reform despite the similarity in Japan's and Thailand's fiscal conditions as well as electoral systems?

JAPAN'S USE OF INSTITUTIONAL REFORM: THE POLITICAL FINANCE REFORM (1975)

The Official Reasons for the Reform: Reducing Corruption

Under the postwar Political Finance Regulation Law (*Seiji Shikin Kisei Hou*), firms and industry associations could donate unlimited amounts of money to both individual politicians and political parties.[3] The factional fights within the LDP over multimember district (MMD) seats and campaign resources also fueled legislators' incentives to mobilize campaign donations and engage in corruption. Especially visible was the LDP's intimate relationship with big business conglomerates, who were the drivers of postwar economic growth. Indeed, Table 4.1 shows the list of major corruption scandals revealed after the World War II. The corruption scandals that were revealed before the 1975 political finance reform involved "globalization winners," that is, export-oriented industries and big business conglomerates (*zaikai*) in shipping, steel, and textile sectors.

The LDP's close relationship with big businesses was most visible to voters during the 1974 Upper House election, which the media sarcastically called the "money politics election" (*kinken senkyo*). The LDP mobilized large contributions from corporations and assigned industry conglomerate the task of mobilizing votes for each of the candidates listed in a national tier.[4] Left parties criticized the LDP as a "sell-out" to capitalists and export-oriented industries. The public's discontent with the LDP's campaign further accelerated the decline of the government's approval rate.

To address this discontent, Prime Minister Miki of the LDP initiated a revision of the Political Finance Law in 1975. The revision limited the amount of political donations that a single firm, industry association, or labor union could give to individual politicians to a mere 1.5 million yen ($5,000 at the 1975 exchange rate). An individual legislator was allowed to receive a total

---

[3] Iwai (1990).

[4] Eda Satsuki's (1991) memoir, chapter 1. In 1974, Japan's Upper House had a two-tiered electoral system: 100 seats were allocated to the national level, MMD system (*dai-senkyoku sei*), and 152 seats were allocated to MMDs in each of the forty-seven prefectures. Every three years, a half of Upper House legislators end their six-year terms and are eligible for reelection. Although voters cast a single nontransferable vote at both tiers, the number of candidates running differed between the two tiers (e.g., one hundred for the national tier, seven for the prefectural tier).

Helping Losers Survive Elections

123

TABLE 4.1. *Major Corruption Scandals Involving Business and Legislators in Postwar Japan*

Year	Scandal Names	Sector	Position in the International Economy (W: winners, L: losers)
1948	Showa Electricity	Electricity	Protected and regulated
1954	Ship Manufacturing	Ship manufacturing	(W) Export-oriented
1957	Prostitution	Sex industries	Regulated
1961	Yahata Steel	Steel	(W) Export-oriented
1961	Bushu Railroad	Transportation	Protected and regulated
1966	Taxi industry	Transportation	Protected and regulated
1967	Kyowa Seitou	Sugar	(W) Import-dependent
1975	**Political Finance Reform**		
1976	Lockheed Scandal	Airbus	Protected and regulated
1985–86	Textile Industry	Textile	(L) Import-competing
1988–89	Recruit Scandal	Real estates	(L) Scarce factor
1988–89	Meidenkou scandal	Construction	Protected and regulated
1991	Kyowa	General contractor	Protected and regulated
1992	Sagawa Express	Shipping/mailing	Protected and regulated
1993	"Zenekon" scandal	General contractor	Protected and regulated
1998–02	Suzuki Muneo scandal	General contractor/ Official Development Aid (ODA)	Protected and regulated

Source: Iwai (1990), p. 6, *Yomiuri Shimbun*, Onkochi Database "60: Seiji Shikin-Kenkin no arubeki sugata ha," April 2, 2009, and *Asahi Shimbun*, various years.

of only 75,000 to 10 million yen ($2,500 to $3.3 million dollars) from firms, industries, and labor unions.

This revision was puzzling in light of existing domestic explanations of political finance reform. First, the LDP was *the* primary beneficiary of campaign donations from firms and organized interests. Yet, it was the opposition party politicians who voted against the bill to limit contributions from organized interests, and the majority of the LDP politicians supported it. The LDP's willingness to limit donations from organized interests poses a puzzle to the "revenue-maximizing" argument that incumbents' incentive for political finance reform is to maximize their revenues.[5] Another puzzle is why the left parties would oppose a bill that appeared to create a more level playing field for opposition parties. The roll-call votes in the Japanese Upper House were absolutely evenly split (117 Yea votes and 117 Nay votes), which was the first and last time this occurred in Japanese Diet history.[6]

---

[5] Scarrow (2007).

[6] See Eda (1991), chapter 1. Ultimately the bill was passed because of the final vote that the chairperson, Kono Kenzo, exercised. House of Councilors, the National Diet of Japan, information available at http://www.sangiin.go.jp/japanese/goiken_gositumon/faq/a05.html.

124 *Empirical Evidence*

The Upper House deliberations and the roll-call votes over this legislation give us a better clue to solve these puzzles. The LDP's motivation for the reform was to help the LDP's urban legislators survive the competition with left parties by limiting labor unions' contribution. All of the opposition party politicians opposed this bill because of its inclusion of labor unions on the list of organized interests, on which the ceiling on donations was imposed. In particular, the two powerful left parties, the Socialist and Democratic Socialist Parties, who had depended on campaign donations from labor unions, became concerned that the passage of this bill would lead to a vast reduction in their campaign resources. During the Diet deliberations, these parties made the argument that: "How can you treat political donations from capitalists, who translate excessive profits into political influence, and donations from labor unions, who contribute from the wages they earn with sweat, in a same way?"[7] The LDP's initiative to limit corporate as well as associational contributions could be seen as a strategy to contain the rise of left parties while appealing to urban voters with a cleaner party image.

The pattern of roll-call votes also confirms the LDP legislators' motivations for supporting the bill. Although the majority of roll-call votes in the Japanese Diet, especially in the Upper House, had been strictly along party lines, the ruling legislators' decision to abstain or be absent from the voting provides important information on who was against the bill. This inference is particularly reasonable for the case of 1975 Political Finance Reform Bill, as the votes were expected to split completely along partisan lines and the LDP leaders were desperate to make every vote count. Yet, twelve LDP legislators, which constituted 9.3 percent of all LDP legislators, either abstained or were absent from the voting on the bill.

If the 1975 political finance reform was indeed the LDP party leaders' effort to help urban legislators' win future election in the face of the rise of left parties, then, I predict that two attributes of legislators were associated with their voting behavior on the floor. First, the LDP legislators who had a greater capacity to mobilize campaign donations from large firms and industries should be against the bill. The loss of campaign donations from large industries should have been especially damaging for legislators who belong to the largest, majority faction within the LDP, Tanaka Kakuei's faction, because large factions had better access to campaign contributions from organized interests and used this resource to expand their membership further.[8] Because

---

[7] Testimony by Hata Yutaka (Japan Socialist Party) at the Upper House committee on the Revision of Electoral Campaign Law (Vol. 1), June 28, 1975 and by Wada Haruo (Democratic Socialist Party) at the Upper House's Main Meeting (Vol. 22), July 4, 1975. Available at transcripts of Diet deliberations at the National Diet Library's website: http://kokkai.ndl.go.jp/.

[8] Iwai (1990); Cox and Rosenbluth (1993). This is precisely how the largest faction in the LDP then, led by Tanaka Kakuei, expanded by skillfully mobilizing legal and illegal political donations from organized interests.

Helping Losers Survive Elections 125

TABLE 4.2. *The Predicted LDP Legislators' Voting Decisions on the 1975 Political Finance Bill*

	Access to Campaign Donation	
	Scarce	Plenty
Rural/safe	Loyal	*Rebel (n = 12, 9.3%)*
Votes		
Urban/competitive	Loyal	Loyal

TABLE 4.3. *Who Defected? Access to Donation and Rural Safe Seats*

LDP Elected from Local Districts	Loyalists (%)	Rebels (%)
Money dimension: % Tanaka faction	7.7	80
Vote dimension: ruralness and safe seats		
% Work force in the primary industry	17	24.7
Margin of victory for all districts	0.001	14
Margin of victory for district magnitude = 1	31.4	42.8

Source: I used roll-call vote data from Kabashima (2005), election results of the 1974 Upper House election, and factional information from Za-Senkyo (available at http://www.senkyo.janjan.jp/election/1974/99/00001945.html), and demographic information from Ministry of Agriculture, Forestry and Fisheries' Agricultural Census (1975), and Ministry of Labor's Labor Force Survey (1975). In 1974 Upper House election, the LDP won 62 out of 130 seats, which explains the negative value of margin of victory for all districts.

of the lack of comprehensive contribution data during this period, I use legislators' factional affiliation with the Tanaka faction as a proxy for their access to campaign donations.

The second condition is that those who have safe seats in rural areas are more likely to defect (abstain or be absent from the voting) because these rural legislators do not face the urgent need to contain the power of the left compared to those who run for competitive seats in urban areas. Table 4.2 summarizes this prediction.

Table 4.3 summarizes the actual pattern of defection. Consistent with the prediction, 80 percent of the LDP rebels belonged to the largest majority faction at that time, run by Kakuei Tanaka, who was a former prime minister known for his ability to mobilize campaign donations from firms and industries. As Table 4.3 shows, moreover, the LDP legislators who defected tended to be elected from rural and safe seats, unlike those who stayed loyal to the LDP party line.

In sum, the analysis of roll-call votes suggests that the urban LDP legislators and/or the LDP legislators with scarce access to campaign donations supported political finance reform, whereas the rural legislators and those with lucrative access to campaign contribution opposed it. This lends support to the LDP's

126   *Empirical Evidence*

motivation for political finance reform to help urban LDP legislators survive
the rise of left parties. With 12 defections occurred among 129 eligible LDP
legislators in the Upper House, the party leaders of the LDPpassed the political
finance reform with the bare majority.

The Effect of Political Finance Reform: Rent-Seeking when Pork Barreling Was Constrained

Although the pattern of roll-call votes suggests that the revision would help
urban rather than rural LDP legislators, the revised law also helped rural LDP
legislators mobilize votes and rents from their constituents for their political survival. First, the corporate donation ceiling specified in the revised law
shifted the proportion of campaign donation from the winners to the losers
of the global economy.[9] Because protectionist interests were more likely to
be concentrated in rural areas, this shift helped the LDP's rural legislators'
rent-seeking activities in districts, and hence political survival. Second, two
loopholes embedded in the revised law also helped the LDP's rural legislators'
vote- and rent-seeking activities in their districts and thus their political survival, as discussed later.

The first loophole was that firms and industries were allowed to make
unlimited contributions to local party branches (*shibu*), which were organized
to support LDP candidates in a district. Local party branches are generally
managed by individual legislators and often run by a legislator's local support
group (*koenkai*).[10] This meant that the collection of campaign finance became
decentralized from the LDP leaders, especially factional leaders, to individual legislators.[11] Conventional wisdom about this decentralization was that it
intended to diversify the risk of corruption (and corruption revelation) from
party and factional leaders to individual legislators and to make individual
legislators responsible for corruption scandals.

Yet, this decentralization of political finance also had deeper welfare
implications for Japan's political economy. As individual legislators became
more responsible for raising their own campaign finance from organized
interests in localities, the loophole incentivized the individual LDP legislators to extract rents from geographically concentrated interests in their
districts, which were more likely to be import-competing, rather than
export-oriented, industries at that time.[12] Indeed, a systematic analysis of
interest group lobbying data, discussed in detail later, confirms the 1975
political finance reform increased legislators' mobilization of protectionist and geographically organized interest groups. Table 4.1 also shows that

---

[9] Grossman and Helpman (1994).
[10] Iwai (1990); Sasaki et al. (1999).
[11] Iwai (1990); Cox and Rosenbluth (1993); Naoi and Krauss (2009).
[12] Ray (1981); Busch and Reinhart (2000).

Helping Losers Survive Elections

the nature of corruption scandals involving business had changed after the mid-1970s – import-injured and heavily regulated industries dominated the corruption scandals.

The second loophole embedded in the revision was that subsidized industries (i.e., import-competing industries) were permitted to contribute to individual legislators through the purchase of "party tickets" at fundraising parties without violating the law. After the revision, the LDP's headquarters and prefectural or local branches began organizing official fundraising parties called Political Economy & Culture Parties.[13] The revenues raised at the Political Economy & Culture Parties were split between the LDP headquarters and the local branch. Heavily subsidized agricultural organizations such as Agricultural Cooperatives (*nokyo*) have leveraged this loophole and, in this manner, have made large donations to LDP politicians catering to agricultural interests (i.e., *nousei zoku*).

In sum, the revision of the Political Finance Reform Law was Optimal Use of Institutional Reform to help both urban and rural LDP legislators survive elections in the face of rise of left parties in urban districts and diminishing Pork resources in rural districts.

Using interest group lobbying data in the Diet deliberations, I show that, indeed, the pattern of interest group mobilization by the LDP legislators changed after political finance reform (1975) in two ways: (1) the LDP legislators mobilized more protectionist interest groups after the reforms than free-trading groups; and (2) the LDP mobilized more geographically organized interest groups more after the reforms, compared to sectorally organized, national interest groups. In other words, as the LDP government's *policies* moved toward more open economy and more spending favoring broader interests in the mid-1970s, the pattern of LDP's rent-seeking activities moved toward the opposite: toward more protectionist, more geographically organized groups. In essence, after political finance reform, the party leaders allowed the backbenchers to mobilize political support from protectionist and geographically organized interests to substitute the declining Pork, while making sure that these rent-seeking activities would not intervene in the progress in trade liberalization.

I present two pieces of evidence to demonstrate that the pattern of interest group mobilization changed after the political finance reform in 1975: (1) a structural break (i.e., sudden changes) around the reform in the relative frequency of legislators mobilizing free trade versus protectionist interest groups; and (2) a structural break (i.e., sudden changes) around the reform in legislators' propensity to mobilize geographically organized groups over nationally organized, sectoral or, class-based organizations.

To do so, I leverage a procedure in the Japanese Diet in which interest groups testify before Diet committees only by invitation from legislators. In each

---

[13] See Liberal Democratic Party (1987: 670–671).

128   *Empirical Evidence*

lower-house standing committee, an executive board consisting of five to ten members of parliament has power over committee invitations. The ruling and opposition parties usually invite several witnesses so that different policy positions are well represented in the testimony. As a data source, I used an official document search engine of the National Diet Library of Japan located at http://kokkai.ndl.go.jp, which has transcripts of all the Diet committee discussions and floor debates in the Lower and Upper Houses from 1947 to the present.

After identifying all possible interest group testimony on trade in the lower-house between 1950 and 2002, I coded whether (1) trade policy is actually discussed, and (2) interest groups expressed their trade policy positions.[14] I then identified (1) who testified (i.e., a class, sector, firm, or geographically organized group) before which committee, (2) the commodity or industry, and (3) the trade policy position. The dataset contains 208 instances in which interest groups clearly expressed their trade policy preferences before the Diet committees during this period. The unit of analysis is therefore interest group–testimony–year.[15]

The Overall Pattern of Interest Group Lobbying on Trade in Japan

Figure 4.1 shows the changing patterns in the frequency of trade testimony during the past five decades. It shows that increase in trade testimony by interest groups roughly corresponds with the expansion of trade, measured by the percentage of import and export values per Japan's gross domestic product. Approximately 80 percent of total testimony on trade policy (165 cases out of 208) was given in front of two committees – the Economy, Industry and Trade Committee and the Agriculture, Forestry and Fisheries Committee. These committees have working relations with their corresponding ministries, which have been the major financial sources of compensation for import-injured industries. The distribution of lobbying across committees suggests that the major motive for legislators to invite interest group witnesses is to demand compensation for income losses from liberalization, not necessarily to change the course of trade policy outcomes.

Figure 4.2 describes the changes in the proportion of protectionist testimony per total testimony since 1951, aggregated every five years. It

---

[14] First, I narrowed the search to testimony given by interest groups, not by bureaucrats or politicians. Second, I used different key words to identify all possible interest group testimony on trade policy: export (*yushutsu*), import (*yunyu*), trade (*boueki*), and tariffs (*kanzei*). The search results broadly cover all the statements that used one of these key words, including testimony on different policy issues, such as environmental and security issues.

[15] If testimony was given for the same industrial sector (e.g., textiles) but by different interest groups (e.g., the National Textile Association and the Cotton Yarn Association), I count it as separate testimony to gauge the frequency of the appearance. Because the time allocated for policy debates in the Diet committees is limited, I reason that an interest group given multiple opportunities to voice its trade position is more powerful than one not given such an opportunity.

Helping Losers Survive Elections

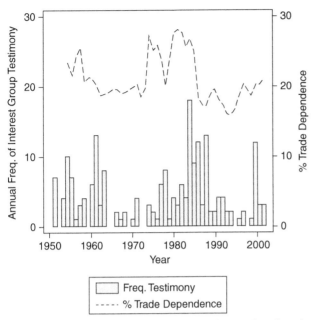

FIGURE 4.1. Trade exposure and the incidence of trade policy testimony before Japan's Lower House, 1950–2002.

Source: Annual frequency of interest group testimony over trade issues in the Lower House is from the author's dataset using the transcript of Japan's Lower House deliberations at the National Diet library. Data on trade dependence from 1960 to 2002 is from World Bank's *World Development Indicators*, various years. For trade dependence data from 1955 to 1959, I used data from the Ministry of Economy, Trade and Industry's Whitepaper (2012), chapter 2 and for the data in 1954, I used Japan's Economic Planning Agency's Annual Whitepaper on the Economy (*Keizai Nenji Hakusyo*) published in 1955. Trade dependence data from 1950 to 1953 were not available.

TABLE 4.4. *Frequency of Trade Policy Testimony by Types of Interest Groups, 1950–2002*

Types	Frequency	Category (%)
Sector	102	49
Geographically organized	89	43
Firm	12	6
National Labor	5	2
Total	208	100

Source: Author's original dataset.

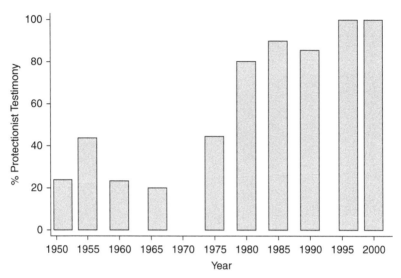

FIGURE 4.2. Proportion of protectionist testimony before Diet committees (%), 1950–2002.
Source: Author's dataset.
Note: Annual data aggregated to every five years from 1950 to 2002. Between 1970 and 1974, interest groups did not give protectionist trade testimony. The eight trade testimonies given between 1970 and 1974 were for free trade, given by textile industries that faced trade conflicts with the United States.

demonstrates that the strong protectionist bias in the testimony began in the mid-1970s. Until then, more than half of the testimony was given for the free trade position.[16] The rise of protectionist bias in the testimony in the 1970s is puzzling in light of the bilateral trade conflicts with the United States, which reached their height around then as discussed previously. Japan's key export industries, such as textile, electronics, and automobiles, were subject to retaliatory tariffs by the United States in the 1970s, which should have mobilized Japanese exporters' interests as the costs of protectionism became more concentrated on particular export-oriented industries.[17] Indeed, between 1970 and 1974, textile industry groups gave testimony all advocating for free trade (Destler, Fukui, and Sato 1979). Yet, after 1975, we see the protectionist testimony dominating the Japanese Diet deliberations.

---

[16] Overall, 70 percent of total testimony was for protectionism, whereas only approximately 20 percent advocated in favor of free trade. The remaining 10 percent of testimony was for export promotion or ambiguous statements.
[17] Using interest group testimony data in the U.S. Congress, Gilligan (1997) has shown that reciprocal agreements empowered exporters' interests by concentrating the benefits of free trade to particular industries and thus lowering the collective action costs for exporters.

Helping Losers Survive Elections 131

Table 4.4 documents that geographically organized groups – such as prefectural and city-level industry and labor organizations – constituted approximately 40 percent of trade-policy testimony in the Diet. Unlike European countries or the United States, the lobbying activities of the three major, nationally organized labor unions on trade issues have been extremely minimal in Japan. In the aggregate, unions testified on trade issues only five times before Diet committees between 1950 and 2002. Among them, there is only one instance of testimony at the Committee on Public Welfare and Social Labor where clear reference was made to trade policy.[18] The proportion of geographically organized groups' lobbying per total lobbying activities also increased substantially around the mid-1950s, after the unification of the two conservative parties and Japan's joining General Agreement on Tariffs and Trade (GATT), and increased further in the mid-1970s.[19]

Evidence: The Timing of the Protectionist and Geographic Turns in Interest Group Mobilization

While Figure 4.2 presents visual evidence of the sharp rise of protectionist lobbying around the mid-1970s, I demonstrate the existence of this structural break more systematically by modeling the proportion of protectionist testimony (a percentage variable theoretically ranging from zero to 100) as a function of a linear trend and allow for a break at the time of institutional changes in politics (i.e., the political finance reform of 1975 and the electoral reform of 1994). To do so, I follow Scheve and Stasavage's test on structural breaks (2009: 243–244) by estimating the following structure: Protectionist $_t$ = $\alpha + \beta T_1 + \gamma T_2 + \varepsilon_t$

T_1 and T_2 refer to pre-reform and post-reform time trends. T_1 takes values equal to t (*e.g.*, 1960, 1965, 1970 … 2000 in five-year intervals) for all years prior to a reform (or chosen structural break) and it is set at $T_1 = 0$ for all years (t) after the reform. $T_2 = 0$ for all years (t) prior to a reform (or chosen structural break) and it is set equal to t for all subsequent years after a reform. If protectionist lobbying increases over time in postwar Japan, the coefficients of β and γ should both be positive. More importantly, however, the size of the coefficients in matrix γ should be larger than in β if there is significant acceleration of this increase, indicating the presence of a structural break.

Table 4.5 reports the results of ordinary least squares (OLS) estimates of the equation. Standard errors are reported in parentheses. The table shows the acceleration (i.e., existence of structural breaks where $\gamma > \beta$) of protectionist lobbying after 1975 continuing the trend until 1985, lending support to

---

[18] Kume (1998).
[19] Rogowski (1989).

TABLE 4.5. *Testing for a Trend Shift in Protectionist Lobbying at Different Break Dates*

Institutional Changes	1960	1965	1970	1975	1980	1985	1990	1995	2000
			↑ Seniority System	↑ Political Finance Reform				↑ Electoral Reform	
β	0.364 (0.120)	0.188 (0.103)	0.074 (0.082)	−0.048 (0.037)	−0.013 (0.031)	0.049 (0.038)	0.081 (0.034)	0.087 (0.029)	0.093 (0.024)
γ	0.121 (0.021)	0.108 (0.026)	0.088 (0.027)	0.058 (0.015)	0.067 (0.015)	0.083 (0.020)	0.091 (0.021)	0.093 (0.021)	0.091 (0.024)

Note: The table reports the results of OLS estimates of the equation, Protectionist $_t$ = α + βT_1 + γT_2 + ε$_t$. T_1 takes a value of t for all years previous to each of the break dates (1960, 1965, 1970...2000 in five-year intervals) and zero otherwise. T_2 takes a value of zero for all years after the break dates and zero otherwise. Standard errors are reported in parentheses. The table shows the acceleration (i.e., existence of structural breaks where γ > β) of protectionist lobbying after 1975 continuing the trend until 1985 (in boldface).

Helping Losers Survive Elections

the LDP's mobilization of protectionist and geographically organized interest groups after the political finance reform.[20]

Contrary to the established wisdom that the adoption of proportional representation system insulates legislators from narrow and parochial interests, the electoral reform of 1994, which introduced a party list, proportional representation system, did not reduce the propensity of legislators to mobilize geographically organized groups.[21] Moreover, the introduction of a single-member district system for 300 Lower House seats did not increase the propensity of free trade lobbying either, which challenges studies linking majoritarian electoral systems with more liberal trade policy.[22] This might be due to the specific institutional designs of Japan's mixed-member electoral system where the double-listing rules between single-member district and proportional representation allow legislators to run from both electoral systems. The mixed system might have blurred the difference between how legislators behave under the two different electoral systems.[23]

In sum, the political finance reform of 1975 was the Optimal Use of Institutional Reform to help co-partisan legislators survive future elections in the face of diminishing fiscal resource and the rise of left parties. The two conditions, that is, the uncertainty about future fiscal resource and the LDP's centralization, facilitated the use of institutional reform. I demonstrated that the revision of political finance law, which governs how wealth translates into political influence, helped urban LDP legislators survive the rise of left parties by limiting labor union contribution, and helped rural LDP legislators survive the diminishing government's resource for pork barrel politics. The political finance reform had a long-lasting effect on how the LDP mobilized interest groups and extracted rents, as seen in the longitudinal pattern of interest group mobilization on trade.

The Lack of Institutional Reforms in Thailand

Despite the fact that Thailand shared the demand-side condition with Japan, that is, fiscal uncertainty, the Thai party leaders did not initiate any institutional reform to help co-partisans survive future elections. Instead, party leaders kept the status quo political finance regulation, which encourages legislators to extract rents from oligopolistic, exporting firms, rather than import-competing industries in localities.

---

[20] I conducted the same structural break test to see whether the proportion of lobbying by geographically organized groups increased after the two institutional reforms. The results lend support.

[21] Rogowski (1987).

[22] Rogowski and Kayser (2002); Park and Jensen (2007).

[23] McKean and Scheiner (2000); Bawn and Thies (2003).

134 *Empirical Evidence*

The Thai party leaders did not have any incentives to change the status quo for two reasons. First, with the fluid multiparty coalition governments where factional and coalition alliances changed quickly, party or coalition leaders did not have incentives to tie their hands to any new rules of the game to help co-partisans' political survival. Second, short-lived and fragile multiparty governments prevented parties from developing institutional relationships with particular financiers of campaign activities.[24] Instead, individual politicians and factional leaders developed personal relationships with the financiers. This differed from the Japanese political parties, where the ruling LDP and opposition parties respectively developed institutional relationships with capitalists and labor. Changing the political finance regulation thus would not help or harm the co-partisan legislators in the Thai case.

The pattern of corruption revelations in Thailand is consistent with the incentive structure provided by the political finance regulation that legislators targeted big businesses for rent extraction. Table 4.6 lists major corruption scandals that involved industries and the resignation or official investigation of ministers between 1992, when Thailand returned to democracy, and 2006, when it reverted back to a military rule.[25] Export-oriented sectors, such as chemical, pharmaceutical, food-processing, and agribusiness industries, were the major bribers of government ministers. The majority of companies involved in these scandals were big business conglomerates such as Charoen Pokphand Group, which was a major campaign financier for several political parties and factions. Another common type of corruption is insider trading of land by ministers, where ministers bought a large patch of land before the information about forthcoming public work projects was released. Although the majority of these corruption scandals were related to public work projects, they differed from the Japanese cases, where heavily regulated and protected industries, such as construction and transportation companies, dominated the corruption scene after the 1975 revision of the Political Finance Reform Law (see Table 4.1). In Thailand, import-competing and regulated sectors rarely entered major corruption scandals except for "policy corruption" cases under the one-party majority of Thai Rak Thai (2001–2005).[26]

---

[24] Farmers are an organized interest group in Japan, owing to their small number and geographic concentration (e.g., constituting only 4 percent of total labor force), but they are a diffused mass group in Thailand (e.g., 68 percent of the Thai population resided in rural areas as of 2000).

[25] The list is limited to scandals that involved industries and ministers because of the rampant smaller corruption cases involving individual legislators. There were also other corruption scandals involving politicians' electoral fraud and under-declaration of assets that did not explicitly involve business or industries.

[26] The exceptions are so-called "policy corruption" cases by Prime Minister Thaksin, in which he adopted policies or changed regulations to benefit companies that he and his family owned. Because of the nature of the policy corruption, industries such as telecom, satellite and media, and airlines that were heavily regulated by the government were involved in the policy corruption.

Helping Losers Survive Elections 135

TABLE 4.6. *Major Political Corruption Scandals Involving Business and Ministers in Thailand*

Year	Event	Ministry	Sector/Company	Positions in International Economy
1992	Mosquito Eradication	Interior	Chemical	Export-oriented (W)
1995	Klong Daan Sewage	Interior	Landowners	Abundant factor (W)
1998	Rural Hospital Project	Public health	Medical/ pharmaceutical	Export-oriented (W)
2003	Thaksin's "Policy Corruption"	Prime minister	Telecom	Regulated/ protected (L)
2003	Thaksin's "Policy Corruption"	PM and Board of Investment	Satellite	Regulated/ protected
2003	Thaksin's "Policy Corruption"	PM and transport	Airline	Regulated/ protected
2004	Seeds Project	Agriculture	Rubber/ agribusiness	Export-oriented (W)
2005	Strengthening Thai Program	Public health	Medical/ pharmaceutical	Export-oriented (W)
2005	Rotten Canned Fish	Human security	Food processing/ fishery	Export-oriented (W)

Sources: Pasuk (1999), Suwanmala (2009), *the Bangkok Post* and *the Nation*, various years.
Note: (W) denotes the winners and (L) denotes the losers of the global economy.

The pattern of corruption incidents in Thailand thus suggests that legislators targeted the beneficiaries of trade and investment liberalization for rent extraction, just as in the Japanese case before the political finance reform of 1975. The public's discontent with these scandals was also high in Thailand, similar to the Japanese case.[27] The subsequent responses to these scandals involving export-oriented capitalists, however, differ significantly between the two countries. First, although there was a major political finance reform in 1999 to reduce corruption in Thailand, the reform did not put a ceiling on corporate donations. Table 4.7 compares the outcomes of political finance reforms in Japan (1975 and minor revision in 1994) and Thailand (1999). Although the Thai reforms increased the transparency of political donations, they did not limit the extent to which organized interests provide donations to legislators.

---

[27] However, Albritton and Bureekul (2002) show that rural voters show much higher tolerance for corruptions and related gift-giving activities than urban respondents.

136 *Empirical Evidence*

TABLE 4.7. *Political Finance Reforms in Japan (1975 and 1994) and Thailand (1999)*

Regulatory Characteristics	Japan	Thailand
Regulation exists?	Yes	Yes
Disclosure provision	Yes to over JPY 50000	Yes to All
Ceiling on party donation	Yes	No
Ceiling on donor	**Yes (fn1), plus per year ceiling**	**No**
Ceiling on total funds a party raises	No	No
Ceiling on party election expenditure	No	Yes, Thai baht million per district
Ban on types of donation	**Yes, corporations that receive subsidies**	**Yes, trade associations and chamber of commerce**
Ban on foreign-owned corporate donation	Yes until the revision in 2006	Yes
Ban on corporate donation	**No, but ceiling exists**	**No, and no ceiling exists.**
Ban on government contractors	No in general, but Yes if subsidized	No

Source: The coding is based on Maja Tjernstrom and Anna Katz, 2003. *The Matrix of Political Finance Laws and Regulation,* International IDEA, with additional information by the author using an internal memo *"Seijishikin Kisei Kankei Nenpyo"* (Chronology of the Revisions of Political Finance Regulation) by the Research and Legislative-Making Bureau of the National Diet Library, March 9, 2009.

Note: fn.1: JPY 7,500,000–100,000,000 (Int'l $ 49,840–664,600) according to the size of capital (corporations), membership (trade unions), and annual expenses (other organizations).

First, firms are allowed to finance electoral campaigns and political parties without any ceiling on the amount. This allows firms with high growth revenues, such as big business conglomerates, to turn economic wealth into political influence. On the other hand, trade associations and the Chamber of Commerce, both of which represent various industrial sectors, have been prohibited from donating or participating in electoral campaigns by the law as have provincial branches of the trade associations and the Chamber of Commerce.[28] This was partly due to

---

[28] Laothamatas (1988). This does not mean that these associations cannot directly lobby (i.e., ask for assistance) the government or politicians. Indeed, Arghiros notes that "some provincial business associations have also become effective sources of pressure," lobbying provincial and central governments for their support in the 1990s (Arghiros 2001: 20). And Laothamatas (1992) has argued that during the late 1980s and early 1990s, many provincial associations became autonomous pressure groups with demands on the provincial and central government for infrastructure and policy.

Helping Losers Survive Elections

the fact that many of these associations were established by the government and considered public agencies.[29]

Although the enforcement of this law has been sporadic, and the smaller and private industry associations often participated in electoral campaigns at the local levels,[30] Laothamatas (1988) reports several incidences where the police caught the participation of the Chamber of Commerce in electoral campaigns.

This regulation has profound implications for the distribution of power between economic winners and losers. The regulation gives a clear advantage to economic winners over losers, because as individual firms, export-oriented firms can expend more resources than import-competing firms. Import-competing firms, moreover, face high barriers to collectively influencing policymaking through associations, because the law prohibits campaign activities by industry associations (see Chapter 6 on the weak political influence of the Chamber of Commerce in Chonburi Province). Because of the personal relationships between legislators and financiers, the political parties do not act as enforcers of exchanges between firm-level contributions and an industry's desirable policy outcome, either.[31] Mirroring these candidate-centered electoral incentives and political finance regulation, Thai trade and industrial policy has been highly decentralized and sporadic, favoring individual firms rather than particular localities or sectors.[32]

To cope with this power imbalance, trade associations and the Chamber of Commerce have sought an alternative way to influence policy, which is to send members of associations directly to Parliament.[33] Although there had been an increasing number of representatives who were former board members of trade and business associations in localities, key party and cabinet positions have continued to be given to those who have owned or have connections with big national conglomerates. As shown in the list of corruption incidents, they have sought to advance parochial firm-specific interests, rather than industry or sectoral interests in policymaking.

---

[29] Laothamatas (1992).

[30] See Arghiros (2001: 223). He discusses how rural industrialists and Sino-Thai merchant-contractors fought the provincial-level election between 1990 and 1995 in Ayutthaya. Rural industrialists with backing from the Brick Manufacture's Association wanted to gain political power by securing seats in the provincial council, but Sino-Thai merchant contractors had more resources and won the election.

[31] Naoi and Krauss (2009).

[32] Rock's (1995) work confirms that industrial policy in Thailand has pro-big firm bias, which consequently contributed to economic growth. Doner and Ramsay also argue that rent-seeking in Thailand has a pro-growth bias, which accounts for the coexistence of clientelism and economic growth.

[33] Laothamatas (1988); Naoi and Krauss (2009); Gelbach et al. (2010).

138   *Empirical Evidence*

Decentralized Thai Party System: A Quota System for the Allocation of Cabinet Posts

Although Thai legislators did not develop a seniority system for allocating cabinet or committee seats (see Chapter 3 on the seniority system in Japan), they have adopted a quota system – an allocation of cabinet posts according to party or factional seat share in the parliament – since the 1975 election.[34] The emergence of a quota system changed the course of Thai politics in two ways.

First, the quota system promoted decentralization and fragmentation of political power to factional leaders away from the party leaders. Gathering seven members of parliament is sufficient to obtain one cabinet position and thirty members per faction is considered the ceiling in terms of obtaining enough spoils for the faction without undermining the benefits for individual members (i.e., minimum winning coalition). The quota system thus discouraged the merger among factions and parties and instead encouraged a fragmented power struggle among factions over membership. Greater numbers of parties in the ruling coalition tend to be associated with inefficient bargains among multiple actors, leading to the government's use of Pork.[35]

Second, because the size of a faction directly translates into political power and access to government resources, factional leaders who obtain ministerial positions have incentives to use government resources to expand the membership or deter current members from defecting to other factions (see Chapter 3 on electoral disconnection between Thai ministers and their constituencies).[36] This creates incentives for ministers to allocate budget resources to the highest bidder in the economic and political market (i.e., money and votes), leading to a resource allocation favoring organized and wealthier interests rather than the diffused poor.

In sum, the quota system of cabinet post allocation functions to translate market power into political influence. Legislators who benefit from the system, that is, those who have access to wealthy financiers, have no interests in changing it. Even legislators in the minority or opposition factions do not have interests in changing the system either, because of rampant opportunities for factional and party switching and mergers.

---

[34] Scholars such as OcKey (1994, 2004) and Connors (1999) have referred to post-1975 election cabinet formation as the time when a quota system was instituted. The original source on this institutionalization, as well as why the quota system was adopted at this particular timing, were not provided in these studies. The reasonable guess is that the 1975 election was one of the earliest democratic election in which parties, not the military, formed the multiparty coalition government.

[35] On average, the effective number of parties in Thailand before the 2000 election was 6.3, well beyond the average in other parliamentary systems with similar electoral systems such as Japan (3.1 in 1984).

[36] OcKey (2004: 38).

Helping Losers Survive Elections   139

In contrast to Thai legislators' long-term commitment to a quota system since 1975, there has been no institutionalization of seniority system of a personnel appointment system in the party or the Cabinet. Although no study to my knowledge has explored why this is so, the lack of seniority system facilitates party leaders' recruitment of "businessmen politicians" to run for elections. "Businessmen politicians" are legislators who own or have owned businesses, often related to public works projects. Party leaders like to recruit local businessmen for political race, because they possess two key resources for winning elections – financial resources and a local vote canvasser network. Yet, the seniority-based allocation of cabinet posts would have made this recruitment harder, because, once elected, businessmen politicians will have to wait for several terms to obtain cabinet positions.

Indeed, without the seniority system, there was an increasing number of political candidates in Thailand who are business owners.[37] From 1975 to the March 1992 elections, the proportion of members of parliament who had a background in owing business increased from 35 percent to 45 percent. The increase was even more dramatic for those who occupied cabinet positions. From the 1975 Kukrit cabinet to the 1991 Chatichai cabinet, ministers with business-owning backgrounds increased from 27 percent to 45 percent. The more resourceful these businessmen politicians are, the more likely it is that they are based in the industrial vicinity of Bangkok.

To conclude, Thai party leaders had no strong incentives to initiate institutional reforms to change how legislators mobilize votes and money, owing to their short time horizon under a fragile, multiparty coalition governments. Consistent with the incentives provided by the political finance regulation, the legislators' rent-seeking targeted the winners of global economy, rather than losers, in contrast to the Japanese case after 1975 Political Finance Reform.

CONCLUSION

When do party leaders have incentives to change the rules of the game, that is, legislators' access to money and rents, to assist co-partisan legislators survive elections in an effort to build the coalition supporting open economy? This chapter has shown that when party leaders' Pork or Policy promises are not credible owing to the uncertainty about fiscal resource in the future (the demand-side condition) and a ruling party is centralized (the supply-side condition), party leaders are more likely to resort to an institutional reform to help backbenchers' political survival and make them stay with the party. Japanese and Thai cases after the energy crises shared the demand-side condition, and varied in their supply-side conditions – Japan had the LDP as a dominant party and Thailand had an unstable, multiparty coalition.

---

[37] Laothamatas (1988).

Japan's LDP initiated the political finance reform that limited contribution from corporations and labor unions to help urban legislators survive the competition with the left parties. The revision as well as loopholes embedded in the law also changed the locus of legislators' rent-seeking from free-trading to protectionist interests, and further strengthened legislators' incentives to mobilize votes and campaign contributions from geographically organized interests in districts. The party leaders allowed the individual legislators' rent-seeking in districts as a substitute to diminishing pork resources since the 1970s, which impacted rural LDP legislators. These rent-seeking activities in districts were operated under the severe budget constraints, and accordingly, did not reverse the LDP's overall commitment to trade and investment liberalization.

On the other hand, Thai's multiparty coalition government did not initiate any institutional reform to help their co-partisan legislators survive future elections in the face of fiscal constraints. They kept the status quo, that is, the political finance regulation which allows firms to give unlimited contribution to political candidates, and prohibits industry associations and labor unions' campaign contributions and involvement in electoral campaigns.

Both governments were able to resist protectionism, yet, their choice of coalition-building strategies shaped how politicians distribute budget and rents – with a deeper welfare implication for citizens. Thailand's continuous use of pork to hold the coalition together consequently favored the organized, urban, and industrial groups, while Japan's institutional reform contributed to legislators rent-seeking with more protectionist and geographically organized interests in rural areas.

5

Japanese Legislators in Rival Regions

> I said "no" to using safeguard provision for our industry. The timing was not right – China has just retaliated against Japan with higher import duties for air-conditioning, cell phones and all that. I got a phone call from President Inamori of Kyosera [cell phone manufacturer] saying "You've got to stop this [protectionist bandwagon], China's retaliation is killing us." So I told my supporters, "Sorry, now is not the right time [for protectionism]." But I brought a big highway construction project their way.
>
> Author's Interview, the LDP Lower House Member of fence-sitting district, March, 2006

This chapter provides case study findings on how Japanese legislators representing two sets of rival regions – areas with similar industry profiles but one area with unified protectionist interests and another with intraindustry split between free trade and protectionist interests – took trade policy positions in 1990–2006. Two of these regions, the cities of Senshu and Imabari, specialize in the towel industry,[1] while Okayama and Kumamoto Prefectures specialize in the production of tatami mats.[2] Both industries faced a deluge of imported products from China in the 1990s, and thus all four regions were affected.

---

[1] The towel industry in Japan has been highly dependent on corporate clienteles that purchase towels as gifts to customers rather than individual consumers. It is a custom in many Japanese companies to give towels (often with their company's name printed) for free to customers or clients during two "gift seasons" in August (*ochugen*) and December (*oseibo*) every year. Another common use of towels as a gift is when people move into a new house. It is a custom to visit neighbors to introduce oneself bearing fresh towels.

[2] Tatami mats are a traditional type of Japanese flooring made from woven straw. Japanese people started using tatami mats during the eighth century (Nara Period). Japanese traditional houses usually have rooms with tatami mats and even modern apartments often have one room with tatami flooring. During the past fifteen years or so, though, hardwood floors became more popular among younger people and, as a result, the use of tatami mats has been declining.

	LDP Incumbent	
	No	Yes
Fence Sitting		Imabari: Free Trade w/ Pork
		(Final Policy Outcome)
Unified Protectionism	Senshu: Protectionism without Pork	
	(Not Chosen Outcome)	

FIGURE 5.1. Towel industry – predicted legislator positions.
Note: The final government decisions are summarized in parentheses.

Yet legislators representing the rival regions expressed opposite trade policy positions. For the towel industry, a legislator representing Imabari City advocated for free trade while a legislator representing Senshu region lobbied for protectionism. For the tatami mat industry, politicians representing Kumamoto Prefecture lobbied for protectionism, while politicians representing Okayama Prefecture advocated for free trade. If politicians are merely transmitting the constituents' demands for protectionism or free trade, we would not expect to see this divergence in politicians' policy positions among districts with similar industrial profiles. This divergence makes sense when we consider legislators' trade policy positioning as part of a larger, national effort to build an open economy coalition.

Figure 5.1 shows predicted legislators' policy positions for the two towel-producing regions. Consistent with the optimal allocation of Pork developed in Chapter 1, I predict that Liberal Democratic Party (LDP) politicians representing "fence-sitting" districts, such as Imabari City, where there is a split among firms' policy positions on trade within the same industry, would take a free trade position and receive particularistic projects. The district with a more unified preference for protectionism, such as Senshu region of Osaka, received fewer particularistic benefits despite the fact that the towel industry's net loss from China's export deluge was much larger than that of Imabari.

Globalization as Legislation accounts for this puzzle – to recap, it is more efficient for ruling parties to target particularistic benefits to a legislator representing small net losers to change his or her mind about trade policy than a legislator representing big net losers. Moreover, consistent with the ruling party's incentive to minimize the electoral loss of choosing free trade, party leaders are more likely to target particularistic benefits to co-partisans, that is, the LDP district (Imabari) than the opposition district (Senshu).

Figure 5.2 describes predicted legislators' policy positions for the two regions that produce tatami mats. Again, I predict that the LDP politician representing the "fence-sitting district" (Okayama fourth district) would take a

Japanese Legislators in Rival Regions

	LDP Incumbent	
	No	Yes
Fence Sitting		Okayama: Free Trade w/ Pork
		(Not Chosen Outcome)
Unified Protectionism	Kumamoto: Protectionism without Pork	
	(Final Policy Outcome)	

FIGURE 5.2. Tatami mat industry – predicted legislator positions.
Note: The final government decisions are summarized in parentheses.

free trade position and receive particularistic benefits, while the LDP politician representing a district with unified protectionist position (Kumamoto fifth district) would receive fewer such benefits.

The key difference between the towel and tatami mat industry cases, however, is the government's final decisions. For the towel industry case, the government decided *not* to use safeguard provisions, and opted for free trade with Pork for Imabari region. The outcome was consistent with the Optimal Use of Pork hypothesis. By contrast, the government chose to use safeguard measures to protect the tatami industry. This was the first time that the Japanese government used safeguard provisions to protect import-injured industries (Kuno 2006; Naoi 2009). Because protectionism was a chosen policy outcome, I would expect that the government gave no side payment for fence-sitting Okayama Prefecture. I will explore the source of divergence between the two cases later.

CASES AND PREDICTED LEGISLATORS' POLICY PREFERENCES

WHY FOCUS ON THE POLITICS OF *NOT* USING SAFEGUARD PROVISIONS?

I focus on the period between 1990 and 2006 when China's export deluge became a major concern for the domestic towel and tatami producers.[3] Especially during the years since 2000, whether or not the government should adopt the World Trade Organization (WTO) legal safeguard provision (also known as the "escape clause") to protect the two industries became the center of public debates.

---

[3] See "Sweater and Sheets–Industries in Crisis," *Nihon Keizai Shimbun*, June 4, 1994; "Towel Producing Region of Senshu, Osaka, Faces the Rapid Rise of Import," *Nihon Keizai Shimbun*, July 1, 2000.

There are three advantages to focusing on politicians' policy positioning regarding the use of safeguard protections. First, with this provision, governments can raise tariffs *unilaterally*. Under safeguard provisions specified by the WTO, WTO member states are allowed to raise tariffs temporarily for import-injured industries without violating General Agreement on Tariffs and Trade (GATT)/WTO principles (Article XIX). The new WTO rule also specifies that exporting countries cannot retaliate against this specific form of protectionism for the first three years since the adoption. Focusing on politicians' policy positioning regarding the use of unilateral, safeguard protections provides me a cleaner case to identify legislators' and industries' policy positions and why they often diverge, compared to trade policy negotiated at international organizations or bilateral trade agreements.

Second, the domestic decision-making procedure of this policy instrument allows me to identify which legislators were *eligible* for protecting their constituents, but decided to commit to free trade instead. Under the Japanese Customs Tariff Law, two or three ministers are collectively authorized to make two-stage decisions regarding a safeguard protection.[4] At the first stage, these ministers are authorized to investigate whether a given industry is eligible for a safeguard protection by establishing facts that imports were "a substantial cause of serious injury" for the Japanese industry in question for the past three years. Which industry cases to investigate are solely up to ministers, because the Customs Tariff Law does not give private actors such as industries or firms the right (legal standing) to file complaints and request investigations into the adoption of safeguard protection. After official investigations and monitoring of import activities, ministers collectively decide whether to grant a safeguard protection at the second stage.

Despite that an executive, not a legislative, body decides a safeguard protection, legislators have ample room to influence the decision-making process at each stage. Because elected legislators who represent their constituents' interests occupy ministerial positions,[5] industries and farmers lobby legislators to "let ministries know" that they deserve a serious look.[6] For instance, in 2001, ministers collectively decided to investigate nine industry cases for potential safeguard protection (see Table 5.1 for the comprehensive list). Among these nine cases, they chose three commodities – tatami mat, scallions, and fresh shiitake mushrooms – for the protection. This investigation process allows me to identify what industries "made the first cut" (i.e., passed the initial evidentiary

---

[4] Naoi (2009). Three ministers are the Minister of Finance (MOF), the Minister of Economy, Trade, and Industry (METI) and the Minister with a jurisdiction over a given commodity (e.g. Minister of Agriculture, Forestry and Fisheries for agricultural and fishery commodities).

[5] In rare circumstances, ministers are appointed from academia or bureaucrats (e.g., economist Heizo Takenaka's appointment to Minister of Economic and Fiscal Policies and Minister of Monetary Affairs).

[6] On how the LDP's "agricultural policy tribe" politicians pressed the MAFF to adopt a safeguard measure, see Takii (2001).

Japanese Legislators in Rival Regions

hurdle set by bureaucracies to start an official investigation), yet did not receive the protection. I could infer from the two-stage decisions whether legislators voluntarily passed up the opportunity to use the protection for industries in their districts and why legislators chose to pursue free trade for some industries but not for others.

Finally, despite the fact that the government's decision to use safeguard protection does not require majority support from the parliament, the two additional characteristics of safeguard protection in Japan fit the Globalization as Legislation (GL) approach. The first is that the Japanese government needed to strictly limit the use of safeguard protection because it has provoked retaliatory actions by foreign governments and China[7] and opened a floodgate of lobbying by import-injured industries. Japanese exporters also lobbied for the restrictive use of this measure to maintain their access to foreign markets. Thus, just like legislation to raise or lower trade barriers, the politics of safeguard protection directly pitches the interests of import-injured industries against exporters. Intraparty disagreements were also prevalent regarding whether or not and for which industries safeguards should be used.

LDP party leaders thus could not respond to all the backbenchers' requests for the safeguard investigations and adoption. Instead, party leaders had to encourage members to pass up the opportunity to use it even if industries in their districts clearly deserved the protection. We can thus view this political process – that is, the party leaders' efforts to limit the protectionism – as the leaders' efforts to build a majority coalition for free trade.

CASE STUDY 1: TOWEL INDUSTRY – SENSHU VERSUS
IMABARI CITIES

Background

The Senshu region of Osaka Prefecture and Imabari City of Ehime Prefecture are two rival sites for towel production. Senshu and Imabari represented 40 percent and 50 percent of the total domestic towel sales in the year 2000.[8] The rivalry between the two regions dates back to the mid-1930s.[9]

---

[7] WTO's new rule specifies that WTO member countries should not retaliate against the use of safeguard protections for the first three years, and this new rule partially accounted for the surge of Japanese legislators' interests in using the safeguard provision (see Naoi 2009). Yet, WTO member countries have "legal" means for retaliation, such as accusing a country of unfair trade practices and levying antidumping duties. China retaliated against Japan's safeguard adoption a few months before its accession to WTO (the accession date was December 11, 2001 and China retaliated during the summer of 2001).

[8] "Towel Producing Region of Senshu, Osaka, Faces the Rapid Rise of Import," *Nihon Keizai Shimbun*, July 1, 2000.

[9] Osaka Prefectural Government, http://www.pref.osaka.jp/kogyo/jiba/seni/3–06.html (accessed April 10, 2005). The first towel import to Japan occurred in 1872 from England as a result of the opening of Japan's trade in 1859 and England's industrial revolution. After a decade since

146 Empirical Evidence

1990s: Facing Deluge of Imports from China

During the 1990s, Japan experienced a significant increase in imports of textile products from China, including towels. The quantity of towel imports more than quadrupled in the fifteen-year period after 1988 from 16,622 tons to 72,609 tons. The import penetration ratio, calculated by dividing total domestic sales by total imports from China, increased significantly, from 14.9 percent in 1990 to 63.4 percent in 2001.[10]

The two rival regions, Imabari City and Senshu region, were severely hit by the deluge.[11] During the period between 1990 and 2001, the number of towel companies decreased from 461 to 203 and the number of employees declined from 3,535 to 2,862 in Senshu region.[12] Imabari City of Ehime Prefecture experienced a similar industry decline between 1990 and 2000. The number of towel companies decreased from 390 to 219 and the number of employees fell from 6,533 to 4,237.[13] The Towel Industry Associations in the two regions jointly organized demonstrations during the summer of 2000 to advocate for regulation of towel imports. Around 2,700 people participated in the demonstration in Imabari. The city-level legislatures in Imabari and Senshu regions also unanimously passed a petition letter (*ikensho*) to be submitted to the Ministry of Economy, Trade and Industry (METI) for the safeguard adoption. In the following year, the National Towel Industry Association finally filed a formal request to initiate safeguard protection at the METI. The Shikoku Towel Association organized another demonstration during the summer of 2001 and, this time, it drew a larger turnout of 4,800 people.

Despite these organized interest group activities as well as city governments' support for protecting the towel industry, however, the Lower House politicians representing the two regions expressed different trade policy positions.

Senshu Region of Osaka Prefecture: Big Net Losers and Protectionist Legislators

Representatives of Senshu region unanimously supported the protection and use of WTO legal safeguard measures that temporarily raise tariffs for three

---

the first import, Japanese manufacturing companies began making domestic towels. See Shikoku Taworu Kogyo Kumiai [Shikoku Towel Industry Association], http://www.stia.jp/navi/history/index.html.

[10] See towel database at Shikoku Towel Industry Association, available at http://www.stia.jp/data/. Japanese Towel Industry Association 2001.

[11] "Towel Industry in Osaka, Senshu City, Suffers from the Rise of Imports." *Nihon Keizai Shimbun*, July 1, 2000.

[12] Table 6 in Chusho Kigyo Sougou Jigyo Dan (2001).

[13] Imabari City (2014).

Japanese Legislators in Rival Regions

years. In the year 2000, Lower House incumbent Matsunami Kenshiro of the Conservative Party began lobbying the METI for the adoption of safeguard protection of the towel industries.[14] Although his lobbying was unsuccessful, the safeguard issue came up for Senshu region again during the Lower House election campaign in the year 2003. During this campaign, all the parties, in one way or another, expressed support for the declining towel industry. While the incumbent, Matsunami Kenshiro of the Conservative Party, supported the adoption of WTO legal safeguard protection, Nagayasu Yutaka of the Democratic Party advocated for the creation of a large factory complex on Osaka Bay for suffering small and medium-sized firms to revitalize local industry. Finally, Yasuda Yoshihiro, who was endorsed by the LDP, advocated for cooperation among towel companies to differentiate their products from the cheap Chinese products.[15] The Communist Party candidate argued for a more generous financial loan system for small and medium-sized firms. Although these positions differed slightly in how they wanted to save the towel industry, none of them advocated for free trade or encouraged local companies to outsource their production activities abroad.

The cross-partisan support for the decline of the towel industry in Osaka was also seen among the members elected from the proportional representation (PR) list.[16] The three Lower House members with different party affiliations – Kagita Setsuya (*Shinshin-tou*, later Democratic Party), Yoshii Hidekatsu (the Japan Communist Party), Kubo Tetsuya (*Shinshin-tou*, later *Kōmeito*) – all testified before the Diet committees between 1996 and 1997 in support of protecting the declining towel industry.[17]

In sum, politicians in the ruling coalition as well as those in the opposition unanimously supported protection for the declining towel industry in Osaka. Political candidates who were elected from the single-member district (SMD) as well as from the PR list supported protectionism.

---

[14] "*Naniwa no Sentaku*" [Choices that Osaka faces], *Osaka Nichi Nichi Shimbun*, November 7, 2003. The Osaka Towel Industry Association as well as two towel companies in Izumisano City donated campaign funds for the Conservative Party's brunch in the 19th district of Osaka prefecture in the year 2003. This was probably to reward Matsunami for his efforts to realize safeguard protection for the towel industry. See Osaka Senkyo Kanri Iinkai (2003), *Seiji Shikin Syushi Houkokusyo* (Osaka Election Commission, Report, *Revenue Reports of Political Funds*, 2003).

[15] "*Naniwa no Sentaku*" [Choices that Osaka faces], *Osaka Nichi Nichi Shimbun*, November 7, 2003.

[16] The lack of major partisan difference among policies advocated by candidates elected from the PR list is interesting given how existing theoretical works in political economy predict that the PR should lead to stronger partisan differences in policies than majoritarian systems.

[17] Kagita Setsuya, Testimony before the Budget Committee, March 4, 1997; Yoshii Hidekatsu, Testimony before the Budget Committee, February 29, 1996; Kubo Tetsuji, Testimony before the Agriculture, Forestry, and Fishery Committee, May 22, 1997.

148   *Empirical Evidence*

Imabari City: Small Net Losers and Fence-Sitting Legislators

Compared to Senshu region, where there was cross-partisan support for protecting the towel industry, in Imabari City, the incumbent, LDP member Murakami Seiichiro has never taken the protection of the towel industry seriously. On the contrary, he explicitly took the position of encouraging local towel industries to relocate their production to China to become internationally competitive. During the period of heated discussion in the Diet on the use of safeguard provisions to protect the towel industry, MP Murakami, as Vice Minister of the Committee of Finance and Monetary Issues, argued in support of free trade:

I believe there are three reasons our country's economy has not been good in the past decade. One is the borderless and globalizing economy, and the other is marketization of China and Russia ... these things brought the safeguard issue for the towel industry ... The underwear I am wearing today, for instance, usually cost 2000 Yen in Japan. But cheap ones [imported or outsourced ones] cost only 500 yen. I believe that, to make firms competitive internationally, we need to make steady progress ... for instance, like the towel industry in my home district, outsourcing their production abroad is one of the options.[18]

Both Imabari City government officials and the opposition party politician, Haruna Naoki of the Japan Communist Party, confirmed the low level of involvement of Murakami Seiichiro of the LDP in protecting the Imabari towel industry.[19] The city government official thought that MP Murakami was trying to please both domestic and internationalized towel producers by not taking a clear position on the safeguard issue.[20] MP Murakami's lukewarm attitude toward protecting the towel industry continued even when there was a large demonstration organized by the Towel Industry Association in September 2001. Initially, both the LDP representative and the mayor of Ehime Prefecture (endorsed by the LDP during the election) were reluctant to attend the demonstration. But because of the large attendance it drew (4,800 people) they eventually decided to show up and give speeches.

In sum, in the two rival regions that suffered similarly from the deluge of imports from China, politicians' policy positions and lobbying behaviors differed. In the Senshu region representatives lobbied for protectionism, such as the adoption of WTO legal safeguard for the towel industry, while in Imabari

---

[18] Murakami Seiichiro, Testimony before the Committee of Finance and Monetary, May 31, 2001. Translation by the author.

[19] The only Communist Party seat in the four prefectures of Shikoku region was in Imabari district, except for the 1996 election when the party obtained two seats – one from Kochi Prefecture and the other from the PR Shikoku regional block. Haruna Naoki of the Japan Communist Party was a strong advocate of the adoption of safeguard to protect towel industries since 1991.

[20] Interview with the Imabari City government official on April, 2005. Also see Haruna Naoki's diary on his official website at www.haruna-naoki.jp/library/kouen/article/930802-170335 .html (accessed April 14, 2005).

Japanese Legislators in Rival Regions 149

City, LDP politicians advocated for free trade and the relocation of towel factories abroad. Why did this divergence occur?

Why Divergence? Fence-Sitters and Electoral Benefits of Side Payments

Based on the theory developed in Chapter 2, I show that two factors account for the divergence in legislators' trade policy positions: (1) whether firms' policy positions are heterogeneous (i.e., fence-sitters) or unified within a given industry and (2) whether a legislator belongs to the ruling party. Regarding the heterogeneity of firms, towel companies in Imabari were polarized into free trade and protectionism, making the LDP legislator Murakami a fence-sitter. By contrast, towel companies in Senshu region had unified interests in protectionism and thus mobilized cross-partisan support for protectionism among legislators. Regarding the legislators' party affiliations, Imabari representative Murakami was a senior and powerful member of the incumbent LDP, while Senshu representative Matsunami was a member of the opposition, Conservative Party. The LDP's coalition government had no incentive to compensate Senshu, the big net losers of China's export deluge, more than the fence-sitting Imabari, the small net losers.

Fence-Sitters versus Unified Protectionists

Towel companies' interests were divided between free trade and protectionism in Imabari and they were united and protectionist in Senshu. The divide among Imabari firms emerged along where they produced their goods: factories abroad or at home, consistent with Melitz's (2003) theory of heterogeneous firms. Firms that relocated their production activities to China opposed protectionism whereas firms that stayed in Japan supported protectionism.

In Imabari, seven towel companies began relocating their production activities to China in the early 1990s. In less than a decade, the seven firms invested a total of 14 billion yen in China[21] and sold 50 percent of total towel sales from Imabari City and 25 percent of total towel sales in Japan in the year 2000.[22] Thirty-eight percent of total towel export values from China were produced by Japanese subsidiaries, most notably from Imabari. Despite these initiatives by the towel companies to establish foreign subsidiaries in the rival Imabari City, companies in Senshu City of Osaka have continued to produce

---

[21] Data published by Shikoku Towel Industry Association Statistics and the survey done by "Association of Towel Industry with Subsidiary in China" (*Chugoku Shinshutu Towel Kigyo Renraku Kyogikai*) both available at www.rieti.go.jp/jp/columns/a01_0003_rd.html (accessed April 13, 2005).

[22] See Harada Seiichi's article at www.rieti.go.jp/jp/columns/a01_0003_rd.html.

their products domestically.[23] Among the 148 member companies listed as members of the Osaka Towel Industry Association, none had established factories abroad.[24]

The Osaka Towel Industry Association was instrumental in mobilizing a large demonstration calling for the adoption of safeguard statutes in September 2001. The Towel Industry Association of Shikoku region, which includes Imabari City, on the contrary, was split into pro-safeguard and anti-safeguard groups reflecting the international–domestic divide in their production sites (i.e., China or Japan). The seven firms in Imabari City strongly petitioned against the adoption of safeguard statutes using national media and lobbying to the Ministries. On the other hand, the Imabari City government issued a petition letter (*Iken-sho*) to the parliament and the METI advocating the adoption of safeguard measures against Chinese towel products.

The city government's decision to support domestic producers rather than the seven major firms that had invested in China was both economically and politically motivated. A city government official reported that the mission of the city government was to ensure local employment and that the government also has an incentive to secure tax revenues from local companies – the City's individual and corporate tax revenues experienced a 63 million yen decline between 2001 and 2002. The City official said: "those firms that invest in China did so at their own risk. But those firms that remain producing towels here do not have other options."[25]

In sum, Imabari's divided position made it a fence-sitter of the open economy coalition, evidenced by a legislator's position-taking and Regional Industry Association's lack of collective action to lobby for the safeguard protection. Senshu's position was unified in support of protectionism as evidenced by cross-partisan support among legislators and candidates and the collective lobbying efforts by the Regional Industry Association. The intra-industry divides accounts for why the LDP incumbent Murakami was seen as "lukewarm" and "fence-sitting" on the safeguard issue (the first dimension of Figure 5.1). Whether an industry is fence-sitting or not, however, remains insufficient to explain why a legislator representing a fence-sitting district ended up siding with free-trade interests. To answer this question, we need

---

[23] Two examples of these seven firms are Toyo Terry, which established a subsidiary in China in 1991 and Hartoweru, which established a subsidiary in 1992. See www.rieti.go.jp/jp/columns/a01_0003_rd.html (accessed April 10, 2005).

[24] For the complete list of members, see http://www.rinku.or.jp/os-towel/. Senshu Bank in Senshu region, which finances local small and medium-sized firms, published reports in 2003 that suggest that there were two firms in Senshu that began investing in China. From the member list of Osaka Towel Industry association, however, this information was unidentified. It could be that the two firms were "outsiders," those that are not members of the association.

[25] Interview with Imabari City government official at Business and Commerce Section, April, 2005.

Japanese Legislators in Rival Regions

to look into the supply side of trade policy, namely, parties' and legislators' incentives.

Compensating Co-Partisans

Why did the LDP legislator Murakami side with free-trade interests in Imabari? The theory of optimal use of Pork developed in Chapter 1 suggests that the ruling party can use particularistic benefits to entice a co-partisan fence-sitting legislator to support free trade. Why co-partisans? From the perspective of party leaders, they prefer to use the budget to reduce the chances of their co-partisan's electoral defeat in the next election, rather than to give the opposition an opportunity to claim credit for obtaining compensation. From the perspective of individual legislators in fence-sitting districts, particularistic projects can help them reduce the electoral costs (loss of votes and campaign contributions from protectionist groups) they must incur as a result of taking the side of free-trade groups. Co-partisan legislators in fence-sitting districts can also legitimately request such projects to the party leaders as a reward for the sacrifice they made for the collective benefits to the party, that is, commitment to an open economy.

The LDP incumbent, Murakami Seiichiro, has enjoyed overwhelming victory over opposition candidates in Imabari, which is the second SMD in Ehime Prefecture. The safe seat enabled the LDP legislator, Murakami, to advocate unpopular policies to promote globalization and outsourcing in Imabari City, without incurring many electoral costs.[26] On the other hand, Senshu region, which was the nineteenth SMD of Osaka Prefecture under the new electoral system, had an opposition party legislator. The Conservative Party's Matsunami occupied the seat during the heated discussion on safeguarding the towel industry. Thus, from the LDP party leader's perspective, either using the safeguard protection or targeting particularistic projects to Senshu did not make political sense because either way it would have given an opposition legislator an opportunity to claim credit in the next election.

Policy Outcomes: Free Trade and Highway Project to Imabari Region, a Small Net Loser

In response to the lobbying by the towel and other textile industries facing an import deluge from China, the METI proposed a budget bill for "Revitalizing

---

[26] At that time, the LDP generally collected 800 million yen per year in Ehime Prefecture (approximately US$7.3 million using the average exchange rate of ¥110/$ during 2003), and Murakami's local support group *Shinseikai Touyo-shibu* was also resourceful. It reported 41 million yen (approximately US$3.8) in political revenue for fiscal year 2003, when there was a general and local election. This was the highest political revenue among all the nonparty political organizations among four prefectures in Shikoku Island.

152   *Empirical Evidence*

Local Industries."[27] of which 400 million yen was specifically set aside for textile-producing regions in the year 2002. The textile-producing regions' quota was expanded in the following year to 560 million yen. Senshu region was the major recipient of this package, in addition to becoming a major recipient of the Emergency Measure for Revitalization of Industrial Clusters,[28] the measure that aims to stop deindustrialization. With these compensation packages, Osaka prefectural government had built tax-exempt towel factory complexes on the coast of Osaka. Thus, a policy measure to directly address the hardship of towel industry seemed to favor the big net losers, that is, Senshu region.

Yet, in the shadow of these policy measures, Imabari received a 85 billion yen budget, which was twentyfold that of textile revitalization measures, from the national government to extend the Imabari–Komatsu Express Way. The Imabari–Komatsu Express Way connects with two other existing highways, Nishi–Seto Express Way and Shikoku–Juukan Express Way, and runs through Imabari City.[29] The Imabari–Komatsu Express Way project was originally approved and funded by the national government in 1988, and the first phase of construction was completed and was open to traffic in July 2001, just around the time that industry groups' lobbying for safeguard protection was at its peak. With a new announcement made in 2001 by the LDP prime minister Koizumi Junichiro to cut down the public work expenditures by one trillion yen, Imabari City was concerned about whether or not it would obtain a new round of the national budget to start the second phase of the project to extend the highway further to the city's west. Despite Koizumi's announcement and urban residents showing overwhelming support to cut public expenditures, Imabari's request to obtain the budget was successful. The government approved a multiyear budget of more than 80 billion yen to extend the Imabari–Komatsu Express Way.

Given Murakami's high position in the cabinet as well as within the LDP, flexing the muscle to obtain the budget was not too difficult. Murakami was a senior LDP politician who was promoted to Vice Minister of the Ministry of Finance in 2001 under a new prime minister,[30] Koizumi. Since Murakami first ran for the Lower House election in 1986, he has held major positions in ministries and in the LDP such as Deputy Secretary General of the Liberal Democratic Party. Later Koizumi also named him a Cabinet-Appointed Special Minister of Deregulation and Industry Revitalization.

---

[27] The Law is called Jiba sangyo tou chiiki kassei sochihou in Japanese.
[28] The Law is called Tokutei sangyo syuseki no kasseika ni kansuru rinji sochi hou in Japanese.
[29] Ministry of Land and Transportation's Shikoku Regional Development Bureau, "Ippan Kokudou 196-gou Imabari Douro Jigyo Saihyoka" (The Project Reevalution of General National Road, No.196, Imabari Road), December 1, 2010.
[30] Murakami was a third-generation LDP legislator who inherited his father's and grandfathers' local support network in Imabari. Murakami's committee assignments in the Diet ranged across Finance, Budget, Coal Mining, and Construction.

Japanese Legislators in Rival Regions 153

In sum, Murakami pursued free trade and obtained the highway extension budget for Imabari. As predicted earlier, free trade was the final policy outcome and the small net losers, Imabari region, obtained the particularistic benefits. The big net losers, that is, Senshu region of Osaka, obtained only a small budget – approximately 5 percent of Imabari's highway project – to "revitalize" textile industry. Consistent with the theory of optimal use of Pork in the global economy, the particularistic benefits were allocated to the co-partisan fence-sitters of globalization.

CASE STUDY (2): *TATAMI* MAT INDUSTRY – KUMAMOTO AND OKAYAMA PREFECTURES

Background: *Tatami* Mat and Rival Regions

Tatami mats are a traditional type of Japanese flooring made from woven straw. Each tatami mat is generally sized 91 centimeters by 182 centimeters (35.8 inches by 71.6 inches) and Japanese citizens and realtors to this day use one tatami mat (*ichi jo*) as a unit to describe the square footage of a house. A recent survey of homeowners by Tokyo Gas Company in 2009 found that 82 percent of respondents have at least one tatami room,[31] yet domestic consumption of tatami mats has been declining due to wood flooring taking over tatami mat in newly built homes. Still, the tatami mat occupies a special place in Japanese hearts, as reflected in the famous Japanese saying, "I want to die on tatami mat." It refers to a person's desire to age and die at home instead of spending one's final days in a hospital bed.[32]

There are three stages of manufacturing tatami mats, which are important to understanding the characteristics of the two "rival" tatami manufacturing regions, Kumamoto and Okayama. The first stage is harvesting the straw (*igusa*), which is farming. The second stage is to make a semifinished woven mat called *goza* and the final stage is to hem the four edges of the *goza* with a belt woven with either synthetic or cotton yarns (tatami mat). Some companies do all three production stages in-house, while others outsource one or two stages, especially the farming and the intermediate stages.

Between 1955 and 1965, the domestic market shares of tatami mats were about equally divided between Okayama and Kumamoto Prefectures.[33] The geographical distribution of the tatami industry has changed since the 1970s

---

[31] Internet survey conducted by Tokyo Gas Company with 1,606 homeowners older than the age of 20. Report available at: http://blog.tokyo-gas.co.jp/mystyle/enquete/page01.html (accessed June 22, 2011).

[32] Another recent usage of this saying is to describe the desire of Japanese citizens living and working abroad to return to Japan after the retirement. In this context, the tatami mat is a symbol of a Japanese home.

[33] Imports of tatami mat and its material (*igusa*) were liberalized in 1961.

154   *Empirical Evidence*

as Kumamoto increased its share of production and Okayama Prefecture – once known as the home of tatami production – decreased its share as a result of industrialization initiated by the LDP government, such as the building of the Mizushima Petrochemical Complex. With higher wages, industrial sectors absorbed *igusa* growers and tatami manufacturers as a new labor force in Okayama. As a result, the two tatami regions' business strategies diverged. The majority of Kumamoto companies continue to grow *igusa* and manufacture tatami mats in-house in Japan, while the majority of Okayama firms specialize in selling semifinished products (*goza*) and outsource most of the production stages to China.

As of 2001, Kumamoto produced more than 90 percent of *igusa*, most notably in the Yatsushiro region. Okayama produced less than 1 percent of *igusa* in Kurashiki City, which is the only remaining *igusa*-producing region in Okayama.[34] On the other hand, Okayama continues to occupy around 50 percent of domestic market share of semifinished products, *goza*, and Kumamoto and Fukuoka Prefectures followed the lead.[35]

1990s: Facing the Deluge of Imports from China

From 1996 to 2000, the quantity of tatami and *goza* imports, as well as its import penetration ratio, doubled as a result of imports from China. The domestic sales price of *igusa* fell sharply during this period to 25 percent of the price in 1996 (from 2,840,000 yen to 750,000 yen). Responding to the rise of tatami imports from China, tatami mat industry associations organized demonstrations and lobbied members of the parliament and prefectural-level representatives. The responses of the parliament members to the rise of lobbying by the tatami industry, however, differed between Kumamoto and Okayama Prefectures.

Kumamoto Prefecture: Unanimous Support for Protectionism

Two senior legislators from Kumamoto Prefecture had worked hard to protect the tatami industry, yet interestingly, neither of them represented the major *igusa* and tatami-producing region, Yatsushiro area. During the early phase of tatami-industry lobbying in 1999, then-Liberal Party politician Noda Takeshi was a strong advocate for protecting the industry.[36] Noda represented the

---

[34] As of 1999, four families farm *igusa* in Okayama in a total of 15 hectares of land. Kurashiki City site has 7.6 hectares and is known for producing high-end tatami. Kurashiki City, http://www.city.kurashiki.okayama.jp/dd.aspx?menuid=4121 (accessed June 22, 2011).

[35] Miyake Kunio (2002), "Okayama-ken no jiba sangyo no hensen to kadai" Hiroshima University, Research Center of Regional Economic System, Research Report, 14, 2002: 101–112.

[36] Noda was previously with the LDP, then moved to the Liberal Party, and in 2005, he was at the Conservative Party.

Japanese Legislators in Rival Regions 155

second district of Kumamoto Prefecture – where fruit and vegetable growers are the main constituents – for eleven consecutive terms. During his tenure as the Minister of Local Governance since 1999, Noda was able to obtain a 2.8 billion yen budget package that specified that schools nationwide buy tatami mats for their playrooms. The package was generous enough to keep the tatami industry in Kumamoto quiet for a while. Yet, surprisingly, Noda's SMD was not one of the main *igusa*-producing regions at all. The municipality-level data on *igusa* production report less than one hectare of land used in this district for *igusa* production.[37]

When the second wave of protectionist lobbying by the tatami industry emerged around 2001, the strongest advocate of safeguard protection for the tatami industry was the LDP representative, Toshikatsu Matsuoka. He has represented Kumamoto's third district for five terms since 1990. The district's main industry is vegetable farming, with a particular focus on growing tomatoes, peppers, and asparagus.[38] Reflecting largely agricultural constituents, Matsuoka's platform has consistently been one of protecting farmers in Kumamoto. He has held important positions in the LDP, as well as in the Diet, such as Deputy Secretary General of the Liberal Democratic Party and Vice Minister of the Ministry of Agriculture, Forestry, and Fisheries (MAFF). In the year 2001 when the tatami industry won safeguard protection, Matsuoka was a Minister of Agriculture, Forestry, and Fisheries. Matsuoka's heavy involvement in achieving temporary safeguard protection for the tatami industry in 2001 is well documented by journalists.[39] Government officials at MAFF also confirmed that, owing to Matsuoka's high position in the Ministry, the tatami industry was selected as one of three commodities that were granted safeguard protection in 2001. Yet, curiously, the numbers of *igusa* growers as well as tatami manufacturers were negligible in Matsuoka's SMD – just like in Noda's second district, less than one hectare of land in the district was used for *igusa* production. On the other hand, in 2001, non-LDP legislator Kaneko Yasushi occupied the seat at the fifth SMD where the majority of *igusa* growers and tatami manufacturers reside.

What did these two powerful LDP legislators gain from their effort to protect the industry, given that the two districts did not have sufficiently large tatami industry clout? One could argue that the two powerful legislators lobbied for the tatami industry in the hope of signaling their largely agricultural constituents that they care about farm protection. Yet, this argument quickly falls apart

---

[37] Ministry of Public Management, Home Affairs, Posts and Telecommunications' *Toukei de miru Shikuchoson no sugata* 2003 [Statistical Outlook of Municipalities], based on 2000 National Census.
[38] Ministry of Agriculture, Forestry and Fisheries, Yasai Shukka Toukei [Statistics on Vegetable Shipment], 2001a.
[39] Takii Hiroomi, *Korekara dousuru seifu-gaado* [What to Do with Safeguard Measure?]" *Ronza*, October, 2001.

considering that these two legislators had given up on two commodities grown in their districts that passed the initial evidentiary hurdle at the ministries and thus similarly deserved safeguard protection – tomatoes and eggplants. Both tomatoes and eggplants faced China's import deluge and they were two of the fourteen products for which the Minister of Agriculture, Forestry and Fisheries had requested the government to monitor the levels of import competition with China in 2001. However, the government decided not to adopt safeguard protection for these two commodities, and instead adopted protection for *igusa* and tatami grown and manufactured in the non-LDP district.

Okayama Prefecture: Fence-Sitters

Many tatami companies in Okayama Prefecture started to invest in China in 1979. Hagihara Inc., one of the oldest tatami companies in Okayama, started investing in China in 1978 and had nine production sites in China as of April 7, 2005.[40] Another local company, Tokura Shoji, also began investing in Ninpo City of China in 1993. In Okayama, many tatami production companies have their own in-house trading section or subsidiary to coordinate production in Japan and China. Tokura, the major tatami production company in Okayama Prefecture, for instance, imported around 70 percent of its domestic sales from China in 2003.[41]

In response to lobbying by these companies in Okayama with high foreign direct investment and subsidiary rates in China, the Okayama Prefectural Diet passed a local measure to redefine the production category of "tatami" so that semifinished products that companies import from China would not be charged safeguard tariffs.[42] Hayashima Town Council in Okayama Prefecture, moreover, unanimously approved a petition letter asking that safeguard measures not be adopted. Tatami companies in Hayashima town found the safeguards to be against their interests because more than ten years ago, they began importing cheaper materials and semifinished products from China to be more competitive in the domestic market.[43]

Reflecting the constituents' interests for free trade, the LDP representative in Okayama Prefecture, Hashimoto Ryutarou, remained detached from the safeguard debates. Only lower tier local governments became politically active, and they advocated free trade, not protectionism.[44] The only potential protectionist

---

[40] Information available at Hagiwara Inc.'s official website (http://www.e-hagihara.co.jp).
[41] MJSHP Business Report 2003.
[42] The MAFF, "Opinions Expressed during Safeguard Investigations for Scallion, Fresh *Shiitake*, and Tatami-mat." Available at http://www.maff.go.jp/mlet/sgiken.pdf (accessed May 29, 2005).
[43] Information available from Hayashima town's official webpage at http://www.town.hayashima .okayama.jp/townoffice/kikaku/syuho/rekisi/h13/daije0801.html (accessed April, 2005).
[44] Ministry of Finance, "*Negi, Namashiitake oyobi Tatami omote ni kansuru seifugaado chosa ni oite hyomei sareta iken oyobi saiiken ni tsuite*" [Summary of Opinions Expressed or Re-expressed Regarding Safeguard Survey on Scallion, Fresh Shiitake Mushrooms and Tatami-mat], September 4, 2001. http://www.mof.go.jp/customs_tariff/trade/plan/kinkyu/kao37a.htm.

Japanese Legislators in Rival Regions 157

forces in Okayama was the *igusa*-producing region in Kurashiki City, yet there was no trace of protectionist lobbying by the four families engaged in *igusa* farming.

Final Policy Outcome: Protectionism

The government decided to use safeguard measures for the first time in its history on April 23, 2001. Tatami was one of the three commodities, together with fresh shiitake mushroom and scallions, chosen for the safeguard protections. In addition to 200 days of temporary tariffs on imports, the legislature passed a compensation package called the "Special Grant for Promoting Competitiveness of Tatami/Igusa Production Regions" which amounted to one billion yen, of which the Yatsushiro region was the major recipient. Other compensation policies adopted by MAFF involved enforcing the rules to indicate the national origin of production on the products,[45] which disproportionately favored tatami companies in Kumamoto Prefecture, where tatami mats were still produced domestically.

The remaining puzzle is given that both LDP legislators representing Kumamoto and Okayama held high positions in the cabinet and the LDP, why did the government ultimately respond to the protectionist Kumamoto lobby instead of the free-trading Okayama lobby? Here is the answer to the puzzle. The LDP gained one more Lower House seat without winning an election by selecting the tatami industry for protection. A nonpartisan legislator in the fifth district, Kaneko Yasushi[46] joined the LDP seven months after the safeguard was initiated and just around the time the 200 days of temporary tariff for tatami industry had expired. Although there is no direct evidence to suggest that the senior LDP legislator's assistance for tatami industry convinced Kaneko to join the LDP, it is reasonable to think that Kaneko saw the benefits of being affiliated with the LDP after the safeguard adoption. Because of Matsuoka's ministerial position and renowned influence over agricultural policy, the LDP credibly claimed credit for safeguard protection for the tatami industry. Kaneko continued to run and won subsequent elections with the LDP nominations.

To lend more systematic support to this conjecture, I analyze why the LDP chose to protect three commodities among the list of nine commodities that passed the evidentially hurdle at three ministries: Ministry of Finance; Ministry of Economy, Trade and Industry; and Ministry of Agriculture, Forestry and Fisheries. Table 5.1 lists nine commodities that ministries officially investigated for potential safeguard protection in 2001 and the final policy outcomes. Using Vegetable Production and Shipping Statistics,[47] I matched each commodity

---

[45] MAFF, A memorandum prepared for press release on September 17, 2001.
[46] Yagami Masayoshi ran from the LDP in 2000 election, yet he was with Shinshin Party before.
[47] The MAFF, Vegetable Production and Shipping Statistics (*Yasai Seisan Shukka Toukei*).

158   *Empirical Evidence*

TABLE 5.1. *Protectionism Was Chosen for Non-LDP, Single-Member Districts*

Commodity	Safeguard	Prefec/SMD	LDP Incumbent	Switch to LDP	Prediction Correct?
Tatami mat	Yes	Kumamoto, 5	No	Yes	Yes
Fresh shiitake	Yes	Tokushima, 1	No	No	Yes
Scallion	Yes	Saitama, 11	No	Yes	Yes
Scallion	Yes	Chiba, 6	No	No	Yes
Onion	No	Hokkaido, 12	Yes	N/A	Yes
Pepper	No	Miyazaki, 2	Yes	N/A	Yes
Towel	No	Ehime, 2	Yes	N/A	Yes
Tomato	No	Kumamoto, 3	Yes	N/A	Yes
Eel	No	Kagoshima, 5	Yes	N/A	Yes
Seaweed	No	Iwate, 2	No	N/A	No

Source: Vegetable Production and Shipping Statistics (*yasai seisan shukka toukei*) of the Ministry of Agriculture, Forestry and Fisheries.

with a single-member electoral district where a given commodity had either the highest shipping volumes or the largest geographic areas of harvesting across the nation in 2001.[48] I also matched information on whether these Lower House electoral districts were represented by LDP incumbents or members of the opposition.

The pattern is unmistakably clear: the government used safeguard measures to protect commodities produced in districts where non-LDP incumbents held seats, and chose free trade for commodities produced in districts where LDP incumbents were in control. This pattern holds for eight out of the nine investigated commodity cases.[49] Among the three commodities and four "top producing" electoral districts that received the safeguard protection, party switching from nonpartisan to the LDP occurred in 50 percent of the cases, that is, two districts (Kumamoto fifth and Saitama eleventh) between 2001, when the temporary safeguard measure was adopted, and the subsequent Lower House election in 2003.

In sum, the LDP party leaders kept overall commitment to free trade by giving up protectionism for their core constituencies. Instead, the LDP incumbents

[48] Using the statistics, I first narrowed down a top producing prefecture for each commodity, and then used the statistics and other sources such as "Vegetable Total and Aggregate Information Network" (*bejitan*) database, available at http://vegetan.alic.go.jp/ and a given prefecture's Japan Agricultural Cooperative's website to identify the prefecture's top producing electoral district. The Bejitan database was published by Agriculture and Livestock Industry Corporation (ALIC), a government-affiliated organization. Table 5.1 includes two districts that produce scallion, because their shipping volume was about the same.

[49] Seaweed and eel industries were able to negotiate voluntary export restraints agreements with China without much government intervention, which accounted for the lack of safeguard adoption despite the opposition party held the seat. See Naoi (2007, 2009).

Japanese Legislators in Rival Regions

used the safeguard protection to increase its chances of winning more seats in the next election. Those LDP incumbents who gave up protectionism for collective benefits of the party received particularistic benefits to mitigate the electoral costs, confirming the Optimal Use of Pork hypothesis.

CONCLUSION

The evidence presented in this chapter lends strong support to the Optimal Use of Pork hypothesis developed in Chapter 1. Overall, evidence from the "rival region" case studies challenged the conventional wisdom that legislators simply transmit their constituents' interests into their trade policy positions. Even when legislators represented districts that similarly faced competition with Chinese exports, their trade policy positions as well as behavior differed. The party strategies to maintain free trade with Pork allocation explained this "electoral disconnection," that is, why some legislators passed up the opportunity for protectionism even when their constituents demanded them. In particular, the LDP's "fence-sitting" legislator, who represented the district with intra-industry divides over trade policy (e.g., Imabari), supported free trade and received Pork from the government. Party leaders, however, did not allocate Pork to Senshu region, where the opposition party held a seat.

The findings also challenge the existing explanation for trade policy, which emphasizes the collective action capacity of interest groups (Olson 1965). The collective action capacity of interest groups did not account for the policy outcome, as legislators representing divided districts were more likely to receive more particularistic benefits than those who represent unified districts. Party leaders' allocation of Pork was not based on the sheer size of needs of industries that were affected by globalization either, contrary to the prediction from the compensation literature. Consistent with Optimal Use of Pork hypothesis, the biggest losers of China's export received only small compensation (e.g., the case of Senshu region), whereas the small net losers (e.g., Imabari) received big particularistic benefits.

Finally, case study evidence suggests that legislators in the global economy are concerned not only about reelection and rent-seeking. Legislators can also be concerned about a policy (i.e., commitment to an open economy) and increasing seat shares of co-partisans in the parliament, that is, "collective goods" for the party and the national economy. The policy and seat share concerns were more prominent among senior legislators who held important positions in the government and the party. Senior politicians with safe seats, for instance, such as the LDP's Murakami have taken a risk of losing some votes and campaign contribution from import-competing industries to avoid China's retaliation and to keep the government's commitment to an open economy. Murakami was also able to use public works projects to offset the electoral loss.

6

Thai Legislators' Position-Taking on Foreign Retail Investment Liberalization

This chapter provides case study findings on the determinants of Thai legislators' position-taking on foreign retail investment into their constituencies in Chonburi and Buri Ram Provinces after the Asian Financial Crisis (1997). The regulation of foreign retail investment was a highly divisive and political issue in constituencies and national policymaking in Thailand, especially after the crisis, which makes an appropriate test case for Globalization as Legislation (GL). Moreover, foreign retail investment is a hard case to test GL, because Prime Minister Thaksin and his cabinet ministers (2001–2006) took positions to restrict foreign retail investment, while many backbenchers opposed it. This pattern is a reversal of the premise of this book – that party leaders support globalization and backbenchers oppose it. I leverage this reversal to test whether an underlying logic of Optimal Use of Pork – that is, party leaders buying off support from fence-sitting legislators for policymaking – still holds even if we reverse the preference of party leaders and backbenchers.

Despite the fact that foreign retail liberalization had been estimated to drive half of small mom-and-pop shops out of business after the crisis (Isaacs 2009; Kanchoochat 2009), the majority of legislators showed very little sympathy for the local retail storeowners in their constituencies. The electoral disconnection is a puzzle, because 14 percent of the labor force has been employed in the retail sector in Thailand and elections in these provinces were competitive. Legislators spent vast monetary and human capital resources to win elections, yet only a few sided with organized anti-foreign retail campaigns in their provinces, and many supported more investment.

I compare legislators' position-taking on foreign retail investment in Chonburi and Buriram Provinces in Thailand, because the two provinces ensured the variations in legislators' policy-positioning: legislators representing Chonburi supported foreign retail investment *against* the prime minister's protectionist position, while legislators representing Buriram Province opposed

160

Thai Legislators' Position on Foreign Retail Investment

	In Ruling Coalition	
	No	*Yes*
Fence Sitting		Chonburi: Protectionism with Pork
		(Not Chosen Outcome; Pro-FDI with Pork)
Unified Protectionism		Buriram: Protectionism without Pork
		(Not Chosen Outcome; Protectionism with Pork)

FIGURE 6.1. Predicted legislators' position-taking and side-payment allocation. *Note*: The government's final decisions are described in parentheses. Prime Minister Thaksin Shinawatra of Thai Rak Thai supported protectionism. Both Chonburi and Buriram legislators belonged to the Chart Thai Party, a key coalition partner of a major ruling party, Thai Rak Thai.

foreign retail investment *with* the prime minister.[1] The two provinces also share key political characteristics. Legislators in the two provinces belonged to the same party, Chart Thai Party, which was a critical coalition partner of the ruling Thai Rak Thai Party between 2001 and 2005. In both provinces, legislators were coherent and well-organized around family ties, creating what was called Chonburi and Buriram factions. This allows me to identify why legislators in the two provinces took different policy positions while holding their political attributes relatively constant.

Figure 6.1 shows predicted legislators' policy positions for the regulation of foreign retail investment. Consistent with the Optimal Use of Pork hypothesis developed in Chapter 1, I predict that legislators in ruling coalitions who represent "fence-sitting" districts, where there is a split among industries' policy

---

[1] Chonburi is located in central Thailand, a two-hour drive from Bangkok, and is industrial. Buriram is located in the northeast, and is largely agricutural. Ideally, I would have wanted to compare Chonburi with another province that faced similar levels of foreign retail competition, and its representatives supported protectionism. Kanchoochat's (2008) study suggests that an anti-foreign retail campaign was mobilized and successful in Chumphon, Phrae, Kanchanaburi, and Chanthaburi Provinces, although the study reported no involvement by their members of parliament. Indeed, my research assistant's interview with Chumphon's Department of Commerce suggests that legislators were not involved or took no visible position on this in the four provinces with a successful protectionist campaign. Kanchoochat suggested that the commonality among the four protectionist provinces was that local-level politicians had ties with the local retail business through ownership and family relationships (personal communication, Veerayooth Kanchoochat on June 23, 2014). Interviewing with Thai officials, legislators, and local scholars as well as searching all the newspaper archives in English (*Bangkok Post* and *The Nation*), I was able to identify only one legislator who visibly took a protectionist position on the retail issue – Newin Chidchob from Buriram. I thank Chayathorn Termariyabuit for her help with the interviews with provincial government officials.

162   *Empirical Evidence*

positions on foreign direct investment (FDI), took a protectionist position with the prime minister and received particularistic benefits. Districts with a more unified preference for protectionism, such as Buriram Province, took a protectionist position and received no major particularistic benefits.

As I show in the text that follows, however, the actual outcomes differed from the predictions. In Chonburi, legislators supported the expansion of foreign retail investment *against* the prime minister's position, but received Pork nonetheless for staying with the ruling coalition. Party leaders rewarded Chonburi legislators for their loyalty to stay in the multiparty coalition, despite their policy disagreement. In Buriram, one legislator (Newin Chidbob) visibly supported protectionism, and he also received Pork for supporting the prime minister's protectionist campaign. Party leaders thus used Pork for two distinct purposes, both of which ensured majority coalition-building: one was to keep the coalition intact by preempting an exit by unhappy legislators, and another was to reward legislators' policy loyalty.

FOREIGN RETAIL LIBERALIZATION

The retail industry is an important sector in Thailand, accounting for 8 percent of its gross domestic product (GDP) and 14 percent of the total labor force (McKinsey 1999 and Thai Labor Force Survey, 2001 to 2008).[2] Although the Thai government adopted retail trade liberalization a year after its accession to General Agreement on Tariffs and Trade (GATT) in 1982, foreign retail investment was fairly limited in size and geographic scope until the 1997 Asian financial crisis. As of 1996, only eighteen branches of foreign-owned mega retail stores invested in Thailand, and they were concentrated in Bangkok and its vicinity (Kanchoochat 2008: 85).

After 1997, however, by taking advantage of the falling Thai baht and land price during the Asian financial crisis, English and French megastores such as Tesco and Carrefour also expanded their investment (Isaacs 2009). Within nine years, foreign mega retails opened 130 new branches in 41 out of 76 provinces in Thailand, mostly in provincial capital cities. These foreign-owned retail stores became popular among consumers and have driven out half of local Thai stores since the crisis (Isaacs 2009).[3] As of 2006, 45 percent of Thai

---

[2] Official labor force surveys available at National Statistics Office: http://web.nso.go.th/en/survey/lfs/lfs2009_tab.htm (accessed September 2011) suggests that from 2001 to 2008, a stable 14 percent of the labor force in Thailand has been employed in wholesale, retail, and hotel and restaurant businesses. McKinsey reports that around one-third of this employment, which is 4.2% of the national labor force, was employed in the "pure" retail sector (i.e., excluding hotels, restaurants, and wholesalers) as of 1999.

[3] "Thai Mom-and-Pop Grocery Stores Fight Losing Battle against Hypermarkets," *Associated Press,* January 14, 2002.

Thai Legislators' Position on Foreign Retail Investment

retail stores are so-called "modern" mega-stores owned by large foreign and Thai companies, and 55 percent are small local stores. Thai local retail stores organized to lobby legislators and bureaucrats in electoral districts as well as in Bangkok. Yet, legislators' responses to the protectionist lobby differ among provinces.

Chonburi Province: Landowners and Labor Supported FDI – Capitalists Were Split

In Chonburi Province, the expansion of foreign mega stores polarized the residents. Labor and landowners supported foreign investment and local shop owners opposed it.[4] Thai capitalists who own business related to land development, such as construction companies and industrial estates owners, also supported the investment. Even among Thai retail storeowners, policy position was divided, pitching the interests of franchise store owners versus small shop owners.[5] For instance, Thai oligopolistic company owners, such as the Charoen Pokphand group supported the expansion owing to the group having a franchise agreement with Japan's convenience store 7-Eleven. In sum, the conflict that emerged in Chonburi was that a coalition with big capitalists, landowners, and labor supported FDI, and local shop owners opposed it.[6]

At the elite level, the Chonburi Chamber of Commerce[7] represented the protectionist interests of local retail stores, whereas the members of Parliament,

---

[4] Interviews with the chair of Chonburi Chamber of Commerce, officers at the Provincial Administration Office and the Tambon Administration Organization (a lower tier of local government), summer, 2001.

[5] The Thai Retailers Association (TRA) was established in 1991 and comprises of 126 members, many of which are large Thai retail stores and their joint ventures with foreign retail stores. The President of the TRA has been the chairman of large chain retail stores, owned by oligopolistic Thai companies with many joint-venture agreements with foreign firms, such as the Charoen Pokphand Group. Thus, the TRA's policy position has been to support the expansion of foreign retail stores. While small retail owners' demonstration and lobbying continued, the TRA continued to appoint pro-foreign investment presidents and promote self-help rather than government protection. ("Retailers Advocate Government Control," *The Nation*, August 2, 2000.)

[6] The pattern of an interest group coalition in Chonburi differs from the prediction from the factor-based trade theorem, such as Hechscher–Ohlin theorem. It would predict the emergence of class conflict, i.e., labor supporting foreign direct investment and capital-land coalition supporting protectionism. Another class-based prediction would be that skilled labor supports FDI, and unskilled labor opposes it (Pandya 2010). I don't have direct survey evidence to test this claim within the Thai context, yet evidence from migration studies in Thailand suggests that many foreign-owned factory workers in industrial cities such as Chonburi and Rayong were unskilled migrants from north and northeast (or from Burma and Cambodia) (Anantarangsi and Walsh 2012). This means that FDI projects might be benefiting both skilled and unskilled workers.

[7] The Chamber of Commerce is a provincial charter of the Thai Chamber of Commerce, which represents domestic commercial interests.

the Thai Federation of Industry,[8] and some of the lower tiers of local governments supported the expansion of foreign-owned retail stores. Chonburi's Chamber of Commerce organized small retail stores to campaign against the investment of foreign mega retail stores such as Britain's Tesco-Lotus and France's Carrefour in the late 1990s. The Thai Federation of Industry, another business association that represents industrial interests, supported the investments by foreign retail stores.

The conflict between the Chamber of Commerce and the Thai Federation of Industry became visible at various meetings in the budget planning committee at Chonburi's Provincial Administration Office (PAO). In the past, the provincial government invited both associations to participate in the budget planning committee. The Chamber of Commerce and the Federation of Industry expressed their needs during budget planning, which were reflected in the proposals. As the conflict between the two organizations grew, the Chamber of Commerce was excluded from the meeting. The director of the budget committee began inviting regional field officers appointed by the Ministry of Interior, who supported foreign investment projects.[9]

The chair of the Chamber of Commerce confessed that the members of parliament in Chonburi did not show any signs of caring about the suffering of local retail stores, never mind supporting them. Members of parliament as well as politicians at local government levels[10] supported and promoted FDI into the province.[11] The lower tiers of local governments (such as Tambon Administrative Organizations under the provincial-level) supported the increasing foreign direct investment because they collected more corporate tax from having land contracts with new investors.[12] In theory, local governments should be indifferent between foreign and domestic investment projects, as the land contracting tax does not distinguish between contracts with domestic or foreign firms. In reality, however, domestic small retailers rarely expand their businesses, and the majority of new investment projects that require large land contracts were foreign-owned. At the Bang Samet Tambon Administration Organization in Chonburi, for example, the town gained more revenue from its land rental contracts with foreign investors than through local agreements.[13]

---

[8] The Federation of Industry is a nationally organized business association for manufacturing industries. The Federation of Industry has provincial-level chapters established around the late 1980s.

[9] Interview with the chair of Chonburi Chamber of Commerce, summer, 2001.

[10] Local governments here refer to the provincial government as well as lower tier local government called the Tambon Administration Organization (the TAO). The TAO is the equivalent of "prefecture" or "county."

[11] Interview with the head of Chonburi's Chamber of Commerce and Federation of Thai Industries.

[12] Interview with TAO officer at Bang Samet, summer of 2001, Chonburi. The Thai tax system allowed local governments to collect corporate tax through land contracting with companies.

[13] Interview with the officer at Bang Samet TAO, summer of 2001, Bangkok. Moreover, with the Decentralization Act, which granted more budgetary resources and policymaking power to local governments, mega retail stores pay corporate taxes directly to the local authority instead of to

Thai Legislators' Position on Foreign Retail Investment 165

The lack of responses from legislators forced Chonburi's Chamber of Commerce to adopt a more "noisy" strategy such as organizing demonstrations and parading in Bangkok with other provincial Chamber of Commerce offices.[14] Why did members of parliament and some of the lower tier local governments support the interests of international capitals over those of domestic capitalists given that half of local retail stores were driven out of business since 1997?

Buriram Province: Only Protectionist Legislator in the Coalition, Newin Chidchob

There were only a few legislators who visibly stood to support retail protectionism: the most vocal was Newin Chidchob under Thaksin's cabinet (2001–2006) elected from Buriram Province.[15] Newin was a force behind a draft Foreign Retail Act, which aimed to empower provincial governments in approving the opening of new foreign retail branches. The draft law also contained zoning and work hour regulation for foreign retail stores to protect domestic small retail shops. Newin said: "The heart of the draft bill is to allow communities and local authorities to decide if they want or do not want large discount stores."[16] In his position as a deputy agricultural minister, Newin also promoted "one village ("tambon"), one retail" project that was to help at least one small Thai retail store survive or open in 70,000 villages across the nation.[17]

Newin's protectionist policy position seems odd, given that his district Buriram Province was overwhelmingly agricultural and the workers in the service industry constituted less than one percent of the labor force.[18] As of 2001,

---

the central government. The TAO will obtain a considerable increase in tax revenue from foreign companies.

[14] In April 2002, president of Chonburi's Chamber of Commerce also participated in the 200 business people's parade in Bangkok, submitting the proposal to freeze any further opening of foreign retail branches and to tighten the foreign business regulations. See "Call for Freeze on Superstores," *The Nation*, April 4, 2002.

[15] Juti Krairerk, the opposition legislator from the Democratic Party representing Phitsanulok Province, also supported retail protectionism. See "Retail Business Bill: Confusion over Govt's Next Move," *The Nation*, April 3, 2002.

[16] "Thailand Deputy Agriculture Minister Criticizes Move to Scrap Retail Law," *Bangkok Post*, November 20, 2002. Juti Krairerk, the opposition legislator from the Democratic Party representing Phitsanulok Province, also criticized Thaksin for scrapping the draft legislation. See "Retail Business Bill: Confusion over Govt's Next Move," *The Nation*, April 3, 2002. I could not find more evidence, in addition to this press comment, to support that Juti actively complained to protect Thai retail stores. Thus, I focus here on Newin Chidchob from Buriram.

[17] Thaksin also promoted this idea, by promoting his famous "one village, one product" program whereby each village would have at least one product that is competitive in the national or international market. See ibid.

[18] McKinsey (1999).

Empirical Evidence

no foreign mega store had opened a branch in Buriram Province.[19] Briram's Chamber of Commerce had not organized protectionist lobby or demonstration at that time, contratry to Chonburi's counter-part.[20] Newin's commitment to protecting local retail stores, despite the lack of protectionist lobby and political clout, is a puzzle.

Why Divergence? Fence-Sitters and Electoral Benefits of FDI

Given the polarized constituents' opinions toward FDI in Chonburi and the lack of a protectionist lobby in Buriram, why did legislators in Chonburi support foreign retail investment, and legislators in Buriram opposed it? The key to answer this question is to start with the observed structure of interests: the emergence of the land-labor coalition supporting FDI in Chonburi and the lack thereof in Buriram. FDI projects, particularly for heavy industries (e.g., shipping, steel, and petrochemicals) and large retail stores, require a large patch of land. Landowners benefit from foreign investment projects because they increase the price of land. Labor also increases income from FDI, especially if they generate new employment for high-skilled workers (Pinto and Pinto 2008; Pandya 2010).

From politicians' perspectives, therefore, FDI projects are desirable to the extent to which they increase the income of landowners, labor, and any capitalists who own business related to land development. Furthermore, having new foreign investment allows legislators to extract additional rents by acting as brokers of small landowners. Both the income effects and legislators' rent-seeking incentives with FDI are stronger in urban and industrial areas than in their rural counterparts precisely because land is scarce and thus more expensive.[21]

Indeed, major financiers of legislators in Chonburi Province were a business tycoon who owned a steel company and industrial estate (Swasdi Horrungruang)[22] and local construction companies including several owned by Chonburi legislators themselves. Furthermore, Chonburi's three out of

---

[19] The first foreign retail store opened in Briram in 2004, after Newin had resigned from the Deputy Commerce Minister position.

[20] In 2009, after several foreign retail stores opened their branches in Buriram, the industry minister reportedly discussed the retail protectionist issue with Buriram's Chamber of Commerce. "Thailand Buriram and Chiang Rai to Be Promoted as Border Trading Points," *Thai Press Reports*, November 10, 2009.

[21] This is why applying the factor-based, Stolper–Samuelson theorem to account for FDI coalitions remains insufficient – in developing economies, it is scarcity of land, not its abundance, that accounts for why landowners might demand FDI.

[22] Sawasdi Horrungruang owns Nakornthai Strip Mill (NSM) steel company, which declared debt during the 1997 financial crisis. The NSM merged with Siam Iron and Steel and Siam Construction Steel, and its debt was restructured by the state-owned Thai Asset Management Corporation.

Thai Legislators' Position on Foreign Retail Investment 167

seven Lower House seats have been occupied by the three sons of the local "godfather" figure, Somchai Khunpleum, who built its business empire in real estate, construction and illegal businesses.[23] As Thailand industrialized and the government expanded infrastructure investment in Chonburi in the 1970s,[24] Somchai's business grew by contracting with the government's public works projects. When the government built Eastern Seaboard industrial complexes in Chonburi with funding from The World Bank and the Japanese government in the 1980s (see Chapter 2), Somchai played an important intermediary role in negotiating with small landowners to secure the large area of land needed for the government-funded projects (Shatkin 2004).

In sum, the members of the parliament in Chonburi are likely to promote foreign investment rather than oppose it, because of its positive income effects on organized voters (such as big capitalists and landowners) and its rent-generating opportunities. The economic gains the members reap from the foreign investment will feed back to the Chart Thai Party's electoral campaign activities in Chonburi and its activities in the parliament such as factional expansion and coalition log-rolling.[25] Local shop owners, by contrast, have no political clout. As one of the junior officers at the Bang Samet Tambon Administration Organization in Chonburi, playfully said: "The only role that the members of Parliament play in this province is to give souvenirs or a champion cup at sports competitions."[26]

In sum, interest groups in Chonburi were split into liberalization and protectionist forces and legislators chose to stand on the side of the liberalization group. Legislators' motivation for this electoral disconnection was vote-seeking and rent-seeking. The policy-seeking motivation, which was one of the critical sources of electoral disconnection in Japan, seemed absent in Chonburi legislators' decisions to commit to an open economy.

Explaining Newin's Protectionism: The National-Level, Majority Coalition Building

If individual legislator's vote and rent-seeking incentives accounted for their policy positioning on FDI in Chonburi, how do we explain the protectionist positioning of Buriram's legislators? To understand this puzzle, we need to locate the retail regulation in Buriram province in a context of national policymaking: when the Thai Rak Thai Party came into majority power in 2001,

---

[23] McVey (2000); Shatkin (2004).

[24] Arghiros (2001).

[25] Indeed, with Somchai's profits from business and a local support network he cultivated for forty years, he was reported to control fifteen to twenty seats in the parliament by funding the Chart Thai Party and its candidates.

[26] Interview with a junior government official at the Bang Samet Tambon Administration Organization in Chonburi, summer, 2001.

168   *Empirical Evidence*

Prime Minister Thaksin initiated a protectionist campaign to limit the foreign retail stores. It was the party leaders' efforts to build a majority coalition for lawmaking at the national level shaped Buriram legislators' policy-positioning. Contrary to the Japanese case in which the party leaders worked hard to build a majority coalition for an open economy, however, Thai party leaders struggled, in vain, to build a protectionist majority coalition to regulate the expansion of foreign retail stores. The struggle was due to the majority of legislators supporting foreign retail investment, as explained earlier.

Protectionist Turn in Retail Policy (1): Thai Rak Thai's One-Party Dominance

Thai Rak Thai won a landslide victory in the first election under a new electoral system with a policy platform for diffused losers from the financial crisis, such as farmers, urban workers, and small shop owners (see Chapter 4). Consistent with the platform, key members of the party began indicating that a new government would amend the existing Alien Business Law to protect Thai-owned retail businesses. An economic adviser to Thai Rak Thai, Pramond Guna-kasem, informed the press that the government planned to create a zoning policy to limit the entry of foreign-owned stores or to limit the business hours of such operations. Thai Rak Thai also considered another amendment to the Alien Business Law to reduce the power of the Commerce Ministry, which is pro-FDI, to approve foreign business entry. Instead, the planned amendment was to increase the power of provincial governments and local communities in approving the entry of foreign retail stores into a given province.[27] The content of the proposed amendment very much resembled the Japanese "Large-Scale Retail Store Law,"[28] which was legislated in 1973 to protect small Japanese retail stores against the large Japanese and foreign retail stores (Tatebayashi 2004). Thai small retailers expressed their support of the protectionist legislation.[29]

Thaksin's policy appealing to diffused losers, including the Thai retail store owners, appeared to be a textbook adaptation to a new electoral system defined by the 1997 Constitution. Since the 2001 election, the Thai electoral system transformed from a multimember district (MMD) system to a combination of single-member districts (SMDs) and proportional representation systems (PR).

---

[27] The decentralization of FDI regulation to local governments would have served two goals. One was that the government expected the majority of provincial governments to be pro-FDI, given the land-labor coalitions described above as well as legislators' rent-seeking incentives. Second was to avoid violating WTO rules because local governments, not the central governments, make decisions about FDI. "Hypermarkets: Retail Bill Empowers Local Govts," *The Nation*, August 9, 2002.

[28] The Law is called *Daikibo Kouritenpo Hou* in Japanese.

[29] "Small Retailers Back Plan for Zoning Help," *The Nation*, January 11, 2001.

The shift from MMD to SMD was expected to increase legislators' incentives to respond to unorganized voters through two mechanisms. First, under the SMD, legislators had to cater to a larger geographic region with more heterogeneous interests than under the MMD. With more voters to please, targeting particularistic projects to organized interests becomes prohibitively expensive. Instead, legislators have to come up with a less expensive way to mobilize votes, such as strengthening their policy appeals for median voters ("Policy" over "Pork"). Second, because voters cast votes for political parties under the PR portion, it increases party leaders' incentives to establish the party's brand and reputation. Finally, the 1997 Constitution mandates that electorates participate in voting. As a result, the turnout rate has increased from 62 percent in 1996 to 70 percent in 2001 and to 75 percent in 2005 (Institute for Democracy and Electoral Assistance 2014).[30] The idea of compulsory voting is to reduce vote-buying practices by political candidates by increasing the number of potential vote sellers (i.e., eligible voters who will actually turn out to vote) and thus make vote-buying prohibitively expensive for legislators. The higher voter turnout should also empower diffused losers, as organized votes matter less for the final electoral outcomes.

In addition to the electoral reform, Thaksin seemed to have all other conditions paving his way to pass the protectionist retail legislation. Thai Rak Thai occupied 49 percent of House seats alone and 65 percent of seats with its coalition partner, and building a majority coalition appeared easy. Among 248 Thai Rak Thai legislators, 40 percent were freshmen/women who were more dependent on the party nomination and party's financial assistance to run for the next election. Therefore, they should be Thaksin "loyalists."

Second, with personal wealth and business financiers, Thaksin had more resources to distribute to backbenchers than other factional leaders. The resource asymmetry weakened the power of factional leaders. Finally, Thaksin and his party, Thai Rak Thai, were vastly popular among the public. Given Thaksin's power to appoint ministers and nominate candidates in the next election, incumbent legislators were concerned about whether they could run under Thai Rak Thai's nomination in an upcoming election. This should allow Thaksin to discipline legislators who did not follow his policy. Given these conditions, building a majority coalition to pass the Foreign Retail Act seemed like it should be a breeze. But it was not.

Thaksin's effort to build a majoritarian coalition to pass this amendment completely failed. First, as soon as the announcement of draft retail law was made, the stock market fell and foreign investors raised concerns. Thaksin had to announce to the press that: "My government is not protectionist ... Our government is new and we haven't had time to sit down to explain things to

---

[30] Data available at http://www.idea.int/vt/countryview.cfm?CountryCode=TH (accessed June 17, 2014).

them. I would like to see more foreign investment in our stock market, and in the economy."[31] Owners of Thai chain stores with joint-venture projects and the TRA also opposed the bill. Finally, as the Chonburi's case study has shown, despite the one-party majority of Thai Rak Thai and the centralization of political power with Prime Minister Thaksin, few legislators followed his lead. Except for the prime minister, there was one more legislator who explicitly stood for protecting small Thai retail stores among the members of the ruling coalition: a deputy Commerce Minister, Newin Chidchob.

There are several reasons why Newin, who was elected from Buriram province in the northeast, supported protectionism. In addition to the district-level explanations discussed previously (i.e., negligible political clout of foreign-owned or joint ventured retail investment and cheap land in labor-abundant Buriram), Thaksin's efforts to build a national-level policy coalition shaped Newin's policy-positioning. Newin badly needed to win trust from Prime Minister Thaksin, because Thaksin appointed Newin as Deputy Commerce Minister in 2002, even though it was highly controversial among legislators, media, and voters. Newin was involved in a major vote-buying scandal in his province before this appointment and he gained a reputation as a corrupt legislator. Although eventually Thaksin appointed Newin as a deputy commerce minister, he initially told the Chart Thai Party not to nominate Newin to any cabinet posts, as his bad public image would affect how voters and investors evaluated Thaksin's Cabinet. To regain Thaksin's trust, Newin indeed showed unwavering loyalty to his protectionist retail policy.[32]

Yet, without more legislators following his lead, Thaksin ultimately gave up on the legislative route to protect Thai retail stores and, instead, decided to ask the Ministry of Commerce to modify the law using a ministerial ordinance procedure. The Ministry of Commerce followed Thaksin's request by first ordering large foreign retail stores to suspend all expansion plans until the new retail business law had been enacted.[33] It also drafted Retail Law to impose zoning regulation on foreign retailers. Thai retailers also sought help from a supra-legislative body and appealed to King Bhumibol.[34] Thaksin's delegation to the ministry was intriguing, as the Japanese Liberal Democratic Party (LDP) has sometimes used the delegation to bureaucracy and ministerial ordinances to commit to open economy in the face of protectionist lobby. Yet, in the Thai

---

[31] "Thaksin: We Are Not Protectionist," *The Nation*, April 2, 2001.

[32] Newin's protectionist policy position seemed unchanged even after Thaksin gave up the legislative route to pass the amendment. Thus, his policy positioning was not just to please Thaksin. The promotion to an Allied Retail Trade Co. (ART) advisor might also have made Newin stick to his protectionist position, as he electorally and personally benefited from overseeing the agency.

[33] "Tough Challenge for Sector's New Chief," *The Nation*, September 11, 2006.

[34] "Thailand Acts to Halt Foreign Retailers' Expansion: Move Comes as Dissent among Mom-and-Pop Shops Grows," *The Business Times Singapore*, September 12, 2006.

Thai Legislators' Position on Foreign Retail Investment

case, the delegation was used to implement protectionist policy without polarizing the parliament.

Side Payment for the Policy Loyalty: Newin's Double Promotion

Although Thaksin's protectionist initiative failed to build a majority coalition in the legislature, Thaksin rewarded Newin for his policy loyalty with two personnel promotions: first, to an adviser position for the government-funded private company,[35] Allied Retail Trade Co. (ART), and then to a Deputy Agricultural Minister (2005–2006). First, Newin was given the authority to set up an Allied Retail Thai initiative in 2002, right before the retail legislation was forwarded for Cabinet approval. The initiative was to increase the competitiveness of small Thai retailers by centralizing their transportation logistics, transactions with suppliers and distribution under the government-led franchise agency, the ART.[36] The franchise arrangement was expected to lower the transaction costs of small retailers and increase their bargaining power vis-à-vis large domestic and foreign-owned suppliers. The initiative received some government support, which amounted to 395 million baht.[37] Thaksin said: "I fully support all small and traditional retail shops to operate well-organized and well-structured businesses next door to all Thai neighborhoods."[38]

Small retailers quickly signed up to become ART members, and the membership increased to 28,000 within the three months of its inception in September 2002 and then to 40,000 by 2005.[39] The Thaksin government promised a generous credit package from two banks[40] for ART members, interest-free for the first 45 days and 14.5 percent interest rate, the lowest in the industry.[41]

After the cabinet reshuffle in the fall of 2005, Thaksin promoted Newin to Deputy Agricultural Minister. This promotion was highly controversial, again because the media, legislators, and voters were concerned that Newin would abuse this position to cater to his core supporters, that is, agricultural constituents in Buriram. Indeed, Newin quickly turned this opportunity into vote-, money-, and rent-seeking activities. He created a new "ART-A," a government-funded franchise of retail stores that sold farmers cheaper agricultural supplies and purchased farm products to distribute through the government-funded retail network.[42]

---

[35] The ART is co-owned by the office of Small and Medium-sized Enterprise Promotion and the SMPE Bank. The government spent 395 million baht to fund this project. "Small Business Opportunity," *The Nation*, September 6, 2004.

[36] "Govt Retail Body: AR Thai 'Will Raise Bt2.1 bn,'" *The Nation*, July 3, 2002.

[37] "Allied Retail Trade Co.: Alliance to Use Franchise Chain," *The Nation*, August 22, 2002.

[38] "Small Retailers Close to PM's Heart," *The Nation*, November 20, 2002.

[39] This membership growth was lower than expected. The government estimated the membership to reach 100,000 in a few years. "Art Marketing Revamp," *The Nation*, February 13, 2004.

[40] "ART Members to Get Easier Credit Terms," *The Nation*, December 17, 2002.

[41] Ibid.

[42] "Franchise Stores: Farmers Promised Cheaper Supplies," *The Nation*, February 27, 2003.

172   *Empirical Evidence*

The ART also teamed up with the Thai Chamber of Commerce to support its "one village one retail shop" campaign, which promised to open at least one ART store in each of the 70,000 villages by selling cheaper goods to the rural poor.[43] Thus, by serving dual positions as an adviser to the ART and as a deputy agricultural minister, Newin aligned the interests of small retail owners, whom Thaksin wanted to please, and Newin's main supporters, farmers. The two office perks gave Newin power to implement policies that mobilize votes, campaign contributions, and rents. Newin's initiatives as deputy minister also gave Thaksin a credit-claiming opportunity to build a reputation among diffused losers of liberalization, such as small retail owners and farmers.[44] In addition to these office perks, Newin also reportedly secured large government budgets for infrastructure development projects in Buriram in 2006 before Thaksin was ousted by the military coup.[45]

Although Thaksin failed to build a majority coalition to regulate the foreign retail investments, he was able to build a party reputation among small retail owners by using the power to appoint deputy ministers. Approving the government's budget to financially assist small retail owners, through the establishment of ART, was also less polarizing than restricting the entries of foreign investment.

Side Payment for Coalition Loyalty but Policy Dissent: Double-Track Railway Construction Project to Chonburi

With his party's one-party dominance and popularity among voters, why did Thaksin not purge ministers and coalition partners who did not follow his protectionist lawmaking? Indeed, for some legislation such as the controversial State of Emergency Decree, the Thai Rak Thai party whips made it clear that any party members who failed to vote for the decree would face severe disciplinary action.[46]

For the retail bill, however, it would have been difficult, if not impossible, for Thaksin to use political appointments and nomination power to discipline the policy dissents. This was because the strongest opposition to the protectionist

---

[43] "One Tambon, One Shop Scheme to Start in Tak," *The Nation*, August 21, 2003.
[44] Newin was later promoted again to Minister of the Prime Minister's Office in 2005. See Wongpreedee (2007).
[45] Wongpreedee (2007), p. 462. The size of actual budget given to Newin was not clear.
[46] Yet, the disciplined Thai Rak Party caused increasing resentment among its backbenchers who felt like they had no freedom to express their views or deliberate on policy issues on the floor. The resentful legislators often chose not to attend the sessions. As a result, on numerous occasions especially since 2004, Thai Rak Thai failed to meet the Constitutional quorum at the House of Representatives, which required that at least half of the members should attend to make the votes valid. The party leaders even discussed giving the members financial incentives to attend the sessions. See "Editorial: Emergency Decree to Sail Through," *The Nation*, August 24, 2005.

bill came from representatives from urban and industrial constituencies, many of which belonged to the Chart Thai Party, the most coherent and critical coalition partner in the Thai Rak Thai's ruling coalition. Chart Thai legislators were known to use a threat of coalition breakaway to induce policy or personnel concession, and they often followed through on the threat and broke away from the ruling coalition. On the other hand, Thai Rak Thai loyalists, such as legislators who were elected to the House for the first time with Thaksin's electoral and financial support, were predominantly from rural areas, which had fewer stakes in regulating the foreign retail investment via the Foreign Retail Act. The geographic distribution of coalition loyalists (i.e., rural) versus the coalitional fence-sitters (i.e., urban) accounts for why Thaksin was not able to discipline the backbenchers to pass the protectionist retail legislation.

Then, how did Thaksin respond to the lack of policy loyalty of its coalition partner, Chart Thai politicians from Chonburi province? Despite the policy disagreement, Thaksin gave them side payments to make them stay in the ruling coalition. He gave them the Laem Chabang double-track railway project. The railway project was part of Thaksin's pledge to make Thailand a transport and shipping hub in Asia. The parliament approved a 400,000 million baht budget to expand a railway from Chachoensao Province to Chonburi's Laem Chabang port from a single to a double track during a five-year period.[47]

Table 6.1 describes the major infrastructure development projects initiated by Thaksin and the distribution of House of Representative's seats across parties in each province.

The table shows that on a monetary basis, the highest beneficiaries of these projects were Bangkok and industrial and manufacturing centers near Bangkok, such as Chachoengsao and Chonburi Provinces. In addition to the railway project, Thaksin also rewarded Chonburi legislators with ministerial positions, such as Sontaya Khunpluem's appointment of long-sought Minister of Tourism and Sports in the cabinet reshuffle in October 2002.[48] The Minister of Tourism and Sports, despite how it may sound, is a popular position among legislators because of the large budget and infrastructure development opportunities.[49] The coalition loyalist, Chonburi legislators, received particularistic benefits even though they did not follow Thaksin's lead on protectionist legislation.

---

[47] "Thailand's Status as Logistics Hub Creates Opportunities for Entrepreneurs," *Thai Press Reports*, January 16, 2007. Also see "Thailand Transport Ministry Asks Cabinet to Permit New Bids for Dual Tracks to Laem Chabang," *Financial Times*, April 30, 2007. Thaksin had a memorandum of understanding with Chinese government on September 2005 that China would build a 78-km track. Later, the interim government overturned this memorandum.

[48] See official website of Thai parliament and cabinet, http://www.cabinet.thaigov.go.th/eng/bb_main11.htm (accessed September 2, 2011). When Thaksin originally formed the cabinet in 2001, Sontaya was appointed as Minister of Science, Technology and Environment, a relatively powerless ministry with a small budget.

[49] "Chonburi Power Joins Pheu Thai Coalition after Election Triumph," *Pattaya Mail*, July 8, 2011.

Beyond Chonburi, the table shows the clear pattern that Thaksin targeted infrastructure development projects in provinces where oppositions held more than 50 percent of the seats, in particular, Democrats. Except for Chiang Mai province, Thai Rak Thai's strong hold in the north and northeast did not receive major infrastructure projects. Instead, Thaksin used Policies for diffused losers such as generous credit to small retail owners and debt moratorium for farmers to please northern and northeastern legislators, who were loyal to Thai Rak Thai (see Chapter 3), and used Pork to entice fence-sitting legislators into his coalition (see Chapter 2).

The differentiation of Pork versus Policy to build a majority coalition is consistent with the theory of Optimal Use of Pork versus Policy developed in Chapter 1. Pork was used for the fence-sitting, small net losers of liberalization, such as urban and industrial provinces facing the foreign retail competition – Chonburi, Chachoengsao, Bangkok, and Pathum Thani.[50] Policy programs were used to mobilize electoral support from diffused and mass losers, such as farmers and small business owners in Thailand.

What diverges from the prediction of optimal allocation of pork developed in Chapter 1 is whom the two governments targeted Pork. Thaksin targeted opposition districts for infrastructure development projects, not co-partisans. By contrast, the LDP targeted infrastructure development projects to co-partisan, and targeted protectionism (i.e., safeguard measures) to opposition districts (see Chapter 5). The contrast is a puzzle, because the two prime ministers (Koizumi Junichiro of Japan's LDP and Thaksin Shinawatra of Thailand's Thai Rak Thai) shared key similarities, such as high popularity among voters, one party holding nearly 50 percent of the seats in parliament, and more centralized personnel appointment power than the previous prime ministers under the new electoral systems (i.e., combination of single-member district system with closed, party-list proportional representation system).

There are two possible explanations for this puzzle that are observationally equivalent, and thus I cannot say that one is superior to the others. First, Thaksin's use of infrastructure projects might have served a similar function as the LDP's use of protectionism (i.e., safeguard adoption) to encourage the opposition legislators' party switching to the ruling party. Because the Thai government is much more concerned about foreign investors' response to protectionism than the Japanese government, Thaksin might have substituted protectionism with infrastructure projects as a tool to encourage party switching.

To lend support to this possibility, in Table 6.1 the right column shows the pattern of party switching that occurred between 2003 (i.e., announcement of infrastructure projects) and the general election in 2005 among provinces

---

[50] Pathum Thani also had well-organized legislators built around the Chucip Hansawat's family and formed Wang Nam Yen faction. Thaksin rewarded Chucip with not only the infrastructural project described earlier, but also with the Minister of Agriculture and Cooperatives position. See Wongpreedee (2007: 456–457).

Project	Project Name	Budget (million baht)	Province	%Thai Rak Thai	% Chart Thai	%Opposition	Party Switch to TRT
			Ruling Coalition				
1	The new city project	100,000	Nakhon Nayok	0	50	50	1:Wuttichai Kittitanasuan
2	Khlong Prapa elevated roadway	20,000	Pathum Thani	50	0	50	0
3	Laem Pak Bia Bridge	56,000	Surat Thani	0	0	100	0
4	Bangkok Public Transport	397,800	Bangkok	81	0	19	1: Ong-art Klamphaibul
5	High-speed railway expansion	400,000	Chonburi	14	86	0	6: Former Chart Thai
			Chachoensao	50	0	50	1: Suchart Tnancharoen
6	Chiang Mai Aviation Hub	28000	Chaing Mai	90	0	10	0
7	Phuket Science Park	100000	Phuket	0	0	100	0
8	Kra Isthmus Canal	35,000 ($USD)	Ranong	0	0	100	0
9	Expressways etc	44728	Multiprovincial				N/A
10	New canal and river routes (eleven projects)	7899	Multiprovincial				N/A
11	Chao Phraya River bridges (four projects)	11060	Multiprovincial				N/A
12	Motorways (ten projects)	119	Multiprovincial				N/A
	National average (2005 election)			50.00	8.75	34.25	

Note: This table builds on Table 4.4 in Pasuk and Baker (2005), p. 128. The author added columns "Province," "% Thai Rak Thai," "% Opposition," "% Chart Thai," and "Party Switch to TRT" and rows 7 to 12 from the author's dataset. The percentage refers to seat shares for the single-member districts of House of Representatives in each province.

176 Empirical Evidence

TABLE 6.2. *Probability of Party Switching to Thai Rak Thai, 2003–2005 by Region*

Region	Probability of Party Switch to Thai Rak Thai (%)			
	Thaksin's Policy	Thaksin's Pork	Received Infrastructural Projects	No Major Projects
North	Favor	1	100	22.2
Northeast	Favor	0	N/A	64.2
Central	Didn't favor	5	50	3.4
South	Didn't favor	3	0	0
National avg.			34.6	23.3

Note: The north and northeast regions are agricultural and Thaksin's (and his Thai Rak Thai Party's) stronghold. The central provinces are mostly urban and industrial, and Thaksin's coalition partner, Chart Thai Party, controlled fifteen single-member seats. The southern provinces have long been loyal to Democrats, the major opposition party. The author collected information on party switching by comparing 2001 and 2005 election results by constituencies in Adam Carr's election archive, available at: sephos.adam-carr.net (accessed June 24, 2014).

that received the major infrastructure projects. Among provinces that received major infrastructure development projects, nine out of twenty-six opposition legislators switched to Thai Rak Thai before the 2005 election, which was a 34.6 percent success rate for Thaksin. This success rate is substantially higher than the national average of party switching to Thai Rak Thai, which was 23.3 percent, yet the difference is much more dramatic if we compare the party switching rate for each of the four regional clusters in Thailand.

Table 6.2 summarizes the results. It shows that Thaksin used Policies favorable to diffused losers in the north and northeast where Thai Rak Thai received the majority of support. His policies were particularly successful in inducing other party legislators to switch to Thai Rak Thai in the Northeast (64.2 percent). Policies seemed to substitute Pork and hence no big infrastructure development project was given to the northeast. In contrast, he targeted pork barrel projects to the central plain such as Bangkok, Chonburi, and Pathum Thani, yielding a 50 percent success rate of party switching among the opposition party legislators. Among provinces in the central plain that did not receive major infrastructure projects, such as Ang Thong, Chanthaburi, and Rayong, the party switching rate was slightly above 3 percent. Despite Thaksin's effort to mobilize support from the south, his pork allocation was not able to induce party switching in southern provinces because of their strong loyalty to the opposition, Democratic Party.[51]

---

[51] Southern provinces have been block-voting Democrats and the support has been very stable over the past two decades. Because of this block-voting, the south received very few infrastructural

The second possible explanation for this puzzle is that Thaksin adopted a grand coalition strategy, to increase the size of the coalition, not to limit the size of the coalition to ensure a sufficient share of the spoils among legislators and parties (i.e., a strategy of minimum winning coalition). To expand the coalition, the government's budget was used to entice outsiders to join the coalition rather than to reward the coalition loyalists. The LDP of Japan at that time, on the other hand, formed a minimum winning coalition with the Clean Government Party (New Kōmei), and thus targeted government's resources for co-partisans, rather than opposition.

Another Protectionist Turn in Retail Policy (2): Post-Coup, Interim Government

The military coup of 2006 overthrew Thaksin's government and Thailand reverted back to autocracy. The interim government, chosen by the Council for National Security (CNS), appointed Prime Minister Surayud, who was a former general. The council also appointed 242 members to the National Legislative Assembly with various backgrounds in politics, academia, the military, and bureaucracy.

The Sarayud government adopted a protectionist position on foreign investors in two areas: foreign ownership regulation and foreign retail investments.[52] With respect to the former, the government revised the Foreign Business Act to limit foreign investors to hold no more than 50 percent of the equity or voting rights in companies as of January of 2007. The addition of the voting rights provision aimed to reduce the loopholes in the previous Foreign Business Act, which defined "foreign" companies only by their ownership share.[53] With respect to the retail regulation, the government proposed a Retail Business Act, which gave power to the Ministry of Interior, which oversees local government activities, to regulate foreign retail investments. Both bills passed the first stage of voting at the National Legislative Assembly.

The National Legislative Assembly voted in support of the protectionist retail legislation by ninety-seven votes. Only six members voted against it and another six members abstained.[54] Despite the overwhelming support in NLA for the draft legislation, however, the government set up a new twenty-member subcommittee to screen "certain aspects of the bill" and added two more NLA members who were widely known as opponents of the foreign retail regulation. One was Darmp Sukotasap, who was a senior vice president of foreign-owned retail store Tesco-Lotus at that time, and another was Ammar Siamwalla, who

---

projects until Thaksin, compared to the central region where the Chart Thai Party was organized to join the ruling coalition and received particularistic benefits.

[52] It is important to note, however, that the Sayurd government moved quickly with free trade agreements with Japan.

[53] "Foreign Business Act: Reconsider Amendment, Envoys Urge," *The Nation*, February 10, 2007.

[54] "Retail Business Act: Current Govt Unlikely to Pass Law," *The Nation*, November 15, 2007.

was the strongest opponent of the bill. Shop owners from several provinces lobbied the government to eliminate the two opponents from the committee, noting the conflict of interests.[55] These shop owners commented that if the law did not pass under the interim government, there would be a slimmer chance of passage by the next democratically elected government.

In the end, the NLA could not pass the two bills because the parliamentary session ran out of time before the general election of 2007. The government's majority coalition-building to regulate foreign retail stores continued to fail even under the interim government with appointed, not elected, legislators. The Democratic government returned to Thailand in 2007 and subsequent elected governments also continued to favor foreign retail expansions.

CONCLUSION

Thai legislators' position-taking on foreign retail investment in Chonburi and Buriram Provinces demonstrated three points. First, legislators supported the expansion of foreign retail investment in Chonburi as a result of legislators' vote and rent-seeking incentives, not of the national-level effort to pass legislations. Where land was relatively scarce and expensive, such as in Chonburi, electoral benefits of FDI outweighed the costs (i.e., loss of votes from local retail owners). Thus, legislators had incentives to support FDI and the party leaders did not have to work hard to build an open economy coalition. In Buriram, lawmaking incentives of the coalition leader (Prime Minister Thaksin) as well as Newin Chidchob's necessity to demonstrate his loyalty to Thaksin played a key role in his protectionist policy position. Buriram's case is thus consistent with this Globalization as Legislation approach.

Second, the party leaders used side payments to achieve two interrelated goals: to keep the multiparty coalition intact and to build a majority coalition for lawmaking. Both goals are consistent with the premise of this book that party leaders need a majority coalition to survive politically and make laws. Yet, because of the fragility of the multiparty coalition in Thailand, the party leaders put greater importance on coalition survival than on lawmaking. Thus, the coalition fence-sitters – that is, legislators who were in the ruling coalition and could pose a credible threat of exit – obtained a high portion of particularistic benefits. Legislators' policy positioning did not appear to affect the party leader's distribution of particularistic benefits – both Chonburi and Buriram legislators, despite their differences in policy positions (pro and anti-FDI respectively), were rewarded for their decisions to stay with the coalition and for policy loyalty.

Finally, even though the centralization of power achieved by the electoral reform and one-party dominance facilitated Thaksin's policy initiatives for

---

[55] "Retail Business Act: Drive to Speed Up New Law," *The Nation*, November 20, 2007.

diffused losers, limiting foreign investment was deemed too costly electorally and economically. Thaksin's effort to establish party reputation among small retail owners failed, as few legislators followed his lead. Backbenchers were already captured by the beneficiaries of foreign retail expansion and feared losing the organized votes and major financier of electoral campaign. The evidence thus suggests that the centralization of power to party leaders via changes in electoral and party systems is a necessary, but not sufficient, condition for policy change. In the retail case, party leaders were forced to resort to supralegislative means, such as ministerial regulations, to regulate foreign retail investment.

PART III

DISCUSSION

7

The Political Foundations of an Open Economy

Discussion

This book has asked what accounts for the vast reduction in trade barriers after World War II across countries with different political institutions. The two facts about trade liberalization documented in Chapter 1 – that is, a bulk of liberalization was achieved unilaterally and the majority of trade barriers had been removed despite the difference in political institutions – forced us to flip the economists' puzzle (why protectionism prevails despite the economic inefficiency). Instead, we should ask *how* governments achieved liberalization even though protectionism seemed politically optimal, namely, the political foundations of an open economy.

This book demonstrated the role of party leaders as builders and gatekeepers of an open economy, contrary to the conventional wisdom emphasizing the role of insulation of trade policymaking from legislators. Party leaders in Japan and Thailand used the three strategies of majority coalition-building for open economy: *Pork*, *Policy*, and *Institutional Reforms*, which bought off support from legislators who otherwise opposed liberalization. Rather than insulating the trade policymaking from the political pressures, these party leaders mobilized the open economy coalition by fueling legislators' rent-seeking incentives with side payments and by helping their political survival. Pork, Policy, and Institutional Reforms served as a glue to hold the coalition together, when trade and investment liberalization imposed electoral costs to backbenchers.

The reminder of this chapter discusses broader implications of the findings presented in this book beyond the studies of trade liberalization. In particular, I focus on three research programs: (1) legislators' position-taking on economic policies, (2) compensation politics in the global economy, and (3) political institutions and economic policies. I elaborate the contribution of this book to each of these research programs in the text that follows.

LEGISLATORS' POSITION-TAKING ON ECONOMIC POLICIES

Many studies have considered that legislators' economic policy positions reflect constituents' interests; namely, legislators are the delegates of voters. The evidence summarized in Chapters 2, 5, and 6 challenge this view. Legislators often took policy positions that diverged from the constituents' interests to help the party leaders secure majority support for economic policies. The party leaders rewarded these legislators with side payments, such as public works projects and ministerial appointments, to mitigate the electoral costs of liberalization.

Chapter 2 has shown that Japanese and Thai party leaders used Pork to buy off fence-sitting legislators' support to build support for trade liberalization. Chapter 2 demonstrated that even when liberalization went through executive routes (i.e., it did not require a majority support on the floor), party leaders' concerns for keeping the majority status (i.e., not letting unhappy backbenchers break away from the party) and ensuring backbenchers' political survival dictated which commodities were liberalized and when. The evidence in two countries was consistent with the Optimal Use of Pork hypothesis developed in Chapter 1 and held up to even the case of semidemocratic Thailand in the 1980s, where an unelected, military-backed prime minister had to build the majority coalition with elected legislators.

The case study findings presented in Chapters 5 and 6 on rival regions further lend support to the Optimal Use of Pork. The LDP leaders with high-rank positions in the government passed up the opportunities to protect their own constituents, and instead, used safeguard protection selectively for non-LDP districts to increase seat shares. The party leaders handsomely rewarded fence-sitting legislators with ministerial appointments and public works projects for their support for open economy.

The evidence presented in Chapters 2, 5, and 6 have further shown that it is often more optimal for the government to liberalize the organized industries than to liberalize diffused interests. This is so because from the party leaders' perspective, Pork will be more cost-effective to buy off support from legislators representing organized interests than diffused interests. By contrast, selective use of protectionism is optimal for diffused interests because the use of Pork would be too expensive. This was the case for shielding Japanese farmers from trade liberalization in the early 1960s and relieving Thai farmers' income losses in the 1980s under Thaksin cabinet.[1] The finding is contrary to the established view that more organized and concentrated interests win protectionism because of their higher collective action capacity.

These findings together call scholars to consider legislators' policy positioning in the context of national-level policymaking and availability of fiscal resource, not just a mere reflection of constituents' interests and demands.

---

[1] Farmers constituted around 30 percent of the labor force in Japan during 1960s and they constituted 90 percent of the Thai labor force in 1980s and 40 percent under Thaksin cabinet.

Globalization as Legislation: Discussion

COMPENSATION POLITICS IN THE GLOBAL ECONOMY

This book has demonstrated that the party leaders' concerns for lawmaking and majority coalition building can influence the government's budget allocation, not necessarily the strength of the demands or needs of constituents. The systematic findings presented in Chapters 2, 5, and 6 suggested that the governments allocated resources to compensate legislators' loss of votes and rents from liberalization, not necessarily to compensate income loss of industries and voters. Because party leaders' incentive is to maintain the majority coalition on the floor with the smallest costs possible, the governments' resource allocation favored the fence-sitting legislators, whose districts incurred small net losses from liberalization, not legislators whose districts incurred big net losses.

The welfare implication of the optimal use of Pork to build the coalition is that urban and industrial bias in budget allocation can occur in early phases of liberalization, such as in Japan and Thailand after their accession to General Agreement on Tariffs and Trade (GATT). The finding challenges the conventional view that pork barreling is a rural phenomenon because legislators can buy rural votes at a cheaper price than from urban voters. By contrast, Chapter 2 has shown that urban bias in side-payment allocation occurred in Japan in the 1960s because it was cheaper for party leaders to buy support from legislators representing urban and industrial districts, where the net loss from liberalization was smaller. The urban and industrial bias in side-payment allocation also occurred in Thailand in the past three decades, due to the better organized urban legislators and the higher rents generated in urban districts where industries are concentrated and the land price is higher.

Chapter 3 explored what influenced legislators' responsiveness to diffused losers when candidate-centered electoral systems encouraged the use of Pork. It has shown that party systems shaped legislators' responsiveness to diffused losers in Japan and Thailand via changing the costs of intraelite bargaining over resource allocation. The one-party majority governments were able to shift resource allocation from Pork to Policy for diffused losers when exogenous economic shocks (energy crises and Asian financial crisis) made the use of Pork prohibitively expensive for the party leaders (Japan in the 1970s and Thailand between 2001 and 2006). There were other periods during which demands for compensation from diffused losers soared, such as Thailand after the 1983 crisis and 1997 financial crisis. Yet, these demands did not translate into government's shift from Pork to Policy, owing to the high costs for the party leaders to strike a bargain over new resource allocation inherent in the multiparty coalition government. These findings force us to rethink the widely claimed and tested Compensation Hypothesis, which predicts that governments will distribute more resources to those who stand to lose from globalization because losers provide more organized political support. Rather than being driven by

186   *Discussion*

the interest group demands, the party leaders' calculation about how much legislative support Pork versus Policy can buy under different party systems influenced the allocation.

Chapter 4 demonstrated that, during economic hard times with fewer fiscal resources, party leaders can use institutional reforms to compensate the electoral loss of legislators from trade liberalization and help their political survival in the future. Changing legislators' access to votes and money via reforms can substitute the use of Pork or Policy. The example of such reforms is the political finance reform in Japan (1975), which limited associational and corporate donations. The reform helped urban Liberal Democratic Party (LDP) legislators compete against left party candidates, and allowed rural legislators to mobilize organized votes and rents in the face of declining Pork resource. Such institutional reforms were absent in the Thai case, however, owing to the short-lived, fragile multiparty coalitions, which inhibited the party leaders' collective strategy to help backbenchers' survival. Consistent with the incentive provided by the political finance regulation, Japanese legislators' rent-seeking after the 1975 reform targeted protectionist, geographically organized interests in districts, while Thai legislators' rent-seeking continued to target export-oriented, oligopolistic firms.

These findings call for more research on a variety of ways in which party leaders can make backbenchers stay with the party when liberalization imposed them electoral costs and their welfare implications for citizens.

POLITICAL INSTITUTIONS AND ECONOMIC POLICIES: THE IMPORTANCE OF PARTY SYSTEMS

The findings presented in Chapters 3 and 4 also challenge the established literature linking electoral systems and economic policies that benefit broader versus narrow segment of societies. I have shown instead that electoral systems are neither a necessary nor a sufficient explanation for the variations or over time changes in the government's economic policies favoring broad versus narrow interests. Rather, party system variations, especially whether they are centralized or decentralized (i.e., a fewer number of parties or factions in the government) account for the government's choice between Pork and Policy by changing the costs of intraelite bargaining over resources.

Japan's LDP shifted from Pork to Policy during the 1970s (see Chapter 3) under the exact same candidate-centered electoral systems and the partisanship in the government. The expansion of welfare spending occurred in the 1970s partially in response to the rise of left parties, yet even after the popularity of the left waned in 1980, the LDP did not revert back to the big pork spending of the 1960s. The reorganization within the LDP in the early 1970s, not an electoral reform, facilitated this shift from Pork to Policy by

Globalization as Legislation: Discussion

lowering the costs of the intraelite bargain over resource. An example of such reorganization was the emergence of policy specialization among legislators ("Zoku" politicians), which strengthened sectoral over geographic representation of interests and facilitated credit-claiming over broader policy programs in policymaking.

The longitudinal study of the Japanese government's budget allocation since 1955 also suggests that the electoral reform of 1994 did not increase the government spending for diffused losers, contrary to the conventional prediction. Instead, the LDP's reorganization that occurred in the early 1970s accounts for this expansion and continued decline of Pork spending after the left party lost their stream in 1980.

By contrast, the expansion of spending for diffused losers occurred in Thailand under Thaksin's one-party majority cabinet (2001–2006) with a mixed-member electoral system (single-member district and closed list proportional representation), a similar to Japan's post-1994 electoral system. These pieces of evidence together suggest that a variation in party systems can affect the government's economic policies more than a variation in electoral systems, although evidence for the Thai case requires innovative identification strategies because of the high correlation between electoral systems and party systems. These findings also challenge the established views that parties in candidate-centered systems are mere forums in which individual legislators advance their vote and rent-seeking incentives.

Second, the findings suggest us to reconsider arguments that the LDP government used targeted benefits to districts (i.e., Pork) to survive the political crises and that pork barreling contributed to the long-term reign of the LDP (Calder 1988; Scheiner 2006). The findings presented in Chapter 3 have shown that the LDP dealt with the crises in the 1970s by shifting resources away from Pork to Policy programs for diffused losers. The evidence summarized in Chapter 4 has suggested that the LDP also dealt with the crises of 1970s by changing the rules of the game, such as the political finance reform of 1975. These policy and institutional innovations contributed to the survival of the LDP, while easing the electoral costs of liberalization imposed on backbenchers. The use of Pork, on the other hand, was prevalent during politically and economically good times, not hard times.

THE FUTURE OF OPEN ECONOMY COALITION BUILDING

In the ever-increasing movement of goods, capital, and labor across borders, will the national leaders' use of side payments to build open economy coalitions be sustainable? In this concluding section, I discuss three major trends in the world economy and politics, and speculate how these new trends will change the national leaders' coalition-building for the open economy.

New Entries of Authoritarian, Hybrid and New Democracies to the World Economy

The first major trend is new entries of developing countries to the world economy with different characteristics of political regimes. Examples of such developing economies are communist and authoritarian China and Vietnam, and former Soviet Union countries, which exhibit hybrid characteristics of democracy and authoritarianism. Moreover, many developing countries have been transitioning to democracies, especially in Africa. How does the national leader's effort to build the open economy coalition differ in authoritarian and hybrid regimes, compared to their counterparts in full-fledged democracies?

First, the national leaders in authoritarian regimes can buy off support for open economy with side payments, just like in democracies, as long as the opposition to liberalization concerns the income loss of the constituents, or the selectorates (i.e., a group of elites who have influence over the survival of leaders). In one-party dominant, authoritarian regimes, such as China and Vietnam, party leaders can also devise Policy to buy off support from diffused losers, or use Institutional Reforms to help co-faction members survive. Shirk (1993) has shown, indeed, that the Chinese Communist Party built a coalition supporting open economy with provinces, by initially granting policy privileges and access to the world economy to coastal provinces. The Chinese Communist Party has also opened its membership to capitalists in 2001 to increase the voice of globalization winners (*New York Times*, August 13, 2001).

Where authoritarian systems differ from democracies, however, is in how the leaders allocate side payments, due to the former's lack of formal majority requirement to make policies. The lack of majority requirement implies that the national leaders' side-payment allocation may not favor "fence-sitting" legislators (or "fence-sitting" selectorates). Instead, the side-payment allocation might favor legislators whose constituents incur big net income losses from globalization as a result of their high levels of grievance and collective action.

Second, in hybrid regimes where there are some degrees of electoral competition, I expect to see that the national leaders help co-partisan (or co-faction) legislators' political survival by using side payments to reduce the electoral costs of liberalization like their counterparts in democracies. Alternatively, party leaders might give backbenchers an electoral advantage through undemocratic means (e.g., suppression and other electoral fraud). Either way, in weak and decentralized party systems, which are often the case for hybrid regimes and newer democracies, party leaders lack means to strike Policy or Institutional Reform solutions with backbenchers. Accordingly, the party leaders are more dependent on the use of Pork to build the open economy coalition (Keefer and Vlaicu 2008).

Finally, democratization should facilitate the party leaders' coalition-building for an open economy through two mechanisms: extension of voter franchise and increase in efficacy of side payments. The extension of voter franchise

Globalization as Legislation: Discussion

from a fraction of elites ("selectorates") to the masses in developing economies means that the median preference among constituents (or "selectorates") shifts from protectionist to free trade (Milner and Kubota 2005). The party leaders' effort to buy off support from protectionist legislators is easier with new entries of free-trading voters. Second, the transition to democracy might change the target of side-payment allocation from big net losers to small net losers ("fence-sitting" legislators) because of the majority requirement in legislatures. This shift will improve the efficiency of side payments, that is, how many legislators' support side payments can buy.

What the preceding discussion implies is that when hybrid regimes and new democracies join the world economy, international organizations should not pressure these governments to implement economic liberalization and fiscal discipline at the same time. Instead of disciplining the use of Pork, international organizations such as World Trade Organization, World Bank, and International Monetary Fund should allow the party leaders' discretion over their use of side payments to build the open economy coalition.

PROTECTIONIST CONSUMERS

Second, a new challenge for the open economy coalition-building might come from protectionist consumers, who prefer to purchase domestically produced food and goods. Consumers today are increasingly sensitive to safety, quality, and ethical issues in international trade beyond the price and variety of goods (Naoi and Kume 2011). These protectionist consumers challenge the premise of this book that side payments can buy legislator support for an open economy as long as legislators and constituents are concerned about the trade's income effects. Allocating side payments to buy off legislators support is harder when trade policy is multifaceted, that is, voters and legislators consider issues beyond its income effects.

Furthermore, these protectionist consumers are inherently diffused and vast in numbers, which warrants the party leaders' use of Policy, especially policies to tighten regulatory standards, to buy off their support for an open economy. The past decade has indeed witnessed that advanced industrialized nations passed policies to tighten safety and quality regulation of food and require the labeling of countries of origin throughout the supply chains: the FDA Food Safety Modernization Act (FSMA) in the United States (2011), "Farm to Fork" movements to increase traceability of food products by the European Union in the 2000s and traceability legislations that require recording and labeling countries of origin of rice in the whole supply chain in Japan (2010). What remains to be seen is whether these new regulatory standards increase consumers' awareness of food safety issues and make them more protectionist, or assure them of the safety of imported goods and make them more free-trading.

Indeed, in the face of a decreasing role of sectoral and class-based organizations and fiscal austerity, new politics of trade are less about organized producers and more about a diffused and unorganized public. Rather than buying off the opposition to globalization with side payments, party leaders' new coalition-building strategy might be informational, such as persuasion and policy campaign. To corraborate with this intuition, we have witnessed the expanding role of media in shaping the minds of the public in advanced industrialized nations during the 2008 recession and during the negotiation of a comprehensive trade agreement with twelve Asia-Pacific countries (including the United States and Japan), the Trans-Pacific Partnership Agreement (Naoi and Urata 2013). A promising line of future research is to examine how communication with elites, such as media and legislators, shapes an economically unorganized public's attitudes toward trade and globalization.

Changing Industrial Geography: Locational Sorting of Productive Firms

Finally, locational sorting of productive versus unproductive firms might directly affect the effectiveness of Pork to buy off support from backbenchers. Consistent with the prediction offered by Krugman and others' new theory of trade (Fujita 1988; Krugman 1991a), scholars have shown that reduced transportation costs have generated locational sorting of productive versus unproductive industries in both developed and developing economies (Kim 1995 on the United States Amiti 1998 on Europe).[2] The theory suggests that productive firms might sort themselves to locate their operations at "the core" – a city that is close to the big market – to leverage the economy of scale and low transportation costs, while unproductive firms sort to locate at the periphery (Melitz 2003; Baldwin and Okubo 2006).

With this increasing locational sorting of productive and globalized firms, party leaders can continue to use targeted side payments (Pork) to buy off legislator support, due to the losers of an open economy being relatively concentrated in some electoral districts. Yet the locational sorting will raise the costs of Pork because there will be a diminishing number of "fence-sitting" legislators on globalization. Instead, we expect to see more polarization of legislators' positions due to some electoral districts disproportionately attracting productive firms, and other districts attracting unproductive ones. The polarization of legislators' positions increases the costs of using Pork to buy off support, as more legislators represent districts that incur big net losses rather than small net losses.

---

[2] There are other empirical tests that did not lend support to Krugman's conjecture. See a survey by Head and Mayer (2004).

References

Acemoglu, Daron, and James Robinson. 2001. "Inefficient Redistribution." *American Political Science Review*. 95(3): 649–661.

Akaneya, Tatsuo. 1992. *Nihon no gatto kanyu mondai – rejium riron no bunseki shikaku ni yoru jirei kenyu* [Japan's Accession to GATT: Case Study from a Regime Theory Perspective]. Tokyo: University of Tokyo Press.

Albritton, Robert B., and Thawilwadee Bureekul. 2008. "Developing Democracy under a New Constitution in Thailand." In *How East Asians View Democracy*, ed. Yuhan Zhu, 114–138. New York: Columbia University Press.

Amiti, Mary. 1998. "New Trade Theories and Industrial Location in the EU: A Survey of Evidence." *Oxford Review of Economic Policy* 14(2): 45–53.

Anantarangsi, S., and Walsh, J. 2012. "Income Distribution and Mobility in Thailand: The Perceptions of Migrant Workers in Bangkok and Vicinity." *NIDA Development Journal* 49(2): 51–78.

Anderson, Kym and Ernesto Valenzuela. 2011. *Estimates of Global Distortions to Agricultural Incentives, 1955 to 2011*. Washington, DC: World Bank. June 2013.

Angrist, Joshua D., and Jörn-Steffen Pischke. 2008. *Mostly Harmless Econometrics: An Empiricist's Companion*. Princeton, NJ: Princeton University Press.

Aramaki, Kenji. 2004. "Shihon torihiki jiyuuka heno siikuensingu: nihon no keiken to chugoku heno shisa." *Kaihatsu Kinnyu Kenkyu-sho hou* 21: 49–77. Japan Bank for International Cooperation.

Arghiros, Daniel. 1992. "Local-level Electoral Politics and Rural Change in Thailand." Paper presented at the Annual Conference of the Association of South-East Asian Studies, April 8–10, 1992, at the School of Oriental and African Studies (SOAS), London.

    2001. *Democracy, Development and Decentralization in Provincial Thailand*. Democracy in Asia No. 8. New York: Psychology Press.

Ariga, Kenichi, and Ejima Shinya. 2000. "Tai oukoku 'Toubu rinkai kaihatsu keikaku sougou innpakuto hyouka' (En-shakkan jigyo jigo hyouka)", *Kaihatsu Kinnyu Kenkyu-sho hou* 2: 81–115. Japan Bank for International Cooperation.

Bailey, Michael A., Judith Goldstein, and Barry R. Weingast. 1997. "The Institutional Roots of American Trade Policy: Politics, Coalitions, and International Trade." *World Politics* 49(3): 309–338.

Bailey, Michael, and David W. Brady. 1998. "Heterogeneity and Representation: The Senate and Free Trade." *American Journal of Political Science* 42 (2):524–544.

Baldwin, Richard E., and Frédéric Robert-Nicoud. 2007. "Entry and Asymmetric Lobbying: Why Governments Pick Losers." *Journal of the European Economic Association* 5(5): 1064–1093.

Baldwin, Richard E., and Okubo, T. 2006. "Heterogeneous Firms, Agglomeration and Economic Geography: Spatial Selection and Sorting." *Journal of Economic Geography* 6(3): 323–346.

Baldwin, Richard E. 2010. *Unilateral Tariff Liberalisation*. Working Paper w16600. Cambridge, MA: National Bureau of Economic Research.

Baldwin, Robert E. 1985. *The Political Economy of U.S. Import Policy*. Cambridge, MA: MIT Press.

1989. "The Political Economy of Trade Policy: Integrating the Perspectives of Economists and Political Scientists." *Journal of Economic Perspectives* 3 (4):119–135.

Baldwin, Robert E., and Christopher S. Magee. 2000. *Congressional Trade Votes*. Washington, DC: Institute for International Economics.

Bates, Robert H 1981. *Markets and States in Tropical Africa*. Berkeley: University of California Press.

Bawn, Kathleen, and Frances Rosenbluth. 2006. "Short versus Long Coalitions: Electoral Accountability and the Size of the Public Sector." *American Journal of Political Science* 50(2): 251–265.

Bawn, Kathleen, and Michael F. Thies. 2003. "A Comparative Theory of Electoral Incentives Representing the Unorganized under PR, Plurality and Mixed-Member Electoral Systems." *Journal of Theoretical Politics* 15(1): 5–32.

Beck, Nathaniel, and Jonathan N. Katz. 1995. "What To Do (and Not To Do) with Time-Series–Cross-Section Data in Comparative Politics." *American Political Science Review* 89:634–647.

Bhagwati, Jagdish, and Vangal K. Ramaswami. 1963. "Domestic Distortions, Tariffs and the Theory of Optimum Subsidy." *The Journal of Political Economy* 71(1):44–50.

Bowie, Alasdair, Danny Unger, and Daniel Unger. 1997. *The Politics of Open Economies: Indonesia, Malaysia, the Philippines, and Thailand*. Vol. 4. Cambridge: Cambridge University Press.

Broz, Lawrence J. 2005. "Congressional Politics of International Financial Rescues." *American Journal of Political Science* 49(3): 479–496.

Busch, Marc L., and Erik R. Reinhardt 2000. "Geography, International Trade, and Political Mobilization in US Industries." *American Journal of Political Science* 44(4): 703–719.

Calder, Kent E. 1988. *Crisis and Compensation: Public Policy and Political Stability in Japan, 1949–1986*. Princeton, NJ: Princeton University Press.

1989. *International Pressure and Domestic Policy Response: Japanese Informatics Policy in the 1980s*. Princeton, NJ: Center for International Studies Woodrow Wilson School of Public and International Affairs, Princeton University.

Callahan, William A. 2005. "The Discourse of Vote Buying and Political Reform in Thailand." *Pacific Affairs* 78(1): 95–113.

References

Calvo, Ernesto, and Edward Gibson. 2000. "Federalism and Low-Maintenance Constituencies: Territorial Dimensions of Economic Reform in Argentina." *Studies in Comparative International Development* 35(3): 32–55.

Cameron, David R. 1978. "The Expansion of the Public Economy: A Comparative Analysis." *The American Political Science Review* 72(4):1243–1261.

Campbell, John Creighton. 1977. *Contemporary Japanese Budget Politics.* Berkeley: University of California Press.

1980. *Contemporary Japanese Budget Politics.* Vol. 25. Berkeley: University of California Press.

Chambers, Paul. 2008. "Factions, Parties and the Durability of Parliaments, Coalitions and Cabinets the Case of Thailand (1979–2001)." *Party Politics* 14(3): 299–323.

Christensen, Scott R. 1992. "The Public Policy Process and Political Change in Thailand: A Summary of Observations." *TDRI Quarterly Review* 7(1): 21–26.

Chusho Kigyo Sougou Jigyo Dan. 2001. Sanchi Kasseika Chosa Kenkyu Bunseki Houkokusho: Koraboreeishon no jittai to kanousei ni tsuite [Report on Investigation and Research on the Revitalization of Industrial Regions]. Available at: http://www.smrj.go.jp/keiei/dbps_data/_material_/common/chushou/b_keiei/keieiseni/pdf/sanchi01.pdf (Accessed January 7, 2015).

Connors, Michael Kelly 1999. Political Reform and the State in Thailand. *Journal of Contemporary Asia* 29(2): 202–226.

Cox, Gary W. 1987. *The Efficient Secret: The Cabinet and the Development of Political Parties in Victorian England.* Cambridge: Cambridge University Press.

1990. "Centripetal and Centrifugal Incentives in Electoral Systems." *American Journal of Political Science* 34(4): 903–935.

1996. "Is the Single Nontransferable Vote Superproportional? Evidence from Japan and Taiwan." *American Journal of Political Science* 40(3): 740–755.

2009."13 Swing Voters, Core Voters, and Distributive Politics." In *Political Representation*, ed. Ian Shapiro, Susan Stokes, Elisabeth Wood, and Alexander S. Kirshner. Cambridge: Cambridge University Press.

Cox, Gary W., and Mathew D. McCubbins. 1986. "Electoral Politics as a Redistributive Game." *The Journal of Politics* 48(2): 370–389.

Cox, Gary W., and Emerson Niou. 1994. "Seat Bonuses under the Single Nontransferable Vote System: Evidence from Japan and Taiwan." *Comparative Politics* 26(2): 221–236.

Cox, Gary W., and Frances Rosenbluth. 1993. "The Electoral Fortunes of Legislative Factions in Japan." *American Political Science Review* 87 (3): 577–589.

Cox, Gary W., Frances M. Rosenbluth, and Michael F. Thies. 2000. "Electoral Rules, Career Ambitions, and Party Structure: Comparing Factions in Japan's Upper and Lower Houses." *American Journal of Political Science* 44(1): 115–122.

Cox, Gary W., and Michael F. Thies. 2000. "How Much Does Money Matter? "Buying" Votes in Japan, 1967–1990." *Comparative Political Studies* 33(1): 37–57.

Curtis, Gerald L. 1971. *Election Campaigning Japanese Style.* New York: Columbia University Press.

1988. *The Japanese Way of Politics.* New York: Columbia University Press.

1999. *Logic of Japanese Politics.* New York: Columbia University Press.

Curtis, Gerald L., and Ishiwaka Masumi. 1983. *Doken Kokka Nippon: Sekai no yutosei no tsuyomi to yowami [Construction State, Japan: Strengths and Weaknesses of the World's "Honor student"].* Tokyo: Kobunsha.

Davis, Christina L. 2003. *Food Fights over Free Trade: How International Institutions Promote Agricultural Trade Liberalization.* Princeton, NJ: Princeton University Press.

Destler, Irving M., Haruhiko Fukui, and Hideo Sato. 1979. *The Textile Wrangle: Conflict in Japanese-American Relations, 1969–1971.* Ithaca, NY: Cornell University Press.

Devarajan, Shantayanan and Chalongphob Sussangkarn. 1992. "Effective Rates of Protection when Domestic and Foreign Goods are Imperfect Substitutes: The Case of Thailand." *The Review of Economics and Statistics* 74 (4): 701–711

Diermeier, Daniel, and Timothy J. Feddersen. 1998. "Cohesion in Legislatures and the Vote of Confidence Procedure." *American Political Science Review* 92(3): 611–621.

Doi, Takero. 2000. *Chihou zaisei no seijikeizaigaku.* Tokyo: Touyou Keizai Shinposha.

Doi, Takero, and Ashiya Masahiro. 1997. "Kokko shishitsukin bunpai to seiken yotou no kankei." *Nihon Keizai Kenkyu* 34: 180–195.

Doner, Richard F., and Anek Laothamatas. 1994. "Thailand: Economic and Political Gradualism." *Voting for Reform: Democracy, Political Liberalization, and Economic Adjustment* 411–452.

Doner, Richard F., and A. Ramsay 2000. "Rent-Seeking and Economic Development in Thailand." In *Rents, Rent-Seeking and Economic Development: Theory and Evidence in Asia,* ed. Mushtaq H. Khan and Jomo Kwame Sundaram, 145–181. Cambridge: Cambridge University Press.

Duch, Raymond M., and Randolph T. Stevenson. 2008. *"The Economic Vote: How Political and Economic Institutions Condition Election Results, Political Economy of Institutions and Decisions.* New York: Cambridge University Press.

Ebrill, Liam P., Janet Gale Stotsky, and Reint Gropp. 1999. *Revenue Implications of Trade Liberalization.* Occasional Paper 180. Washington, DC: International Monetary Fund.

Eda, Satsuki. 1991. *Kokkai giin: Wakaru seiji he no hasshin.* Tokyo: Koudansha.

Epstein, David, David Brady, Sadafumi Kawato, and Sharyn O'Halloran. 1997. "A Comparative Approach to Legislative Organization: Careerism and Seniority in the United States and Japan." *American Journal of Political Science* 41(3): 965–998.

Esping-Andersen, Gosta. 1990. *The Three Worlds of Welfare Capitalism.* Princeton, NJ: Princeton University Press.

Estevez-Abe, Margarita. 2008. *Welfare and Capitalism in Postwar Japan: Party, Bureaucracy, and Business.* New York: Cambridge University Press.

Evans, Diana. 1994. "Policy and Pork: The Use of Pork Barrel Projects to Build Policy Coalitions in the House of Representatives." *American Journal of Political Science* 38(4): 894–917.

2004. *Greasing the Wheels: Using Pork Barrel Projects to Build Majority Coalitions in Congress.* Cambridge: Cambridge University Press.

Frieden, Jeffry A. 1991. "Invested Interests: The Politics of National Economic Policies in a World of Global Finance." *International Organization* 45(4): 425–454.

Friman, H. Richard. 1993. "Side-Payments versus Security Cards: Domestic Bargaining Tactics in International Economic Negotiations." *International Organization* 47(3): 387–410.

Fujii, Nobuyuki. 2004. *Chiiki kaihatsu no raireki: Taiheiyo beruto chitai kousou no seiritsu* [History of Regional Development: Establishment of Asian-Pacific Belt Plan]. Tokyo: Nihon Keizai Hyoronsha.

References

Fujita, Masahisa 1988. "A Monopolistic Competition Model of Spatial Agglomeration: Differentiated Product Approach." *Regional Science and Urban Economics* 18: 87–124.

Fukao, Kyoji, and Yue Ximin. 2000. Sengo nihon kokunai ni okeru keizai syusoku to seisan yoso tounyu –soroo seicho moderu ha tekiyou dekiruka. *Keizai Kenkyu* 51(2): 136–151.

Fukumoto, Kentaro. 2000. *Nihon no kokkai seiji: zen-seifu rippou-hou no bunseki* [Parliamentary Politics Japan: Analysis of All Legislations]. Tokyo: Tokyo University Press.

Gandhi, Jennifer, and Adam Przeworski. 2007. "Authoritarian Institutions and the Survival of Autocrats." *Comparative Political Studies* 40(11): 1279–1301.

Garrett, Geoffrey. 1998. *Partisan Politics in Global Economy*. Cambridge: Cambridge University Press.

Gibson, Edward L., and Ernesto Calvo. 2000. "Federalism and Low-Maintenance Constituencies: Territorial Dimensions of Economic Reform in Argentina." *Studies in Comparative International Development* 35(3): 32–55.

Gilligan, Michael, James Alt, and Ron Rogowski. 1994. "The Political Economy of Trading States: Factor Specificity, Collective Action Problems and Domestic Political Institutions." *Journal of Political Philosophy* 2(2): 165–192.

Gilligan, Michael J. 1997. *Empowering Exporters: Reciprocity, Delegation, and Collective Action in American Trade Policy*. Ann Arbor: Michigan University Press.

Goldstein, Judith. 1986. "The Political Economy of Trade: Institutions of Protection." *The American Political Science Review* 80(1): 161–184.

1988. "Ideas, Institutions, and American Trade Policy." *International Organization* 42 (1, The State and American Foreign Economic Policy): 179–217.

1996. "International Law and Domestic Institutions: Reconciling North American "Unfair" Trade Laws." *International Organization* 50(4): 541–564.

Goldstein, Judith, and Lisa L. Martin. 2000. "Legalization, Trade Liberalization, and Domestic Politics: A Cautionary Note." *International Organization* 54(3): 603–632.

Goldstein, Judith L., Douglas Rivers, and Michael Tomz. 2007. "Institutions in International Relations: Understanding the Effects of the GATT and the WTO on World Trade." *International Organization* 61(1): 37–67.

Gourevitch, Peter Alexis. 1977. "International Trade, Domestic Coalitions, and Liberty: Comparative Responses to the Crisis of 1873–1896." *Journal of Interdisciplinary History* 8(2): 281–313.

1986. *Politics in Hard Times: Comparative Responses to International Economic Crises*. Ithaca, NY: Cornell University Press.

Grossman, Gene M., and Elhanan Helpman. 1994. "Protection for Sale." *The American Economic Review* 84(4): 833–850.

Guisinger, Alexandra. 2009. "Determining Trade Policy: Do Voters Hold Politicians Accountable?" *International Organization* 63(3): 533–557.

Haggard, Stephan. 2000. *The Political Economy of the Asian Financial Crisis*. Washington, DC: Peterson Institute.

Haggard, Stephan, and Robert R. Kaufman. 1992. *The Politics of Economic Adjustment*. Princeton, NJ: Princeton University Press.

1995. *The Political Economy of Democratic Transitions*. Princeton, NJ: Princeton University Press.

2008. *Development, Democracy, and Welfare States: Latin America, East Asia, and Eastern Europe*. Princeton, NJ: Princeton University Press.

Haggard, Stephan, and Chung-in Moon. 1995. "The South Korean State in the International Economy: Liberal, Dependent, or Mercantile?" In *The Antinomies of Interdependence: National Welfare and the International Division of Labor*, ed. J. G. Ruggie, 131–189. New York: Columbia University Press.

Haggard, Stephan, and Michael Webb. 1994. *Voting for Reforms*. Princeton, NJ: Princeton University Press.

Hallerberg, Mark, and Patrik Marier. 2004. "Executive Authority, the Personal Vote, and Budget Discipline in Latin American and Caribbean Countries." *American Journal of Political Science* 48(3): 571–587.

Head, Keith, and Thierry Mayer. 2004. "The Empirics of Agglomeration and Trade." *Handbook of Regional and Urban Economics* 4: 2609–2669.

Hewison, Kevin, and Maniemai Thongyou. 2000. "Developing Provincial Capitalism: A Profile of the Economic and Political Roles of a New Generation in Kohn Kaen, Thailand." In *Money and Power in Provincial Thailand*, ed. Ruth T. McVey, 195–220. Copenhagen: NIAS Press.

Hicken, Allen D. 2002. "From Phitsanulok to Parliament: Multiple Parties in Pre-1997 Thailand." In *Thailand's New Politics: KPI Yearbook 2001*. Nonthaburi and Bangkok: King Prajadhipok's Institute and White Lotus Press

2004. "The Politics of Economic Reform in Thailand: Crisis and Compromise (January 2004)." William Davidson Institute Working Paper No. 638.

2008. "How Do Rules and Institutions Encourage Vote Buying?" In *Elections for Sale: The Causes and Consequences of Vote Buying*, ed. Charles Frederic Scaffer, 47–60. Manila: Ateneo de Manila University Press.

Hicken, Allen D. 2006. "Party Fabrication: Constitutional Reform and the Rise of Thai Rak Thai." *Journal of East Asian Studies* 6(3): 381–407.

2009. *Building Party Systems in Developing Democracies*. Cambridge: Cambridge University Press.

Hillman, Arye L. 1982. "Declining Industries and Political-Support Protectionist Motives." *The American Economic Review* 72(5): 1180–1187.

Hirano, Shigeo. 2006. "Electoral Institutions, Hometowns, and Favored Minorities: Evidence from Japanese Electoral Reforms." *World Politics* 59(1): 51–82.

Hirschman, Albert O. 1970. *Exit, Voice, and Loyalty; Responses to Decline in Firms, Organizations, and States*. Cambridge, MA: Harvard University Press.

Hiscox, Michael J. 1999. "The Magic Bullet? The RTAA, Institutional Reform, and Trade Liberalization." *International Organization* 53(4): 669–698.

2001. "Class versus Industry Cleavages: Inter-Industry Factor Mobility and the Politics of Trade." *International Organization* 55(1): 1–46.

2002. *International Trade and Political Conflict*. Princeton, NJ: Princeton University Press.

Horiuchi, Yusaku, and Jun Saito. 2003. "Reapportionment and Redistribution: Consequences of Electoral Reform in Japan." *American Journal of Political Science* 47(4): 669–682.

Huber, John D. 1996. "The Vote of Confidence in Parliamentary Democracies." *American Political Science Review* 90(2): 269–282.

References

Ihori, Toshihiro, and Takero Doi. 2000. *Zaisei Dokuhon [Readers on Finance]*. Tokyo: Toyo Keizai Shinpo.

Imaizumi, Shinya. 2012. "Rippou no seido to doutai." In *Tai no rippou katei: kokumin no seiji sanka he no mosaku* [Law-Making Process in Thailand]. Kenkyu Sousho. No. 61.

Inoguchi, Takashi, and Tomoaki Iwai. 1987. *"Zokugiin" no kenkyū: Jimintō seiken o gyūjiru shuyaku-tachi.* [Study on 'Policy Tribe Politicians': The Leaders Who Control the LDP]. Tokyo: Nihon Keizai Shinbunsha.

Institute for Democracy and Electoral Assistance. 2014. "Voter Turnout Data for Thailand." Available at: http://www.idea.int/vt/countryview.cfm?CountryCode=TH (Accessed June 17, 2014).

Irwin, Douglas A., and Randall S. Kroszner. 1999. "Interests, Institutions, and Ideology in Securing Policy Change: The Republican Conversion to Trade Liberalization after Smoot-Hawley." *The Journal of Law and Economics* 42(2): 643–674.

Isaacs, Bronwyn Alison. 2009. "Imagining Thailand in European Hypermarkets: New Class-Based Consumption in Chiang Mai's 'Cruise Ships'." *The Asia Pacific Journal of Anthropology* 10(4): 348–363.

Ishikawa, Masumi, and Michisada Hirose. 1989. *Jiminto: Choki shihai no kozo* [The LDP: The Structure of Long-term Dominance]. Tokyo: Iwanami Shoten.

Iversen, Torben, Tom Cusack, and David Soskice. 2007. "Economic Interests and the Origins of Electoral Systems." *American Political Science Review* 101(August): 373–391.

Iwai, Tomoaki. 1990. *Seiji shikin no kenkyu: Rieki yuudou no seiji fuudo*. Tokyo: Nihon Keizai Shimbunsha.

Johnson, Chalmers. 1982. *MITI and the Japanese Miracle: The Growth of Industrial Policy: 1925–1975*. Stanford: Stanford University Press.

Johnson, Harry G. 1965. "An Economic Theory of Protectionism, Tariff Bargaining, and the Formation of Customs Unions." *The Journal of Political Economy* 73(3): 256–283.

Jongwanich, Juthahip, and Archanun Kohpaiboon. 2007. "Determinants of Protection in Thai Manufacturing." *Economic Papers* 26(3): 276–294.

Saito, Jun. 2009. "Infrastructure as the Magnet of Power: Explaining Why Japanese Legislators Left and Returned to the LDP." *Journal of East Asian Studies* 9(3): 467–493.

Kabashima, Ikuo. 2000. "Chihou no oukoku to toshi no hanran [Kingdom of the rural, rebellion of the city]." *Chuo Kouron* (September): 130–143.

Kahler, Miles, and David Lake, eds. 2003. *Governance in a Global Economy: Political Authority in Transition*. Princeton, NJ: Princeton University Press.

Kajisa, Kei, and Takamasa Akiyama 2005. "The Evolution of Rice Price Policies over Four Decades: Thailand, Indonesia and the Philippines." *Oxford Development Studies* 33(2): 305–329.

Kanchoochat, Veerayooth. 2008. "Services, Servility and Survival: The Accommodation of Big Retail." In *Thai Capital after the 1997 Crisis*, ed. Pasuk Phongpaichit and Chris Baker, 85–104. Chiangmai: Silkworm Books.

Kato, Junko. 1998. "When the Party Breaks Up: Exit and Voice among Japanese Legislators." *American Political Science Review* 92(4): 857–870.

Katzenstein, Peter. 1985. *Small States in World Economy*. Ithaca, NY: Cornell University Press.

Kaufman, Robert, and Alex Segura-Ubiergo. 2001. "Globalization, Domestic Politics, and Social Spending in Latin America: A Time-Series Cross-Section Analysis, 1973–1997." *World Politics* 53(4): 553–587.

Kawato, Sadafumi. 1996a. Jimintou ni okeru yakushoku jinji no seidoka. *Hougaku* 59(6): 933–957.

1996b. Shinioriti ruuru to habatsu: Jimintou ni okeru jinji haibun no henka [Seniority Rule and Factions: Changing Personnel Appointment Allocations in the LDP]. *Leviathan*, Special Winter Issue.

2004. *Senkyo seido to seitou sisutemu [Electoral Institutions and Party Systems]*. Tokyo: Bokutakusha.

2005. *Nihon no kokkai seido to seitou seiji*. Tokyo: University of Tokyo Press.

Keefer, Philip, and Razvan Vlaicu. 2008. "Democracy, Credibility, and Clientelism." *Journal of Law, Economics, and Organization* 24(2): 371–406.

Keele, Luke, and Nathan J. Kelly. 2006. "Dynamic Models for Dynamic Theories: The Ins and Outs of Lagged Dependent Variables." *Political Analysis* 14(2): 186–205.

Keen, Michael, and Thomas Baunsgaard. 2005. *Tax Revenue and (or?) Trade Liberalization*. Washington, DC: International Monetary Fund

Keohane, Robert O., and Helen V. Milner. 1996. *Internationalization and Domestic Politics*. Cambridge and New York: Cambridge University Press.

Kim, Sukkoo. 1995. "Expansion of Markets and the Geographic Distribution of Economic Activities: The Trends in US Regional Manufacturing Structure, 1860–1987." *The Quarterly Journal of Economics* 110(4): 881–908.

Kohno, Masaru. 1997. *Japan's Postwar Party Politics*, 108–109. Princeton, NJ: Princeton University Press.

Kohno, Masaru, and Yoshitaka Nishizawa. 1990. "A Study of the Electoral Business Cycle in Japan: Elections and Government Spending on Public Construction." *Comparative Politics* 22(2): 151–166.

Kollman, Ken, Allen Hicken, Daniele Caramani, David Backer, and David Lublin. 2012. *Constituency-Level Elections Archive*. Produced and distributed by Ann Arbor: Center for Political Studies, University of Michigan.

Kondo, Makoto. 2010. *Sekiyu kiki go no keizai kouzou chosei to guroobarizeishon he no taiou* [Adjusting Economic Structure and Responding to Globalization After the Energy Crises]" In *Nihon keizai no kiroku – Dainiji sekiyu kiki he no taiou kara baburu houkai made*, ed. Komine Masao. Cabinet Office, Economic and Social Research Institute. Available at: http://www.esri.go.jp/jp/prj/sbubble/history/history_01/history_01.html (Accessed March 4, 2015).

Kovak, Brian K. 2013. "Regional Effects of Trade Reform: What Is the Correct Measure of Liberalization?" *The American Economic Review* 103(5): 1960–1976.

Krauss, Ellis S., and Robert Pekkanen. 2004. "Explaining Party Adaptation to Electoral Reform: The Discreet Charm of the LDP?" *The Journal of Japanese Studies* 30(1): 1–34.

Krauss, Ellis S. 2010. "The Rise and Fall of Japan's Liberal Democratic Party." *The Journal of Asian Studies* 69(1): 5–15.

Krueger, Anne O. 1974. "The Political Economy of the Rent-Seeking Society." *The American Economic Review* 64(3): 291–303.

Krugman, Paul. 1991a. "Increasing Returns and Economic Geography." *Journal of Political Economy* 99: 483–499.

Krugman, Paul. 1991b. *Geography and Trade*. Cambridge, MA: MIT Press.

References

Krugman, Paul, Maurice Obstfeld, and Marc J. Melitz. 2011. *International Economics: Theory and Policy*, 9th ed. Upper Saddle River, NJ: Prentice Hall.

Kume, Ikuo. 1998. *Disparaged Success: Labor Politics in Post-War Japan*. Ithaca, NY: Cornell University Press.

Kuno, A. 2006. "An Evaluation of Japan's First Safeguards Actions." *The World Economy* 29(6): 763–782.

Laakso, Markku, and Rein Taagepera. 1979. "Effective Number of Parties: A Measure with Application to West Europe." *Comparative Political Studies* 12(1): 3–27.

Laothamatas, Anek. 1988. "Business and Politics in Thailand: New Patterns of Influence." *Asian Survey* 28(4): 451–470.

1992. *Business Associations and the New Political Economy in Thailand: From Bureaucratic Polity to Liberal Corporatism*. Studies of the East Asian Institutes. Boulder, CO: Westview Press.

1996. "A Tale of Two Democracies: Conflicting Perceptions of Elections and Democracy in Thailand." In *Politics of Elections in Southeast Asia*, ed. R. H. Taylor, 201–223. Cambridge, New York, and Melbourne: Woodrow Wilson Center Press and Cambridge University Press.

Lauridsen, Laurids S. 1998. "The Financial Crisis in Thailand: Causes, Conduct and Consequences?" *World Development* 26(8): 1575–1591.

Lawrence, Robert Z., and David E. Weinstein. 2001. "Trade and Growth: Import-Led or Export-Led? Evidence from Japan and Korea." In *Rethinking the East Asian Miracle*, ed., Joseph E., Stiglitz and Shahid Yusuf, 379–408. Washington, DC: World Bank Publications.

Lee, Eddy. 1998. *The Asian Financial Crisis: The Challenge for Social Policy*. Geneva, Switzerland: International Labour Organization.

Liberal Democratic Party. 1987. *Jiyuu minshutou tou shi* [The History of the Liberal Democratic Party]. Tokyo: Shiryohen.

Limmanee, Anusorn. 1999. *Political Business Cycle in Thailand, 1979–1992: General Election and Currency in Circulation*. Research Report Submitted to the Institute of Thai Studies. Bangkok: Chulalongkorn University Press.

Magee, Stephen. 1980. "Three Simple Tests of the Stolper-Samuelson theorem." In *Issues in International Economics*, ed. P. Oppenheimer, 138–153. London: Oriel.

Magee, Stephen, William Brock, and L. Young 1989. *Black Hole Tariffs and Endogenous Policy Theory*. Cambridge: Cambridge University Press.

Mano, Yukichi, and Keijiro Otsuka. 2000. "Agglomeration Economies and Geographical Concentration of Industries: A Case Study of Manufacturing Sectors in Postwar Japan." *Journal of the Japanese and International Economies* 14(3): 189–203.

Mansfield, Edward D., and Diana C. Mutz. 2009. "Support for Free Trade: Self-interest, Sociotropic Politics, and Out-Group Anxiety." *International Organization* 63(3): 425–457.

Mansfield, Edward D., Helen V. Milner, and B. Peter Rosendorff. 2000. "Free to Trade: Democracies, Autocracies, and International Trade." *American Political Science Review* 94(2): 305–321.

Mares, Isabela. 2003. *Politics of Social Risk: Business and Welfare State Development*. Cambridge and New York: Cambridge University Press.

Martin, Will, and Francis Ng. 2004. "A Note on Sources of Tariff Reductions in Developing Countries, 1983–2003." *Background paper for Global Economic Prospects 2005 – Trade Regionalism, and Development*, Washington, DC: World Bank.

Masuyama, Mikitaka. 2003. *Gikai seido to nihon seiji: Giji unei no keiryo seijigaku.* Tokyo: Bokutakusha.

Mayer, Frederick W. 1992. "Managing Domestic Differences in International Negotiations: The Strategic Use of Internal Side-Payments." *International Organization* 46(4): 793–818.

Mayer, Wolfgang. 1984. "Endogenous Tariff Formation." *The American Economic Review* 74(5): 970–985.

Mayhew, David R. 1974. *Congress: The Electoral Connection.* New Haven, CT: Yale University Press.

McCargo, Duncan, and Ukrist Pathmanand. 2005. *The Thaksinization of Thailand* (NIAS Studies in Contemporary Asian History, Vol. 4). Copenhagen: NIAS Press.

McCarty, Nolan, and Lawrence S. Rothenberg. 1996. "Commitment and the Campaign Contribution Contract." *American Journal of Political Science* 40(3): 872–904.

McCubbins, Mathew D., and Gregory Noble. 1995. "The Appearance of Power: Legislators, bureaucrats, and the budget process in the United States and Japan." In *Structure and Policy in Japan and the United States*, ed. P. F. Cowhey and M. D. McCubbins. Cambridge and New York: Cambridge University Press.

McCubbins, Mathew D., and Michael F. Thies. 1997. "As a Matter of Factions: The Budgetary Implications of Shifting Factional Control in Japan's LDP." *Legislative Studies Quarterly* 22(3): 293–328.

McElwain, Kenneth Mori. 2008. "Manipulating Electoral Rules to Manufacture Single-Party Dominance." *American Journal of Political Science* 52(1): 32–47.

McGillivray, Fiona. *Privileging Industries: The Comparative Politics of Trade and Industrial Policy.* Princeton, NJ: Princeton University Press
  1997. "Party Discipline as a Determinant of the Endogenous Formation of Tariffs." *American Journal of Political Science* 41(2): 584–607.

McKean, Margaret, and Ethan Scheiner. 2000. "Japan's New Electoral System: la plus ça change..." *Electoral Studies* 19(4): 447–477.

McKinsey Global Institute. 1999. *MGI Thailand Report: Retail Trade.*

McVey, Ruth, ed. 2000. *Money and Power in Provincial Thailand.* Singapore: Institute of Southeast Asian Studies.

Melitz, Marc J. 2003. "The Impact of Trade on Intra-industry Reallocations and Aggregate Industry Productivity." *Econometrica* 71(6): 1695–1725.

Michio, Muramatsu. 1988. *Chihou Jichi* [Local Governance]. Tokyo: Tokyo Daigaku Shuppankai.

Milner, Helen V. 1988. *Resisting Protectionism: Global Industries and the Politics of International Trade.* Princeton, NJ: Princeton University Press.
  1999. "The Political Economy of International Trade." *Annual Review of Political Science* 2(1): 91–114.

Milner, Helen V., and Dustin H. Tingley. 2011. "Who Supports Global Economic Engagement? The Sources of Preferences in American Foreign Economic Policy." *International Organization* 65(1): 37–68.

Milner, Helen V., and Keiko Kubota. 2005. "Why the Move to Free Trade? Democracy and Trade Policy in the Developing Countries." *International Organization* 59(01): 107–143.

Minesaki, Jun. 2003. "Nihon no doboku wo aruku: Atte atarimae no Tokyo-wan oudan douro." *Kensetu Gyokai.* Available at: http://www.nikkenren.com/archives/doboku/ce/kikanshi0303/aruku1.htm (Accessed April 30, 2014).

References

Ministry of Agriculture, Forestry and Fisheries. 2001a. *Yasai shukka toukei* [Statistics on Vegetable Shipment]

Ministry of Agriculture, Forestry and Fisheries. 2001b. *Yasai tou no seifu gaado wo meguru joukyo.* Available at: http://www.maff.go.jp/j/council/seisaku/kikaku/bukai/01/pdf/h131219_01_07_siryo.pdf (Accessed March 4, 2015).

Ministry of Finance, Zaisei Kin-yu Toukei Geppou [Monthly Reports on Fiscal and Finance Statistics], various years.

Ministry of Health, Welfare and Labor. 2011. "*Jidai no niizu ni taiou shita shakai hosyo seido no hatten wo furikaeru.* [Looking Back on the Development of Social Security System Corresponding to the Social Needs]" Section I of *Heisei 23nen do ban Kousei Roudou Hakusho* (Heisei 23 Health, Welfare and Labor White Paper).

Ministry of International Trade and Industry. 1968. *Senshinkokukan keizai seisaku mondai.* In White Paper on Commerce, [Issues Related to Economic Relations among Advanced Industrialized Nations].

1991. *Tsusho sangyou seisaku shi.* Vol. 8: Period of High Economic Growth. Tokyo: MITI Research Committee.

1994. "Oiru shokku to shigen enerugii seisaku." In *Tsuusho Sangyo Seisaku shi*, Vol. 13, ed. Toshimitsu Imuta.

Miyamoto, Taro. 2008. *Fukushi seiji: Nihon no seikatsu hosho to demokurashii* [The Politics of Welfare: Social Security and Democracy in Japan]. Tokyo: Yuuhikaku.

Muramatsu, Michio, and Ikuo Kume. 2006. *Nihon Seiji Hendo no 30-nen.* [Japanese Politics: Changes in Three Decades]. Tokyo: Toyo Keizai Shinpo Sha.

Myerson, Roger B. 1993. "Incentives to Cultivate Favored Minorities under Alternative Electoral Systems." *American Political Science Review* 87(4): 856–869.

Naoi, Megumi. 2007. "Decentralization, Industrial Geography and the Politics of Export Regulation: The Case of Sino-Japanese Trade Disputes." In *China's Foreign Trade Policy*, ed. Ka Zeng. London: Routledge, 40–58.

2009. "Shopping for Protection: The Politics of Choosing Trade Instruments in a Partially Legalized World." *International Studies Quarterly* 53(2): 421–444.

2010. "Whose Side Do Legislators Take? The Politics of Economic Winners and Losers in the Global Economy." *Journal of Law, Politics, and Sociology (Hougaku Kenkyu)*. March: 502–528.

Naoi, Megumi, and Ellis Krauss. 2009. "Who Lobbies Whom: Special Interest Politics under Alternative Electoral Systems." *American Journal of Political Science* 53(4): 874–892.

Naoi, Megumi, and Ikuo Kume. 2011. "Explaining Mass Support for Agricultural Protectionism: Evidence from a Survey Experiment during the Global Recession." *International Organization* 65(4): 771–795.

Naoi, Megumi, and Okazaki Tetsuji. 2013. "Political Economy of Trade Liberalization: The Case of Postwar Japan." *CIRJE Discussion Papers CIRJE-F-898, Center for International Research on the Japanese Economy (CIRJE)*, 4.

Naoi, Megumi, and Shujiro Urata. 2013. "Free Trade Agreements and Domestic Politics: The Case of the Trans-Pacific Partnership Agreement." *Asian Economic Policy Review* 8(2): 326–349.

Neher, Clark D. 1987. "Thailand in 1986: Prem, Parliament, and Political Pragmatism." *Asian Survey* 27(2): 219–230.

Nelson, Michael H. 2007. "Institutional Incentives and Informal Local Political Groups (Phuak) in Thailand: Comments on Allen Hicken and Paul Chambers." *Journal of East Asian Studies* 7(1): 125–147.

Nemoto, Kuniaki, Ellis Krauss, and Robert Pekkanen. 2008. "Policy Dissension and Party Discipline: The July 2005 Vote on Postal Privatization in Japan." *British Journal of Political Science* 38(3): 499–525.

Ng, Francis K. T. 2011. "Trends in Average MFN Applied Tariff Rates in Developing and Industrialized Countries, 1981–2010." Available at World Bank's Data Bank.

Nielson, Daniel L. 2003. "Supplying Trade Reform: Political Institutions and Liberalization in Middle-Income Presidential Democracies." *American Journal of Political Science* 47(3): 470–491.

Nishio, Masaru. 1977. "Kaso to kamitsu no seiji gyosei" [The Politics and Governance of Depopulation and Over-Population]. *Nenpou Seijigaku* 28: 193–258.

Niskanen, William A. 1975. "Bureaucrats and Politicians." *Journal of Law and Economics* 18(3): 617–643.

Noguchi, Yukio. 1995. *Senkyuhyaku yonjuunen taisei* [1940 Regime], Toyokeizai Shimposha. Tokyo.

Ockey, James. 2003. "Change and Continuity in the Thai Political Party System." *Asian Survey*, 43(4): 663–680.

2000. "The Rise of Local Power in Thailand: Provincial Crime, Elections and Bureaucracy." In *Money and Power in Provincial Thailand*, ed. Ruth T. McVey, 74–96. Copenhagen: NIAS Press.

2004. *Making Democracy: Leadership, Class, Gender, and Political Participation in Thailand*. Honolulu: University of Hawaii Press.

Ohara Shakai Mondai Kenkyujo, *Nihon Roudou Nenkan* [Yearbook of Labor in Japan]. Various Years. Digital Archives available at: http://oohara.mt.tama.hosei.ac.jp/rn/ (Accessed March 4, 2015).

Ohta, Hiroko. 2006. *Keizai zaisei shimon kaigi no tatakai* [The Battles at the Council of Economic and Fiscal Policy]. Tokyo: Toyokeizai Shimposha.

Okazaki, Tetsuji. 2010. *Boueki jiyuuka no seiji keizaigaku: sengo nihon no keisu.* [Political Economy of Trade Liberalization: The Case of Post-War Japan] http://hermes-ir.lib.hit-u.ac.jp/rs/bitstream/10086/18976/1/No5-dp_10_05.pdf (Accessed March 4, 2015).

Okazaki, Tetsuji, and Takafumi Korenaga. 1999. "Foreign Exchange Allocation and Productivity Growth in Post-War Japan: A Case of the Wool Industry." *Japan and the World Economy* 11(2): 267–285.

Olson, Mancur. 1965. *The Logic of Collective Action: Public Goods and the Theory of Groups*. Cambridge, MA: Harvard University Press.

O'Rourke, Kevin H., et al. 2001. "The Determinants of Individual Trade Policy Preferences: International Survey Evidence [with comments and discussion]." *Brookings Trade Forum*. Washington, DC: Brookings Institution Press.

Pandya, Sonal S. 2010. "Labor Markets and the Demand for Foreign Direct Investment." *International Organization* 64(3): 389–409.

Phongpaichit, Pasuk, and Chris Baker. 1995. *Thailand: Economy and Politics*. Kuala Lumpur: Oxford University Press.

Pekkanen, Robert, Benjamin Nyblade, and Ellis S. Krauss. 2006. "Electoral Incentives in Mixed-Member Systems: Party, Posts, and Zombie Politicians in Japan." *American Political Science Review* 100(2): 183–193.

References

Pekkanen, Saadia M. 2003. *Picking Winners? From Technology Catch-Up to the Space Race in Japan*. Stanford: Stanford University Press.

Pempel, T. J. 2010. "Between Pork and Productivity: The Collapse of the Liberal Democratic Party." *The Journal of Japanese Studies* 36(2):227–254.

Pempel, T. J., and Keiichi Tsunekawa. 1979. "Corporatism without Labor? The Japanese Anomaly." In *Trends toward Corporatist Intermediation, ed.* Philippe C. Schmitter and Gerhard Lehmbruch, 231–270. Thousand Oaks, CA: SAGE.

Phongpaichit, Pasuk. 1999. *Civilising the State: State, Civil Society and Politics in Thailand*. Amsterdam: Centre for Asian Studies.

Phongpaichit, Pasuk, and Chris Baker 2002. *The Only Good Populist Is a Rich Populist: Thaksin Shinawatra and Thailand's Democracy*. Southeast Asia Research Centre, City University of Hong Kong.

Prasirtsuk, Kitti. 2007. "From Political Reform and Economic Crisis to Coup d'Etat in Thailand: The Twists and Turns of the Political Economy, 1997–2006." *Asian Survey* 47(6): 872–893.

Punyaratabandhu-Bhakdi, Suchitra. 1983. "Thailand in 1982: General Arthit Takes Center Stage." *Asian Survey* 23(2): 172–177.

Ray, Edward John. 1981. "The Determinants of Tariff and Nontariff Trade Restrictions in the United States." *The Journal of Political Economy* 89(1): 105–121.

Ricardo, David, ed. 1951–1973. *The Works and Correspondence of David Ricardo*, ed. P. Sraffa with M. H. Dobb. Cambridge: Cambridge University Press

Riker, William H. 1962. *The Theory of Political Coalitions*. New Haven, CT: Yale University Press.

Robertson, Philip S., Jr. 1996. "The Rise of the Rural Network Politician: Will Thailand's New Elite Endure?" *Asian Survey* 36(9): 924–941.

Rock, Michael T. 1995. "Thai Industrial Policy: How Irrelevant Was It to Export Success?" *Journal of International Development* 7(5): 745–757.

Rodrik, Dani. 1986. "Tariffs, Subsidies, and Welfare with Endogenous Policy." *Journal of International Economics* 21(3): 285–299.

　1993. "The Positive Economics of Policy Reform." *The American Economic Review* 83 (2, Papers and Proceedings of the Hundred and Fifth Annual Meeting of the American Economic Association): 356–361.

　1994. "The Rush to Free Trade in the Developing World: Why So Late? Why Now? Will It Last?" In *Voting for Reform: Democracy, Political Liberalization, and Economic Adjustment*, ed. S. Haggard and S. Webb, 61–87. New York: Oxford University Press.

　1996a. *International Trade and Big Government*. New York: Columbia University School of International and Public Affairs.

　1996b. "Understanding Economic Policy Reform." *Journal of Economic Literature* 34(1): 9–41.

　1997. *Has Globalization Gone Too Far?* Washington, DC: Institute of International Economics.

　1998. "Why Do More Open Economies Have Bigger Governments?" *Journal of Political Economy* 106(5): 997–1032.

Rogowski, Ronald. 1987a. "Political Cleavages and Changing Exposure to Trade." *The American Political Science Review* 81(4): 1121–1137.

　1987b. "Trade and the Variety of Democratic Institutions." *International Organization* 41(2): 203–223.

204   *References*

1989. *Commerce and Coalitions*. Princeton, NJ: Princeton Univeristy Press.

Rogowski, Ronald, and Mark Andreas Kayser. 2002. "Majoritarian Electoral Systems and Consumer Power: Price-Level Evidence from the OECD Countries." *American Journal of Political Science* 46(3): 526–539.

Rose, Andrew K. 2007. "Do We Really Know that the WTO Increases Trade?" Reply. *The American Economic Review* 97(5): 2019–2025.

Rosenbluth, Frances McCall, and J. Mark Ramseyer. 1993. *Japan's Political Marketplace*. Cambridge, MA: Harvard University Press, 152–160.

Rudra, Nita. 2002. "Globalization and the Decline of the Welfare State in Less-Developed Countries." *International Organization* 56(2): 411–445.

Rudra, Nita. 2008. *Globalization and the Race to the Bottom in Developing Countries: Who Really Gets Hurt?* Cambridge: Cambridge University Press.

Ruggie, John Gerard. 1982. "International Regimes, Transactions, and Change: Embedded Liberalism in Postwar Economic Order." *International Organization* 36(2): 379–415.

Saito, Jun. 2010. *Jiminto choki seiken no seijikeizaigaku – rieki yudo seiji no jiko mujun*. [Political Economy of the LDP's Long-term Rule: Self-contradiction of Pork Barrel Politics]. Tokyo: Keiso-shobou.

Sasaki, Takeshi, Yoshida Shinichi, and Taniguchi Masaki. 1999. *Daigishi to kane: seiji shikin zenkoku chosa houkoku* [Representatives and Money: Report on the Nation-wide Research on Political Finance]. Tokyo: Asahi Shimbun Shuppan.

Sato, Seizaburo, and Tetsuhisa Matsuzaki. 1986. *Jiminto Seiken [LDP Regime]*. Tokyo: Chuo Koronsha.

Scarrow, Susan E. 2007. "Political Finance in Comparative Perspective." *Annual Review of Political Science* 10: 193–210.

Schattschneider, Elmer Eric. 1935. *Politics, Pressures and the Tariff: A Study of Free Private Enterprise in Pressure Politics, as Shown in the 1929–1930 Revision of the Tariff*. Upper Saddle River, NJ: Prentice-Hall.

Scheiner, Ethan. 2006. *Democracy Without Competition in Japan: Opposition Failure in a One-Party Dominant State*. Cambridge: Cambridge University Press.

Scheve, Kenneth F., and Matthew J Slaughter. 2001. *Globalization and the Perceptions of American Workers*. Washington, DC: Institute for International Economics.

Scheve, Kenneth F., and David Stasavage. 2009. "Institutions, Partisanship and Inequality in the Long Run." *World Politics*. 61: 215–253.

Schoppa, Leonard J. 1993. "Two-Level Games and Bargaining Outcomes: Why Gaiatsu Succeeds in Japan in Some Cases but not Others." *International Organization* 47(3): 353–386.

1997. *Bargaining with Japan: What American Pressure Can and Cannot Do*. New York: Columbia University Press.

Selway, Joel Sawat. 2011. "Electoral Reform and Public Policy Outcomes in Thailand: The Politics of the 30-baht Health Scheme." *World Politics* 63(1): 165–202.

Shatkin, Gavin. 2004. "Globalization and Local Leadership: Growth, Power and Politics in Thailand's Eastern Seaboard." *International Journal of Urban and Regional Research* 28(1): 11–26.

Shimano, Takao. 1980. *Shohin seisan yusyutunyuryo ruinen toukei hyo* [Export, Import and Production Statistical Tables for Commercial Product]. Tokyo: Yuukyo Syoin.

Shimomura, Yasutami (Ed.). 2004. *Asian Development Experience, Vol. 2: The Role of Governance in Asia*. Singapore: Institute of Southeast Asian Studies.

References

Shimomura, Yasutami. 2003. "In Search of Endogenous Elements of Good Governance: The Case of the Eastern Seaboard Development Plan in Thailand." *The Role of Governance in Asia* 2: 166–189.

Shinya, Imaizumi. 2012. "Rippou no seido to doutai [Law-making institutions and Changes]." In *Tai no rippou katei: kokumin no seiji sanka he no mosaku*, ed. Shinya Imaizumi. IDE-JETRO Publication, No. 601. Tokyo.

Shirk, Susan L. 1993. *The Political Logic of Economic Reform in China*. Berkeley: University of California Press.

Simmons, Beth A. 2000. "International Law and State Behavior: Commitment and Compliance in International Monetary Affairs." *American Political Science Review* 94(4): 819–835.

Sirikrai, Surachai. 1982. "General Prem Survives on a Conservative Line." *Asian Survey* 22(11): 1093–1104.

Soeya, Yoshihide. 1999. *Japan's Economic Diplomacy with China, 1945–1978*. New York: Oxford University Press.

Soma, Masao. 1977. *Kokusei senkyo to seito seiji –Sougou Bunseki 1945–1976* [National Elections and Party Politics – Comprehensive Analysis from 1945 to 1976]. Tokyo: Seiji Koho Center.

Stiglitz, Joseph E., and Shahid Yusuf, eds. 2001. *Rethinking the East Asian Miracle*. Washington, DC: World Bank Publications.

Stokes, Susan C. 2005. "Perverse Accountability: A Formal Model of Machine Politics with Evidence from Argentina." *American Political Science Review* 99(3): 315–325.

Stolper, Wolfgang F., and Samuelson, Paul A. 1941. "Protection and Real Wages." *Review of Economic Studies* November: 58–73.

Sucharithanarugse, Withaya. 1983. Thailand in 1982: The Year of Living in Anxiety. *Southeast Asian Affairs* 277–295.

Suehiro, Akira. 1989. *Capital Accumulation in Thailand 1855–1985*. Tokyo: The Centre for East Asian Cultural Studies (The Toyo Bunko).

Suehiro, Akira, and Natenapha Wailerdsak. 2004. "Family Business in Thailand: Its Management, Governance, and Future Challenges." *ASEAN Economic Bulletin* 21(1): 81–93.

Suwanmala, Charas. 2009. "Fighting Corruption from the Bottom: A Case of Thailand." Asian Human Rights Commission. Available at: http://www.human-rights.asia/resources/journals-magazines/article2/0901/07fighting-corruption-from-the-bottom-the-case-of-thailand (Accessed March 4, 2015).

Takii, Hiroomi. 2001. "Korekara dousuru seefu-gaado [What to do with safeguard provision]." *Ronza* 77: 100–109.

Tatebayashi, Masahiko. 2004. *Giin Kodo no seiji keizaigaku- Jiminto shihai no seido bunseki*. Tokyo: Yuhikakusha.

Liberal Democratic Party. 1988. *Jiyu minshuto shi* [The History of the Liberal Democratic Party]. Tokyo: The Liberal Democratic Party.

Thies, Michael F. 1998. "When Will Pork Leave the Farm? Institutional Bias in Japan and the United States." *Legislative Studies Quarterly* 23(4): 467–492.

Tomoaki, Iwai. 1990. *Seiji shikin no kenkyu: Rieki yuudou no nihon teki seiji fuudo*. Tokyo: Nihon keizai shimbun sha.

Tomz, Michael, Judith L. Goldstein, and Douglas Rivers. 2007. "Do We Really Know that the WTO Increases trade? Comment." *The American Economic Review* 97(5): 2005–2018.

Topalova, Petia. 2007. "Trade Liberalization, Poverty and Inequality: Evidence from Indian Districts." In *Globalization and Poverty*, ed. Ann Harrison, 291–336. Chicago: University of Chicago Press.

United Nations Center of Transnational Corporations. 1991. *World Investment Report: The Triad in Foreign Direct Investment*. New York: United Nations.

Urata, Shujiro, and Kazuhiko Yokota. 1994. "Trade Liberalization and Productivity Growth in Thailand." *The Developing Economies* 32(4): 444–459.

Uriu, Robert M. 1996. *Troubled Industries: Confronting Economic Change in Japan*. Ithaca, NY: Cornell University Press.

Wade, Robert. 1990. *Governing the Market: Economic Theory and the Role of Government in East Asian Industrialization*. Princeton, NJ: Princeton University Press.

Wallack, Jessica Seddon, et al. 2003. "Particularism around the World." *The World Bank Economic Review* 17(1): 133–143.

Warr, Peter G. 1996. *Thailand's Macroeconomic Miracle: Stable Adjustment and Sustained Growth*. Washington, DC: World Bank Publications.

Warr, Peter G., and Bhanupong Nidhiprabha.1996. *Thailand's Macroeconomic Miracle: Stable Adjustment and Sustained Growth*. Washington, DC and New York: World Bank/Oxford University Press.

Warr, Peter G., and Isra Sarntisart. 2005. "Poverty Targeting in Thailand." In *Poverty Targeting in Asia*, ed. John Weiss. 186–218. Cheltenham: Edward Elgar Publishing.

Weingast, Barry R., and Marshall, W. J. 1988. "The Industrial Organization of Congress; or, Why Legislatures, Like Firms, Are Not Organized as Markets." *The Journal of Political Economy* 96(1): 132–163.

Wongpreedee, Achakorn. 2007. "Decentralization and Its Effect on Provincial Political Power in Thailand (The front of area studies)." *Asian and African Area Studies* 6(2): 454–470.

World Bank. 1993. *East Asian Miracle: Economic Growth and Public Policy*. Washington, DC: World Bank Group.

Index

Agricultural Cooperatives, 127.
  See Nokyo
  accession to GATT, 46
  of Japan, 46
  political donation, 127
agricultural liberalization, 72
  in Japan during 1960s, 46
  in Japan during 1970s, 85
  vs. manufacturing liberalization in
    Thailand, 74
  safeguard protection, 144
  in Thailand, 70–73
Alien Business Law
  Thailand, 168
Allied Retail Trade Co, 171
Asian financial crisis
  Chuan cabinet, 107
  foreign retail investment, 160
  IMF loans, 107
  protest, 24
  Thaksin cabinet, 107
Asia-Pacific Industrial Belts. *See* Law
    to Consolidate and Promote
    Special Areas for Industrial
    Development
autarky
  welfare implications, 19
authoritarianism
  effect on welfare
    spending, 118
  entry to global economy, 188
  selectorates, 188
automobile industry
  infant industry status, 40

big business conglomerates
  corruption in Japan, 122
  family-owned in Thailand, 62
  financiers of the LDP, 58
Bretton Woods system
  end of, 84
Buriram province
  retail investment, 161

Carrefour. *See* retail industry
Chachoengsao province, 173
Chamber of Commerce
  campaign restriction in Thailand, 136
  in Chonburi, 163
  of Japan and Industrial Belt, 57
  Thai elections, 137
Chambers, Paul, 13, 115, 193, 202
Charoen Pokphand group
  retail ownership, 163
  corruption, 134
Chart Thai Party
  coalition behavior, 173
  in Chonburi province, 161f. 6.1.
  retail investment, 161
Chatichai, Choonhaven
  cabinet, 139
Chidbob, Newin
  ministerial appointment, 171
  retail protectionism, 162
China
  export to Japan, 143
  Japan's trade conflicts with, 141
  normalization, 43
  trade retaliation to Japan, 141

Chonburi province, 74–79
  Eastern Seaboard Development
    Program, 167
  infrastructure projects, 173
  party switching, 176
  retail investment, 161
Clean Government Party (CGP), 14t.1.1.
  See also *Komei*
  spending allocation, 100
coalition-building strategies, 11
  bargaining costs for elites, 11
  marginal utility of, 28
  welfare implications, 11
collective action problems
  diffused losers, 23
  over institutional reforms, 27
collective goods dilemma, 9, 19, 24, 28, 30, 86
  trade liberalization, 9
commitment problems
  between party leaders and backbenchers, 120
compensation. *See* Compensation Hypothesis
  allocation criteria, 28
  deviation from the prediction, 28
compensation hypothesis, 10
constituency service
  Pork, 17
Constituency-level Election Archive, 66
Constitutional Reform
  of 1997 in Thailand, 104
consumers
  energy crises, 84
  inflation, 82, 92
  protectionist, 189
  protest, 24
  taxing farmers, 63
co-partisan
  hypothesis in Optimal Use of Pork, 22
core vs. swing
  legislators, 9
  Thai voters, 79
corruption
  approval rate, 122
  major scandals in Thailand, 135
  1974 Upper-House election, 122
  revelation in Japan, 122
coup, 64, 172, 203
  2006 in Thailand, 177

debt-relief program
  for Thai farmers, 82
delegation, 8
  insulation thesis, 36
  to King Bhumibol, 170

ministerial ordinance in Japan, 170
ministerial ordinance in Thailand, 170
to Min. of Commerce, 170
to ministries, 171
RTAA, 30
Democratic Party
  opposition under TRT, 174
  in Southern Thailand, 176
Democratic Party of Japan
  (DPJ), 96, 101, 112
  Agricultural ministers, 112
  ruling party status, 96
  spending allocation, 2009–2012, 101
democratic transition, 188

Eastern Seaboard Development Program, 79
  decision-making, 77n104
  disagreement over, 75
  trade liberalization in, 76
Effective Rates of Protection (ERP)
  robustness check, 65n85
electoral disconnection, 28, 79, 160
  defined, 17
  motivations in Thailand, 167
  retail investment, 167
  safeguard protection in Japan, 159
electoral reform
  budgetary implications of 1994 reform in
    Japan, 102
  Italy, 25
  Japan, 25
  New Zealand, 25
  Thailand, 25, 169
electoral systems
  candidate-centered, 4
  choice of Pork, Policy and Institutional
    Reform, 11
  closed-list PR, 13
  contamination effects, 101
  district magnitude, 12
  empower organized vs. diffused, 101
  geographic size of district, 23
  majoritarian, 101
  multi-member district system, 12
  party-centered, 4
  personalistic, 6f1.3.
    See candidate-centered
  PR and interest group capture, 133
  proportional representation (PR), 11n13,
    13, 83, 96, 101, 113, 147, 168
  single-member district system, 101
embedded liberalism, 13, 18n18
emergency decree, 64, 64n82

Index

209

energy crises, 102
  cancellation of public work projects, 86
  effect on Japan, 102
  effect on Thailand, 102
  escape clause, 143
Estevez-Abe, Margarita, xii, 86n9, 94, 100, 194
Evans, Diana, 9, 9n8, 10, 19, 30, 194
external pressure
  "gaiatsu", 8
  retaliation, 16

factions, 13
  access to donations, 44
  competition in the LDP, 42
  defined, 39
  majority vs. minority status, 89
  oppose liberalization in Japan, 43
  positions on trade policy in Japan, 43
  quota-based post allocation, 89
  Tanaka Kakuei, 125
factor endowment, 12
fence-sitters, 10, 22, 37, 59, 79, 149, 173, 189.
    See also small-net losers
  defined, 20
Fifth National Development Plan, 75
fiscal policy
  centralized system, 31
  decentralization in Japan and Thailand, 31n32
  decentralized system, 31
  Dodge Line, 56
  zero-growth, 103
floating exchange rate system, 84
food control system
  Japan, 93
foreign aid
  from Japan to Thailand, 75
  from the U.S. to Thailand, 62
Foreign Business Act
  revision effort in 2007, 177
foreign direct investment (FDI), 162, 166,
  liberalization in Japan, 85, 120
  retail liberalization, 85
  support from Thai local governments, 164
  of tatami-industry in China, 156
foreign exchange allocation system, 40
Foreign Exchange and Trade Control Law, 42
  Trade Liberalization Plan, 54
foreign exchange restriction
  as protectionism, 41
foreign mega retail stores
  Tesco-Lotus, 162

Foreign Retail Act
  Thailand, 165
free-rider problems
  for firms, 18
  for legislators, 21, 22
  for voters, 21
  with the use of *Policy*, 25
Fukuda, Takeo, 89

GATT
  Occupational Force, 39n13
  Thailand's accession, 35n1
General Agreement on Tariffs and Trade
    (GATT), 3, 8, 35, 82, 131, 144, 162, 185
  accession. *See* GATT
  and free trade, 8
  Japan's accession, 39–41
general interest legislation
  defined, 9
geographic concentration
  import-competing industries, 126
  locational sorting of firms, 190
  rent-seeking, 126
Gilligan, Michael, 8
Globalization as Legislation (GL), 9, 28, 142, 160,
  and towel industry cases, 142
  Buriram case, 178
  defined, 9, 28
  premises, 19
  and retail industry cases, 160
grand coalition strategy
  Thaksin cabinet, 177

hybrid regimes, 188

ideology
  heuristics, 17
Ikeda, Hayato, 42
Imabari City, 145
import liberalization ratio, 35
import-substitution strategies, 3
  and energy crises in Thailand, 103n44
  Thailand, 62
income effects, 17, 81, 167, 189
infant industry status
  in Japan and GATT, 40
  Japan's liberalization in the 1970s, 84
inflation
  Japan, 24
  protest, 24
Inoguchi, Takashi
  and Iwai Tomoaki, 88

I

Institutional Reforms, 10
  defined, 11, 26
  difference from Pork or Policy, 11
  optimal use of, 28
insulation argument, 8
International Monetary Fund
  Asian financial crisis, 107, *See* IMF
  Government Finance Statistics, 103, 115
  1959 General Assembly Meeting, 41
  pressure to liberalize, 8
intra-party competition, 38
  cleavage in Japan, 57
  conflict over posts and policies in Japan, 42
  in post-1955 Japan, 36
intra-party organizations
  in the LDP, 87

Japan-U.S. Security Treaty, 43

Keidanren, 40
Keizai Douyukai, 42
Khunpluem, Somchai
  Chart Thai Party, 167
Khunpluem, Sontaya, 173
Kishi Nobusuke, 42
koenkai, 126
  Murakami Seiichiro's, 151n26
  political contribution, 126
Koizumi Junichiro
  budget, 101
  cabinet, 96
  cut down the public work, 152
  Special Zones for Structural Reforms, 101
Kono, Ichiro, 43
Komei, 96
Krairerk, Kosol
  rice policy, 105
Krugman, Paul
  geography and trade, 190
Kumamoto prefecture
  tatami production, 153
  Yatsushiro region, 154

labor unions
  compensation hypothesis, 80
  Japan, 38
  organizational rates, 100
  political contribution in Japan, 124
  position on Political Finance Reform, 124
  within-enterprise in Japan and Thailand, 13
Laem Chabang double-track railway
    project, 173

Law to Consolidate and Promote Special
    Areas for Industrial Development. *See*
    Asia-Pacific Industrial Belts
Leekpai, Chuan
  cabinet appointments, 110n66
  response to Asian financial crisis, 107
left parties
  policy platforms, 86
  popularity in Japan, 86
  support from small-medium size firms, 86
legislators
  business background and Thai
    ministers, 139
  businessmen politicians, 139
  career background, 39, 57
  former technocrats ("kanryo-ha"), 39
  incentives, 28
  professional ("toujin-ha"), 39
Liberal Democratic Party
  disagreement over *Pork* allocation, 57
  disagreement over trade liberalization, 43
  pork vs. productivity, 57
lobbying
  Diet testimony, 128
  by interest groups in Thailand, 102
  Japanese data, 128
  safeguard protection, 145
  by *tatami*-industry, 154
  by Towel Industry Association, 150
local party branches
  campaign contribution in Japan, 126
losers
  big net, defined, 10
  conditions for the rise of diffused, 23
  diffused and the size of district, 23
  diffused, defined, 23
  small net, defined, 10

majority requirements
  formal vs. informal, 21
  legislators' voting options, 20
  party leaders' options, 20
Martin and Ng, 3
Matsumura Kenzo, 43
Matsunami Kenshiro, 147
MatsuokaToshikatsu, 155
media, 190
Melitz, Marc
  towel industry, 149
Miki Takeo
  oppose liberalization, 43
  political finance reform, 122

Index

Milner, Helen, xi, 3n1, 7n3, 8n7, 9n9, 16, 189, 198, 200
minimum winning coalition, 89, 138
ministerial ordinance
 Thailand, 170
Ministry of Agriculture and Cooperatives
 urban vs. rural constituencies of Thai ministers, 110
Ministry of Agriculture, Forestry and Fisheries
 Minister Matsuoka, 155
 safeguard protection, 156
 urban vs. rural constituencies of Japanese ministers, 112
Ministry of Commerce
 retail regulation, 168
Ministry of Economy, Trade and Industry (METI), 146. See MITI
 of Japan, xvi, 129f4.1, 157
Ministry of Finance
 budget data, 95
Ministry of Interior
 retail regulation, 177
 in Thailand, 164
Ministry of International Trade and Industry (MITI), 41. See METI
Murakami Seiichiro, 148

NESDB, 75
New Industrial Cities
 proposed by the LDP, 58
Noda Takeshi, 154
Nominal Rates of Assistance (NRA), 70, 72, 78, 81
 defined, 70
Nominal Rates of Protection (NRP), 65, 76, 78
 defined, 65

occupational reform, 37
 agrarian reform, 37
 dissolution of oligopolistic firms, 37
 empowered labor unions, 38
OcKey, James, 138n34
Okayama prefecture
 Kurashiki City, 157
 tatami industry, 153
one village, one retail project, 165, 172
outsourcing
 in China, 149, 156

parliamentary system, 30
 dissolution, 30
 party discipline, 30
 vs. presidential system, 30
 vote of no-confidence procedure, 30
party discipline, 12, 25, 26, 87n13, 126, 202
 Thai Rak Thai, 172
party mergers
 Japan, 36
 to Thai Rak Thai, 113
party switching
 infrastructure projects, 174
 to the LDP, 158
 prohibition in Thailand, 113
 safeguard protection, 158
 to Thai Rak Thai, 174
party systems
 centralized, 11
 decentralized, 11
 effective number of parties, 115
 multi-party coalition, 11
 one-party majority, 11
 single-party majority, 13
personnel appointments
 budgetary implication, 100
 and businessmen politicians in Thailand, 139
 ministerial positions, 21
 quota-based allocation in Japan, 89
 quota-based allocation in Thailand, 138
 seniority system, 89
 under PM Koizumi, 101
Plan for Building New Japan, 86
Policy, 10
 defined, 10
 operationalization & data for Thailand, 103
 operationalization & data in Japan, 95
 optimal use of, 26
policy corruption
 Thaksin, 134
policy tribes, 87–89
 agriculture, 88
 construction, 88
 defined, 87
 and energy crises, 88
 medical tribe, 87n12
 welfare tribe, 88
political finance reform, 26, 122
 Japan vs. Thai comparison, 137
 loopholes in Japan, 127
 Political Finance Regulation Law, 122
 why reform in Japan, 122–23

Index

political institutions, 3–4
  electoral systems and trade liberalization, 4
  and post-war liberalization, 4
  protectionism-friendly, 28
  regime types, 4
Pork, 10
  defined, 10
  highway projects, 152
  Imabari-Komatsu Express Way, 152
  Optimal Use of, 22
  Prem's distribution of, 76
  urban vs. rural bias, 29
  welfare implications, 22
pork barrel, 10
  in developed vs. developing economies, 61
  policy tribes (zoku), 87
  "pork-policy compromise", 64
  urban vs. rural bias, 61
Pork, Policy and Institutional Reforms
  predictions, 13
Prem, Tinsulanonda
  cabinet, 64–65
  shift to open economy, 65
price stabilization programs, 82
protectionism
  Japan's agriculture, 61
  and party switching in Japan, 79
  Thailand's agriculture under Prem, 78
Protest,
  Japanese consumers, 24
  retail investment in Thailand, 165
  Thai farmers, 109
  towel industry, 148
Provincial Administration Office
  in Chonburi, 164

quota-based system
  ministerial post allocation in Japan, 89
  post allocation in Thailand, 138

rationality. *See* income effect
recession
  energy crises in Japan, 85
  1983–1986 in Thailand, 103
Reciprocal Trade Agreement Act (RTAA),
    30, 196
rent and rent-seeking, 10
  after 1975 reform in Japan, 186
  and FDI, 167
  and ministerial positions, 171
  motivation of legislators, 167
  related to land sales, 178

and subsidy vs. tariff, 18
  targeting Thai export-oriented firms, 186
  urban bias in Thailand, 185
retail industry
  foreign mega stores in Thailand, 162
  foreign ownership, 163
  liberalization in Japan, 85
  liberalization in Thailand, 160
  partisan support in Japan, 85
  regulation in Japan, 82
  Thailand, 160
  zoning regulation in Thailand, 165
revenues
  tariff, 18
Rodrik, Dani, 18
Rogowski, Ronald
  and Mark Kayser, 101
roll-call votes
  abstention in Japan, 124
  defection, 125
  Japan's Upper-House, 123
  U.S., 16
Rosenbluth, Frances, 25
Rudra, Nita, xii, 10, 204
rural bias
  in public investment in Japan, 56

safeguard protection, 143–45. *See* escape clause
  Customs Tariff Law, 144
  decision-making process, 144
  evidentiary hurdle, 145
Sato, Eisaku, 41
semi-democracy
  Prem cabinet in Thailand, 102
seniority system
  absence in Thailand, 139
  of the LDP, 89
Senshu region, 145
Shinawatra, Thaksin
  use of Policies, 176
Shirk, Susan, 188
side-payment
  legislations in Japan, 54
  in 1960s in Japan, 58
  personnel appointments, 9
  pork, 9
  subsidies, 9
single-non-transferrable-vote (SNTV), 38
small- and medium-size companies, 43
Social Action Party
  coalition entry and exit, 73
  response to the first energy crisis, 56

Index

Suehiro Akira, 62
Surayud, Chulanot, 177

Tambon Administrative Organizations
  retail liberalization, 164
Tanaka, Kakuei, 86
  majority faction, 124
tariff
  reduction around the world, 3
  simple average, 3
  weighted applied, 4
tariffs versus subsidies
  welfare ranking of, 18
tatami-mat industry, 153
  goza, 153
  igusa, 153
Tatebayashi Masahiko, 86
Tesco-Lotus. *See* retail industry
textile industry, 41
Thai Federation of Industry
  retail liberalization, 164
Thai Rak Thai Party
  emergence of, 114
  policies, 114
  policy corruption, 134
Topalova, Petia, 66
towel industry, 146
  Association, 148
trade liberalization, 3, *Also see* tariff reduction
  agriculture in Thailand, 73
  bilateral, 3
  income effect, 17
  Japan's agriculture, 46
  manufacturing industries in Thailand, 65–69
  multilateral, 3
  and political institutions, 4
  post-war pattern around the world, 7f.1.4
  unilateral, 3
  unilateral, defined, 3n2
  and WTO, 4n2
trade theorems
  income effects, 16
  Melitz's heterogenous firms, 149

Ricardo-Viner model, 48
Stolper-Samuelson theorem, 16, 40

United States
  Japan's trade conflicts with, 85
  pressure to liberalize trade, 41
urban bias
  in pork barreling, 37
  in public investment in Japan, 185
  trade protection in Thailand, 63
Uruguay Round
  tariff reduction, 3

Vietnam, 188
vote of no-confidence
  procedure, 30

weighting methods
  Topalova, Petia, 66
welfare implication
  of coalition-building strategies, 140
  of Japan's political finance
    reform, 126
  of the Optimal Use of Pork, 185
welfare programs
  data definition for Japan, 95
  expansion in Japan, 92
  expansion under Thaksin, 118
  IMF data definition, 115
  Japan's left parties, 94
  multi-party coalition, 115
  pension and consumer price indexation,
    Japan, 92
  retrenchment in Japan, 94
  in Thailand, 104
World Bank
  aid to Thailand, 62
  Database of Global Distortions to
    Agricultural Incentive, 70
  World Development Indicators
    Data, 115
WTO
  tariff reduction, 3

For EU product safety concerns, contact us at Calle de José Abascal, 56–1°,
28003 Madrid, Spain or eugpsr@cambridge.org.

www.ingramcontent.com/pod-product-compliance
Ingram Content Group UK Ltd.
Pitfield, Milton Keynes, MK11 3LW, UK
UKHW011316060825
461487UK00005B/104